Communicating in the
Third Space

Routledge Research in Cultural and Media Studies

Communicating in the Third Space

Edited by
Karin Ikas and
Gerhard Wagner

Routledge
Taylor & Francis Group
New York   London

First published 2009
by Routledge
270 Madison Ave, New York, NY 10016

Simultaneously published in the UK
by Routledge
2 Park Square, Milton Park, Abingdon, Oxon OX14 4RN

Routledge is an imprint of the Taylor & Francis Group, an informa business

Transferred to Digital Printing 2009

Typeset in Sabon by IBT Global.

Library of Congress Cataloging in Publication Data
Communicating in the third space / edited by Karin Ikas and Gerhard Wagner.
    p. cm. — (Routledge research in cultural and media studies ; 18)
    Includes index.
    ISBN 978-0-415-96315-2
    1. Intercultural communication. 2. Cosmopolitanism. 3. Culture—Semiotic models. 4. Culture and globalization. 5. Politics and culture. 6. Spatial behavior. 7. Postcolonialism. 8. Bhabha, Homi K., 1949—Criticism and interpretation. I. Ikas, Karin. II. Wagner, Gerhard, 1958–
    HM1211.C649 2009
    301.092—dc22
    2008011421

ISBN10: 0-415-96315-X (hbk)
ISBN10: 0-415-87840-3 (pbk)
ISBN10: 0-203-89116-3 (ebk)

ISBN13: 978-0-415-96315-2 (hbk)
ISBN13: 978-0-415-87840-1 (pbk)
ISBN13: 978-0-203-89116-2 (ebk)

This book is dedicated to
Professor Dr. Dr. h.c. Rüdiger Ahrens, OBE
who inspired this international and
interdisciplinary collection

Contents

Preface
In the Cave of Making
Thoughts on Third Space

Homi K. Bhabha

The cave of making can be a dark and desperate place. From time to time, the darkness is dispelled by flashes that dazzle the obscurity. These sudden impulses are too bright to illuminate an idea or light up a thought; they make the night more impenetrable, the cave more unbearable. And yet, the memory of light lingers on, and leads you further into a darkness that slowly reveals its own geography of insight and ignorance. Then voices begin calling to you from beyond the cave—voices of instruction and encouragement, half inscripted and half intuited, half heard and half imagined. It is these voices, freighted with unresolved conversations and interrupted arguments, that finally help you to "hold" the thought: and in the midst of that movement of ideas and intuitions you discover a momentary stillness. This moment of reflection is never simply the mirror of *your* making, *your* frame of thinking, but a stillness sometimes heard in choral music when several voices hold the same note for a moment—*omnes et singulatum*—as it soars beyond any semblance of sameness. The precarious tension involved in holding the thought—or the note—in common, vibrating beyond the control of any one voice, is the timbre of translation working its way into our thinking. In this act of "holding"—a thought, a note, a tone—the grain of the idea or the concept comes to be revealed through the side-by-side synchrony of different voices. Suddenly, the ungraspable thought is *yours,* but only in the dispossessive spirit of that doubly articulated pronoun. To say that a concept or a thought *becomes yours* is to say that it becomes my thought, my concept; but it is never in my possession, it was never my property, because the thought is also *yours—it belongs to you, too.*

To hold, in common, a concept like third space is to begin to see that thinking and writing are acts of translation. Third space, for me, is unthinkable outside of the locality of cultural translation. It was local knowledge that first led me to the third space by way of some mis-translations in the context of early 19ᵗʰ century Evangelical discourses dedicated to the conversion of Hindus in Northern India. I remember the case of the Biblical mistranslation of the Holy Ghost as *bhoot* (or "spook") by a missionary who was at once affronted and perplexed that his purple proselytizing had not persuaded the affrighted natives to embrace the

Holy Trinity. And then, of course, there were those canny peasants out-side Agra who politely turned down the offer of conversion by fulsomely praising the divine language of Christian catechism while expressing their utter disbelief in a religious system in which the word of God could come from the mouths of meat-eaters. Related more closely to the 1990s, there were groups like the Southall Black Sisters (consisting largely of second-generation migrant and minority women from a wide range of ethnic backgrounds) whose post-colonial, feminist politics opened up a third space of cultural critique and political confrontation founded on a double consciousness: they were as critical of the pluralist prejudices of secular liberals and their reductive stereotypes of faith-based communities, as they were resistant to the patriarchal policing of gender relations and sexual choice within their own traditionalist, status-centered families. Across the threshold of terror and genocide that joins the 20th century to the twenty-first, Truth Commissions provide dialogical third spaces committed to democratic processes of political transition and ethical transformation in societies made wretched by violence and retribution. The traditional grass mat, the *gacaca,* that has provided a name and a place for local practices of post-genocide adjudication in Rwanda—the Gacaca Courts—could also qualify as a third space. The *gacaca* is not simply a neutral area of confession, nor is it principally a space of confrontation and guilt. It is a place and a time that exists in-between the violent and the violated, the accused and the accuser, allegation and admission. And that site of in-betweenness becomes the ground of discussion, dispute, confession, apology and negotiation through which Tutsis and Hutus together confront the inequities and asymmetries of societal trauma not as a "common people," but as a people with a common cause.

The priest who mistook the Holy Ghost for a spook was perhaps a bad translator; the peasants who demanded a vegetarian Bible were, perhaps, shrewd, subaltern strategists. It was, however, neither the question of the accuracy of translation, nor the political uses and abuses of cultural (mis)communication that initially caught my eye. What struck me with some force was the emergence of a dialogical site—a moment of enunciation, identification, negotiation—that was suddenly divested of its mastery or sovereignty in the midst of a markedly asymmetrical and unequal engagement of forces. In an intercultural site of enunciation, at the intersection of different languages jousting for authority, a translational space of negotiation opens up through the process of dialogue. Adapting an idea from Walter Benjamin's essay *The Task of the Translator,* I would suggest that the contingency and indeterminacy of discourse results from a distinction *within* linguistic intention that is made more easily visible by the practice of translation. The living flux of meaning is difficult to pin down (recall Lacan's *points de capiton!*), because the linguistic sign continually shifts from being an "object" of intention—a Hindi "sign," *bhoot,* equivalent (or not) to the English "ghost"—to becoming a "mode" of intention—the cultural and discursive specificity of the "sign" as a repertoire (and reservoir) of meaning that has no equivalence in another language. The specificity of signification cannot be reproduced in an imitative sense; it can only be re-presented as an iterative, re-initiation of meaning that awakens the sign (as mode of intention) to another, analogical linguistic life. Is this not the reason why Benjamin suggests that 'translation, ironically, transplants the original into a more definitive linguistic realm since it can no longer be displaced by a secondary rendering. The original can only be *raised anew* and at other points of time.'[1]

Ironically, it is the 'element that does not lend itself to translation'[2] that makes it possible for discursive authority to be re-negotiated despite the asymmetrical relations of power. Raising the problem of meat eating as a foil to conversion seems to make good political sense, but at the same time may well be theological nonsense. Perhaps the oral transmission of scriptures by Hindu priests might have been mentally transposed, by the North Indian peasants, onto the inscriptive instruction proffered by meat-eating Christian priests, resulting in an imagined pollution of sacred texts. Who knows what exactly happened, or what was precisely meant, at that local point in time? However, what appears from the archive as the strategic advantage of the disadvantaged peasantry over the commanding clerisy is achieved by a strange divergence or displacement of the path of power through an act of signification that emphasizes what semioticians call the arbitrariness of the sign. It is the openness or "emptiness" of the signifier—the untranslatable movement between the intended object and its mode of intention—that enables a speech-act to become the bearer of motivated meanings and deliberative intentions, *in situ*, at the moment of its enunciation. The cipher of meaning—the virtuality and arbitrariness of the sign—is itself a value-system capable of being used, not perhaps to speak truth to power, but to pit an alternative ethical and political authority against the dogmatism of prevailing power. For, at this moment, the openness (rather than emptiness?) of the signifier suddenly drains the charge of power rather than exerting a counter-pressure that would spark it back to life.

How do you attribute value and agency to a voiding, or a draining, of power at the hands of the openness of the arbitrary signifier? In what sense does the "sign" open onto the question of agency and provide an alternative, even antagonistic, form of authority? Consider an incident from Joseph Conrad's *Heart of Darkness*. Conrad's Marlow, the ethical and narrative protagonist of the novel, knows only too well what it means to live in conditions of moral opacity shrouded in a forest of signs that render the conditions of speech and action barely intelligible: 'We were cut off from the comprehension of our surroundings; we glided past like phantoms, wondering and secretly appalled, as sane men would be before an enthusiastic outbreak in a madhouse.'[3] In the midst of this bedlam he sees a French man-of-war shelling the bush, 'firing into a continent' in pursuit of a 'camp of natives—[they] called them enemies!—hidden out of sight somewhere.'[4]

Conrad's theatre of asymmetric warfare is accompanied by a narrative insistence that the knowledge of identity and difference is as much a question of epistemology and history as it is a perceptual and phenomenological problem that relates to *how we see* and *from where we look*. Are natives taken to be enemies because they are hidden, 'out of sight somewhere'? Is this an existential anxiety in the face of what seems alien, or does such alienation mask the annihilatory strategy of the Imperialist? Is it self-protection or self-projection? Where should the ethical line be drawn?

To draw a line that distinguishes friend from enemy, Marlow approaches the "other," shrinks the distance, and enters into a form of ethical proximity. When the 'natives' are observed 'within six inches,' Marlow is convinced of the injustice of naming them enemies or criminals: 'these men could by no stretch of imagination be called enemies. They were called criminals and the outraged law like the bursting shells had come to them, an insoluble mystery from the sea.'[5] As Conrad's narrative destroys the naming frameworks of war ("enemy") and legality ("criminal"), it moves us closer towards identifying with the native's historic situation and his human condition, rather than accepting those projected "identities" and self-serving vocabularies that are shaped for the purposes of war and the laws of conquest: 'half-effaced within the dim light, in all the attitudes of pain, abandonment and despair [. . .] They were not enemies, they were not criminals, they were nothing earthly now—nothing but black shadows of disease and starvation [. . .] Then glancing down, I saw a face near my hand [. . .] and the sunken eyes looked up at me, enormous and vacant [. . .] I found nothing else to do but to offer him one of my good Swede's ship's biscuits I had in my pocket [. . .] *He had tied a bit of white worsted round his neck—Why? Where did he get it? Was it a badge—an ornament—a charm—a propitiatory act?* Was there any idea at all connected with it. It looked startling around his black neck this bit of white thread from beyond the seas.'[6]

Not enemy. Not criminal. Not even native. Having glimpsed the Levinasian face of the other, Marlow can now focus closely on the tiny bit of white worsted whose social origins and cultural significance are ambiguous and enigmatic—open to question. As the arbitrary sign shifts across the open frame of signification, it marks the distance—and the cultural difference—that lies in-between the relative familiarity of a badge and the relative unknowability of a Congolese propitiatory act. Somewhere between the two, Marlow enters a third space. He is now engaged in a translational temporality in which the "sign" of the white worsted from beyond the seas, is an object of intention that has lost its mode of intention in the colonial space, or vice versa. The familiar origin of the worsted as a commodity of colonial trade passes through an estranging realm of untranslatability in the heart of darkness, and emerges ready to be '*raised anew* and at other points of time.' The arbitrary signifier is no longer a linguistic rule or a semiotic process. The openness of the sign to translation—that living flux that marks the "difference" between intention as object and as modality—shifts the balance of discourse from the language of enmity to the language of proximity: 'I saw a face near my hand [. . .] and the sunken eyes looked up at me, enormous and vacant.' But that is not all.

If Marlow's gaze had stopped there, it could have been read as merely an act of pity and philanthropy. But beyond the duality of the silent face-to-face encounter, lies the white worsted, a mediating, material element from the object-world that talks back to Marlow as he probes its origin and function. It is the thread as a mediating third space that designates the dialogical relation between the narrator and the native as contending and contradictory positions within a conflictual discourse. The white thread is a text of signs and symbols that reintroduces, to the reader and the narrator, the silent, dying native as an agent caught in the living flux of language and action: 'He had tied a bit of white worsted round his neck—Why? Where did he get it?' This goes beyond any notion of respect for the other's identity or humanity as a universal subject that has an *a priori* right to representation. It is an identification, in third space, with the thought and action of the other as having an opacity of its own that cannot be simply "read off" the face of things; the thread signifies a "thickness" of culture that is as enigmatic as the obliquity of the signifier through which it is enunciated. Even in his prone state, 'the moribund shape as free as air—and nearly as thin' induces an infectious introjection that comes from outside, from an intuition of the intended act of the other—*Why? Where did he get it?*—in order to drive, as if from the inside, the narrator's decision to make up his own mind against the received wisdom of his wretched times. After all, it is only moments before this incident, in the process of making his deliberate decision to undertake his Dantesque descent into 'the gloomy circle of some Inferno,' that Marlow has this to say of himself and his life: 'You know I am not particularly tender; I've had to strike and to fend off. I've had to resist and to attack sometimes—that's only one way of resisting—without counting the exact cost—according to the demands of such sort of life as I had blundered into. I've seen the devil of violence, and the devil of greed, and the devil of hot desire. . . .'[7] In reaching out to the specific thought of the other and grappling with what is not entirely intelligible within it—rather than acknowledging an "identity"—there lies the possibility of identifying also with the unconscious of the other, and extending oneself in the direction of the neighbor's legible will and his unreadable desire. *Where did he get it? Was it a badge—an ornament—a charm—a propitiatory act?*

The third space is a challenge to the limits of the self in the act of reaching out to what is liminal in the historic experience, and in the cultural representation, of other peoples, times, languages, texts. And it is quite fitting that we should end with a series of questions and interpretations that attempt to decipher the acts of agency. If the white worsted tells a political story of unfair trade and slavery, it is also a figural narrative suggestive of ornamentation, charms and cultural magic. As a shibboleth of the third space, this little piece of thread raises profound questions and awakens important voices. As I hear Marlow's voice probe this symbolic fragment of a third space, I am moved and excited by the various voices in this volume, *Communicating in the Third Space,* that are involved in their own acts of making and mapping: voices that light the way to another darkness, a new cave of making.

NOTES

1. Benjamin, Walter. "The Task of the Translator: An Introduction to the Translation of Baudelaire's *Tableaux Parisiens*," trans. Harry Zohn. *The Translation Studies Reader.* Ed. Lawrence Venuti, 2nd ed. New York: Routledge, 2004 (1923). 74–85. 79 (my emphasis).
2. Ibid. 79.
3. Conrad, Joseph. *Heart of Darkness: An Authoritative Text, Backgrounds and Sources, Criticism.* Ed. Robert Kimbrough, 3rd ed. New York: Norton, 1988. 37.
4. Ibid. 17.
5. Ibid. 19.
6. Ibid. 21 (my emphasis).
7. Ibid. 19.

Introduction

Karin Ikas and Gerhard Wagner

COMMUNICATING IN THE THIRD SPACE

At the turn of the 21st century, globalization has transformed the earth into a planet of nomads. Whether it is empires, states, nations, public spheres, religious communities, ethnic groups, townships, or neighborhoods, today millions of migrants challenge the existing power structures and expose the available self-images as ideologies. Meanwhile, the residents' collective identity is ceaselessly confronted with newly arrived minorities, which bring along their very own traditions. Neither these newcomers nor the changes they bring about can be simply ignored. That is why communication between members of different cultures is such an important affair these days. In fact, it has not only become a world-historical necessity but also a challenge of every day life.

Over the last decades, we have seen the emergence of a growing body of critical works on diverse aspects of inter- or transcultural communication. Interestingly enough, however, we still lack substantial insights as to which social conditions are required to make such communication work. Power relations especially are often neglected. Hence, most scholars engaged in research on inter- or transcultural communications inevitably contribute to the illusion that symmetrical social relations characterize the presently evolving third cultures. It appears that they do not link their approaches to the insights of postcolonial studies. Yet such disregard is not feasible because postcolonial studies have attained global significance as a body of critical works that helps us to come to terms with various notions of power relations as well as inter- or transcultural modes of being in postcolonial societies all over the world. Although a few critics have suggested that this is indeed an increasing problem in inter- or transcultural communication, the majority of these approaches are still written in the tradition of the grounding father, Edward T. Hall. In other words, the question of how to communicate across cultures is primarily approached from an interpersonal point-of-view. Hardly any credit is given to the social and political circumstances in which that communication occurs.

An interdisciplinary approach that combines insights from both post-colonial theory and from studies on inter- or transcultural communication could help to correct these shortcomings in the contemporary critical debate. That is where this critical collection *Communicating in the Third Space* comes in. It takes postcolonial scholar Homi K. Bhabha's thoughts as a starting point because he has fore-grounded the concept of Third Space in his book *The Location of Culture*. Largely, Bhabha conceives the encounter of two social groups with different cultural traditions and potentials of power as a special kind of negotiation or translation that takes place in a Third Space of enunciation. This negotiation is not only expected to produce a dissemination of both cultural traditions that leads to a displacement of the members of both groups from their origins. It is also supposed to bring about a common identity, one that is new in its hybridity; it is thus neither the one nor the other. Bhabha's critical reflections on power relations in negotiations enable us to take into account the displacement and/or replacement of powerfully ascribed identities.

The problem with Bhabha, however, is that his language style and wording is so complex and highly sophisticated that scholars dealing with inter- or trans-cultural communication usually do not apply his concept of negotiation. As the overall notion of third space has gained immense popularity beyond its origin in postcolonial studies in recent years nonetheless, it is high time to launch a critical debate on both its theoretical premises as well as its empirical implications. The volume *Communicating in the Third Space* aims to do exactly this. It clarifies Bhabha's theory by reconstructing its logical, philosophical, psychological, sociological, geographical, and—not to forget—political meaning. Then, it compares it with related concepts such as contact zone or Thirdspace: *Communicating (in) the Third Space*. Afterwards, Bhabha's theory is used as a tool to analyze encounters in which intercultural communication takes place and succeeds from time to time: *Communicating in the Third Space*. Subsequently, it throws light on the scientific reconstruction of concrete processes of inter- or transcultural communication between members of different cultures as well as on the artistic (re-)construction of such processes in literary works.

Understanding inter- or transcultural communication as a process of negotiation that takes place in a Third Space also asks for an interdisciplinary and international research design. Hence, the volume at hand integrates 10 contributions of scholars from the Humanities and Social Sciences.

THE QUEST FOR INTER- OR TRANSCULTURAL COMMUNICATION

The first two chapters are captioned "The Quest for Inter- or Transcultural Communication". Here, Ulrich Beck and Britta Kalscheuer call for theories and concepts that meet the demands and challenges of the quest for inter- or transcultural communication in a globalized world. Beck reconsiders the concept of cosmopolitanism. From the 19th century up to now, cosmopolitanism has been deeply associated with idealism while the real world has spoken the language of realism, which is nationalism. At the beginning of the 21st century, nationalism is becoming unreal and idealistic, cosmopolitanism stands for realism in a world, which has become cosmopolitical in its core. That is what Beck calls cosmopolitan realism. The nation-state is increasingly besieged and permeated by a planetary network of interdependencies, by ecological, economic and terrorist risks, which connect the separate worlds of developed and underdeveloped countries. To the extent that this historical situation is reflected in a global public sphere, a new historical reality arises, a cosmopolitan outlook in which people view themselves simultaneously as part of a threatened world and as part of their local situations and histories. Kalscheuer starts with the premise that the issue of power is not only avoided in intercultural communication debates but strictly speaking also in postcolonial approaches, which do not put enough emphasis on the fact that the suppressed have less power of self-assertion. For her this makes self-evident how tricky any endeavor is that aims at integrating inter- or transcultural and postcolonial approaches. Nonetheless, as her subsequent reconstruction of the history of intercultural communication theory and her coping with its most significant representatives reveals, a critical turn is long overdue; so is the discourse's move towards more self-reflexivity for which, in fact, postcolonial studies are renowned. In her subsequent comparison of Bhabha's notion of the negotiation process with the one put forward in intercultural theories she ascertains that both still neglect power relations and that it might thus be useful to consider an alternative concept to fill the critical void: the so-called concept of transdifference or rather transdifferent positionalities.

THE SPATIAL TURN

The contributions by Edward W. Soja and Julia Lossau, which make up the next section entitled "The Spatial Turn," deal with what appears to be one of the most important intellectual and political developments at the turn of the Second into the Third Millennium, the so-called spatial turn. After critically reviewing its origins and impact, Soja attempts to go beyond the traditional modes of thinking about space and such related concepts as place, location, landscape, architecture, environment, home, city, region, territory, and geography by viewing Thirdspace as an analytical concept that enables us to come to terms with the representational strategies of real and imagined places. He argues that social spatiality functions as form, configured materially as things in space, and mentally, as thoughts about space. Moreover, it is also a process, a dynamic force that is actively being produced and reproduced all the time, and as such it is inseparable from society. Drawing in particular on Henri Lefebvre, Soja proposes a trialectics of spatiality that threads through all subsequent real and imagined journeys undertaken at the turn of the century, and, as a result, it provides new insights for the theoretical journeys undertaken by spatial, feminist and postcolonial critics today. Lossau aims at critically rethinking the complex relations of identity, difference and space. Discontented with binary opposites and cultural essentialisms, postcolonial scholars have long been at work to reconceptualize identity. The related interest in hybrid forms of difference is accompanied by a spatial rhetoric. The subjects of postcolonial discourse position themselves between margin and centre; they live in in-between spaces thereby travelling and eventually crossing—if not transforming—borders, gaps and (different sorts of) oppositional spheres. An important part of what has been called the spatial turn of contemporary social and cultural theory, the use of spatial metaphors—epitomized in Bhabha's concept of Third Space—is meant to highlight difference by allowing for the coexistence of distinct narratives. Lossau argues, however, that the logic of spatial language implies a politics of location, which renders fluidity into spatial fixity. Firstly, she rehearses the main arguments of Bhabha's preoccupation with space in general and Third Space in particular. Although Third Space as a concept is aimed at overcoming the reductionist power of cultural and political fixations, it is hardly capable of avoiding certain shortcomings of the more traditional conceptualizations of identity and difference. By means of system theoretic arguments, Lossau traces the concept's pitfalls back to the ambivalent logic of space. She then considers ways to reach beyond the pitfalls of Third Space and eventually gives us the following questions for further considerations: If spatial semantics pose a threat to difference, is there still space for alternative and truly different approaches to reality and its spatial aspects?

THEORIZING THE THIRD SPACE

The contribution by Robert J.C. Young and the co-authored essay by Karin Ikas and Gerhard Wagner are devoted to what is captioned here as "Theorizing the Third Space" and what aims at reconstructing hidden philosophical and logical dimensions of Bhabha's concept of Third Space. Young argues that Bhabha's notion of Third Space is not a space as such but rather best conceived as a site, which is comparable to the site of enunciation elaborated in Emile Benveniste's *Course in General Linguistics*. He traces the ways in which Benveniste's theory of enunciation was elaborated by Jacques Lacan into a theory of the simultaneous appearance and disappearance of subjectivity at the moment of speech, and argues that Bhabha then develops, as he puts it, the implication of this enunciative split for cultural analysis. In doing so, he places an increasing emphasis on the notion that the moment of splitting also involves a descent into a void.

The psychic anxieties of Bhabha's void are subsequently linked to those of Blaise Pascal, to the experience of *Platzangst* in Sigmund Freud, the void of misgiving in the work of Wilson Harris, and to the ambivalent accounts of masculinity in V.S. Naipaul's *A House for Mr Biswas*. Ikas and Wagner combine Bhabha's question of how postcolonial subjectivity can be defined by the unsettled logic of the third in his concept of Third Space. They take Bhabha's thesis of not operating with Hegel's classical dialectical logic seriously and hence introduce the transclassical logic of the German-American philosopher Gotthard Günther to demonstrate that akin to subjectivity as such, postcolonial subjectivity can be explained with a new logical function called rejection. A person constitutes him-/herself as a subject by rejecting a given—logical or cultural—alternative and thereby marking a third position that is new, neither the one nor the other but something else besides, which contests the terms and territories of both.

LITERIZING THE THIRD SPACE

Bill Ashcroft and Karin Ikas then turn to literature as the classic realm of postcolonial studies in their contributions to the section entitled "Literizing the Third Space." Ashcroft discusses the ways in which inter- or transcultural communication in a third space has occurred successfully in books by postcolonial authors from the former British Empire written in the colonial language English. He demonstrates that not only do writers communicate their culture in another language suggesting that all colonized subjects have discursive agency, but the act of reading itself is a inter- or transcultural interaction in which meaning is constitutively constructed within the message event. Taking Shakespeare's character Caliban and his statement in *The Tempest*: 'You taught me your language and my profit on't is I know how to curse' as the metaphoric model for the resistance to English, he then examines the ways in which the colonized world has transformed dominant languages as well as dominant discourses. Far from simply cursing, that world has used the dominant to transform the nature of power relations. More than any other language users, perhaps, postcolonial writers have successfully demonstrated that culture does not reside in the language, that language can be used as a tool of resistance, by conveying the writer's reality, even though this communication occurs in various forms of textual production. Inter- or transcultural communication can occur most significantly in the appropriation and transformation of a world language by writers and other cultural producers from a very different cultural reality. In this way, inter- or transcultural communication can be seen to be intra-linguistic rather than trans-linguistic as it accommodates the global reality of hybrid identities. Karin Ikas takes the very conversely debated term Mexifornia, one of America's most popular buzzwords in this New Millennium, as an occasion to cast light on the substantial changes currently underway in the United States where the rising number of U.S. Latinos/as in general and Mexican Americans in particular shake up established power structures and expose available self images as ideologies. An identity politics that means a break with sharp contrasts and allows for multiple subject positions to emerge—like the one suggested by the Third Space respective Thirdspace debate originating from Bhabha and Soja—is indispensable to cope successfully with the challenges of this transformation process. Actually, Bhabha and Soja themselves highlight the significance of the Mexican American Borderlands as an exemplary case study for their very own theoretical concepts of the third space, yet both fail to provide any such specific case study. With her contribution, Ikas aims to close this gap. She explores the Southwestern part of the United States bordering Mexico as a classic example for a real and imagined space in-between for the reason that the majority of the protagonists that make up the Mexican-American Borderlands have more than one physical, ethnical and cultural background and thus face the challenge of how to communicate more successfully in a situation in which hybridity is indeed the order of the day. Last but not least, she examines how all this is enacted in Cherríe Moraga's dramatic piece about the Mexican-American Borderlands entitled *The Hungry Woman: The Mexican Medea* where Moraga reinterprets both Mesoamerican mythology and the currently imagined political and social reality of Mexifornia for the modern theatre and audience in our time.

LOCATIONS AND NEGOTIATIONS

In the concluding section with the heading "Locations and Negotiations," the two contributors Frank Schulze-Engler and Gerhard Wagner show that the concept of third space is by no means restricted to postcolonial constellations. Schulze-Engler argues that the idea of third space has largely remained a parochial concept, since it has usually been understood as a subversion of or challenge to conceptually homogenized understandings of culture and society in the West, while similar challenges with regard to non-Western cultures and societies have often gone unheeded. This predicament of third space, Schulze-Engler argues, is symptomatic of a basic predicament of postcolonial theory: its insistence on seeing the contemporary world in terms of colonialism and not of modernity. Since the processes of internal diversification and challenges to a homogenous understanding of nation-cultures that the idea of Third Space grapples with can be perceived in a wide variety of locations, third spaces are, however, a ubiquitous reality. Schulze-Engler looks at a variety of third spaces in literature from non-Western locations and at the way in which these third spaces contribute to the emergence of specific varieties of modernity; examples will be third spaces emerging in reconciliation processes following civil wars (Sri Lanka), third spaces generated in the struggles against dictatorships and the politics of civil society (Nigeria), third spaces implied in the gender politics of gay and lesbian writing (New Zealand) and transsexual identities (the Caribbean), third spaces related to the concept and practice of multicultural societies (Canada), and third spaces created by transnational/transcultural memory (the Middle Passage and modern slavery). Wagner argues that Bhabha has not only inspired cultural theory but also drafted a theory of nation that goes beyond the social sciences' theoretical concept of nation. As Bhabha contends, social sciences concentrate on the perspective of the dominating élite that indoctrinates the people according to its own idea of national identity. For him such an approach is neither valuable to adequately address the situation of the 19th century nor is it useful to assess the current state of affairs in the contemporary world where globalization permanently challenges existing power structures and millions of migrants expose the relevant national self images as ideologies. According to Bhabha, every nation is subject to dissemination. Thus, national identity can only be thought of as the result of a negotiation that emerges in a third space between the dominant élites representative for the majority of the people and the newly arrived minorities. Wagner claims that Bhabha's theory of negotiation need not be limited to the situations of majorities and minorities nor to the ones of residents and migrants. It is useful and can be applied in all those cases in which a dominant definition of identity is challenged by another one, one of those that cannot be ignored any more. Consequently, this entry defines the general social framework and the prerequisites that are needed for negotiations to emerge at all before it carries out a study on the Polish Revolution of the 1980s. By so doing, it is able to present an illuminating case study where the specifics of such a successful negotiation become most obvious.

In concluding, the editors would like to point out that this interdisciplinary and international reader is not only a collection of theorists but also of ideas on the Third Space debate. As such, it is interested in indicating something of the great scope, the rich heterogeneity and the vast energy of the field of postcolonial and trans-/intercultural studies and the challenges and chances the Third Space concept originating from Homi K. Bhabha and Edward W. Soja offers to this field.

Part I

The Quest for Inter- or Transcultural Communication

1 Cosmopolitanization Without Cosmopolitans

On the Distinction Between Normative and Empirical-Analytical Cosmopolitanism in Philosophy and the Social Sciences

Ulrich Beck

INTRODUCTION

Why do we need a cosmopolitan re-definition, re-invention of the social sciences? To cut a long story short—my thesis is: reality is becoming cosmopolitical. There is no pure cosmopolitanism, there is only deformed cosmopolitanization. We, therefore, need a cosmopolitan social science. Cosmopolitanism is a long-sidelined concept recently reactivated by a wide range of social and political theorists.[1] Are they, are we—to put it in ironic terms—self-enclosed, jargon-ridden, hyper-theoretical white men in their late midlife crises, ignoring the excluded and generalizing their own frequent–traveller–cosmopolitanism to be the *conditio humana* at the beginning of the 21st century? No, definitely not. Again my argument is very simple: mainstream social sciences is doing a miserable job. Because of its historical genesis and by its basic framings, concepts and methodologies the social sciences are still prisoners of the nation-state. They misunderstand the realities and dynamics of a globalized world. In order to do their job, they have to overcome methodological nationalism and develop a methodological cosmopolitanism.[2]

In most cases the re-emergence of cosmopolitanism arises by way of a proposed normative or political position. Those positions refer to a vision of cosmopolitan democracy, world citizenship and global civil society. To me these approaches—intimately related to the philosophies of Kant, Habermas and others—are very important.[3] But I believe we have to take a more radical step. The classic attack to this philosophical cosmopolitanism from the 19th century until now has been as follows: it is nice but idealistic. Cosmopolitanism has been deeply associated with idealism. But the real world speaks the language of realism, that is nationalism. At the beginning of the 21st century this has to be turned upside down: nationalism is becoming unreal and idealistic, cosmopolitanism stands for realism in a world, which has become cosmopolitical in its core. That is what I call cosmopolitan realism.[4]

There has been, for example, a heated debate in the United States on off-shoring jobs.[5] The information technology that lets Westerners work from a coffee shop in New York or a pretty village in Bavaria also exposes them to the competition of a smart slum-dweller from Calcutta or Manila, who will gladly do the same day's work for what the Westeners make in an hour. A mouse click can deliver all kinds of services around the world. In the United States, which accounts for 70 percent of off-shoring, the process is climbing the corporate hierarchy, dislodging positions in software design, technological support, programming, and research and development. The reaction in the U.S. is mainly nationalistic and protectionist. Politicians accuse India of stealing American jobs. However, off-shoring is not really a job issue. It is a power issue.[6] More interestingly, it is an issue of power and counter-power: the most powerful democracy of the world, the American globalizer is experiencing (for a change), the out-of-control-feeling (in a tiny dose) which is the dominant feeling of so called third world inhabitants.[7] And this counter-power issue is at the same time an issue of real existing cosmopolitanization, of cosmopolitical realism, which has to become the subject of cosmopolitan social sciences. Therefore, we have to systematically unpack what the black-box known as globalization contains and hides.[8] In the following we will formulate ten theses on the distinction between normative cosmopolitanism and empirical-analytical cosmopolitanism in the social sciences.

THESES

(1) The national gaze is using zombie-categories which do not understand reality. Off-shoring is a good example here, so is jobless recovery. Both presuppose the national container, are partial notions that misunderstand, therefore, the transnational space open to the corporations to locate jobs *beyond* nation borders and national considerations.[9] Managers, even if they are deeply devoted to American patriotism on a personal level, do not have to off-shore but can create jobs in India for Indians. The latter is not because they want to make the world a better place, but because they cannot resist the chances and challenges of the global market economy. And for the same reason jobless growth is only jobless in national categories whereas it might create jobs in a transnational perspective. The excluded non-Western Other is suddenly omnipresent, even right in the center-point of Western national concerns; he or she can no longer be excluded. Therefore it is absurd that Western states heighten their walls against foreigners and point guns at them. So, this is what I mean by saying: reality is becoming cosmopolitical. Remarkably this happens in a non-cosmopolitan way,

in a way no cosmopolitan philosopher would have thought of: without a cosmopolitan public involved, without intention, decision-making, it happens unwanted, unseen, maybe even forced. It is, for sure, not an élite option, not restricted to the rich Western countries and its inhabitants, not addressed to someone who can claim to be a citizen of the world by virtue of independent means, expensive tastes and a globetrotting lifestyle. This is the reason why we do have to make a clear and sharp distinction between cosmopolitanism as a philosophical idea and principle and cosmopolitanization as a reality, which has to be studied by the social sciences. What we have to uncover and understand is the paradox of a *cosmopolitanization without cosmopolitans*.

Why do I use cosmopolitanization and not globalization here? Well, because a real existing cosmopolitanization realizes elements of the cosmopolitan dream, yet in an unexpectedly *deformed* way—involuntary unseen, often non-reflexive, creating ambivalent contradictory realities. What cosmopolitan idealists dreamed of, namely the inclusion of the excluded other, has become (in a specific sense) reality. You can be an alien, a non-citizen living elsewhere and at the same time be a neighbor, a competitor.[10] The inside–outside distinction, the nation–state distinction of who is a citizen and who is an alien, who is a member and who is not a member, who has the right to be recognized and who has no rights and can be ignored— don't work any more. The first modern order, which was built on a combination of universalism, relativism and nationalism, is collapsing. For nations, we might say that the universalism of sameness regulates internal relations while relativism and hierarchical otherness governs external relations. Cosmopolitan realism teaches: we are already mixed up with and against others.[11] Thus, non-interference or purification is no longer a choice for us. Rather, the question is how to get mixed, how to interfere and get interfered. Also, the choice that has to be made is not for off-shoring or high-wage jobs in America, but between off-shoring and immigration (or transmigration).

Cosmopolitanization does not come about as a victory of cosmopolitan ideas, parties, states, organizations, or movements. The cosmopolitanization of reality happens as an unintended result of a confluence of side effects of actions directed at other ends. It is this kind of non-cosmopolitan cosmopolitanization, which we have to come to terms with. In the debate on off-shoring the United States and Europe we suddenly have to include the world outside the United States and Europe. This is true even if the reaction is neo-nationalistic. In fact, protectionism and hate against foreigners may become the dominant reaction to cosmopolitanization.

(2) Cosmopolitanization does not create cosmopolitans. But it creates a new dialectics between cosmopolitanization and anti-cosmopolitanization. We can see this in the United States and even more strongly in Europe where anti-migration movements and politics are significantly on the rise

and gain more and more power The September 11 attacks on the World Trade Center and the Pentagon are another illustration of this complementary dialectics of cosmopolitanization and anti-cosmopolitanization. The massive destruction wrought by a global network of terrorists confirmed the growing importance of new actors and novel relations.[12] National sovereignty, state territory and military power, the traditional trappings of the most powerful state in modern times, succumbed to a surprise attack by non-state actors operating with very modest means on a global scale, and beyond the grasp of sovereign states.[13] Yet, the Al Qaeda network also highlights the dialectics of the anti-cosmopolitical attack enforcing cosmopolitanization. An astonishing diverse coalition of states rallied to the American call for a War on Terrorism. Governments everywhere were intent to defend or consolidate their power against the real or imagined threat of terrorism. But as the cosmopolitan perspective tells us, the dialectics between anti-cosmopolitanization and cosmopolitanization means different things in different world regions. In Washington's view, this was an act of war against the United States, justifying a military response.[14] Although initially European governments went along with this framing of the attack, it soon became evident that in European eyes, 9/11 was a crime that required patient police collaboration, intelligence sharing and quite possibly international legal proceedings. In Asia, finally, governments viewed 9/11 as a big event that made them pay especially careful attention to the U.S. in times of crisis.

(3) The reason for the attraction of the notion cosmopolitical for the social sciences is that it contains a specific model of handling diversity—not the either/or principle but a model or logic of handling diversity in accordance with the also/and realities. Cosmopolis means: every human being is a member of both: the cosmos also/and of the particular polities—cities, nations, ethnicities, religions.[15] And this model preserves through history a positive image which can be lived and politically organized. Referring to this cosmo-polis logic is not merely an intellectual trick. Up until now the either/or principle has been based on an underlying either/or reality of the social world in the nation-state modernity. One was either a member of this nation or that nation. One was in this nation or that nation. It was impossible to be in two places at once. Those once seemingly obvious rules no longer hold. In a cosmopolitized world it is possible to be part of India and part of America at the same time—and to be in India and in Chicago in every socially important way. One's day-to-day, real-time connection to family, friends and workmates, one's connection to the news of local events, one's situation vis-à-vis the future—in all these dimensions, it is quite possible to be in two places in one time. The underlying either/or of social reality is being steadily replaced by an also/and reality where most people have at least one person in another country with whom they are more closely connected than their next-door neighbour. The kind of thinking that can

comprehend this sort of reality without falling into apriories must develop an analogous form of also/and logic. There are quite a few concepts in use, which try to do this—like networks,[16] flows,[17] scapes.[18] But they do not point specifically at this also/and logic. Other notions like hybridity[19] or creolization[20] still depend on the either/or logic they try to overcome. And they are word monsters. Cosmopolitan is a positively named and valued descriptive model for also/and relationships, identities, logistics, responsibilities.

(4) In order to understand off-shoring (or generally speaking cosmopolitanization) in terms of the social sciences we need a cosmopolitan perspective. It sees the increased interdependence of social actors across national boundaries as an unintended and unforeseen side effect of actions that have no normative cosmopolitan intent. This cosmopolitan perspective is not a conquering gaze from nowhere, not a gaze that claims the power to see and not be seen, to represent while escaping representation. It is not a new name for the unwordliness of the Anglo-American and European humanities. For example, if you want to analyse off-shoring (I still use this zombie category) you have to include the excluded external perspective of the different actors in India. You have to follow the actors and integrate their perspective systematically into the sociological methodology. The methodological nationalism from this cosmopolitan outlook can and must be deconstructed and criticized as not only partial but false, universalizing a Euro-centric misunderstanding of reality. This observer's perspective is not global, but rather cosmopolitan because the global *ex*cludes the local, the cosmopolitan *in*cludes the local. Again it is glocal *also/and realities* which the social sciences have to grip.[21] For this I use the metaphor: having wings and roots at the same time.

INTERIM RESULTS

Let me summarize my argument so far. The cosmopolitan realism of the social sciences stands and falls with the distinction between normative cosmopolitanism and actually existing cosmopolitanization. The starting point here is a rejection of the claim that cosmopolitanism is a conscious, voluntary or élitist choice. The term cosmopolitanization of reality is meant to signalize that we are talking also, or even mainly, of a compulsory choice or of a side effect of unconscious decisions. As a rule, the choice to become a foreigner is not freely made but is the consequence of poverty and hardship, of flight from persecution or an attempted escape from starvation. But this forced cosmopolitanization does not yet seem to have moved forward to the state of conscious self-definition, nor has it been seized upon, therefore, as possible means of self-legitimation or self-defense. If the conservatives have been quick to attack the growing sensibility that supports multi-national inclusiveness they have been allowed to keep the term cosmopolitan for themselves. The attack that cosmopolitanism is only available to an élite—those who have the resources necessary to travel, learn other languages and absorb other cultures—therefore, blocks the understanding of reality.

Cosmopolitanization occurs beneath the surfaces, behind the persisting facades of national spaces and sovereignties where the main flags on display continue to proclaim national mentalities, identities and forms of consciousness. This latency makes cosmopolitanization—measurable by the high standards of ethical and academic morality—trivial, negligible or even dubious. This is a first major insight of cosmopolitan realism in the social sciences. A cosmopolitanism that people endure without wanting it, is undoubtedly a *deformed* cosmopolitanism. The existing forms of cosmopolitanization came into the world not as noble achievements that had been fought for and won with all the glittering moral authority of the Enlightenment but as profane deformations carrying the obscurity and anonymity of side effects.

MORE THESES

(5) Reality is becoming cosmopolitical in its core while our forms of thought and consciousness as well as the highways of academic teaching and research cover up the increasing unreality of the world of national states. A critique of the unreal study of the national, which dresses itself up in universalist clothes but can neither deny nor rise above its origins in the horizon of national experience, presupposes the cosmopolitan perspective and its methodological development. But how should the (latent) *cosmopolitanization of reality* be distinguished from a reflexive *cosmopolitan perspective*? The forced mixing of cultures is nothing new in world history—as post-colonialist theory and research have illustrated for so long.[22] On the contrary, it has been the rule through all the plunder and conquests, the migrations, slave trade and colonization, the ethnic cleansing, settlements and expulsions. From its very beginnings, the world market required this global mixing and—as the opening of Japan and China in the 19th century shows—imposed it when necessary by violent means. Capital tears down all national boundaries and jumbles together that which is one's own and that which is foreign.[23] What is new is not the compulsory mélange as such but the fact that it is noticed, becomes self-conscious and is politically shown off, the fact that it is *reflected* and *recognized* in the global public arena of mass media and international news, in the global social movements of blacks, women and minorities, in the popularity of old concepts such as diaspora in cultural theory, and also in projects to achieve a greater degree of self-activity.[24] It is this social and social-scientific reflexivity

which makes cosmopolitan perspective the key concept and issue of the reflexive Second Modernity.[25]

Cosmopolitanization, on this line, must be understood as a *multidimensional* process, which has irrevocably changed the historical nature of social worlds and the status of individual countries within those worlds. It involves the formation of multiple loyalties, the spread of various transnational lifestyles, the rise of non-state political actors (from Amnesty International to the World Trade Organization), and the development of global protest movements against (neoliberal) globalism and for a *different* (cosmopolitan) globalization involving the worldwide recognition of human rights, workers' rights, global protection of the environment, an end to poverty, and so on.[26] All these tendencies may be seen as the, however deformed, beginning of an *institutionalized cosmopolitanism*—paradoxically in the shape of anti-globalization movements or an International Criminal Court or the United Nations. When the UN Security Council passes a resolution, it is seen as speaking for humanity as a whole. And it is true: a cosmopolitan social science will be a part in the social and political construction of an institutionalized cosmopolitanism.

If it is asked who have been the guiding intellectual forces in this inner cosmopolitanization of national societies the names that come up are Adam Smith, Alexis de Tocqueville and John Dewey. And let's not forget the German classical thinkers of the past such as Immanuel Kant, Johann Wolfgang Goethe, Johann Gottfried Herder, Wilhelm von Humboldt, Friedrich Nietzsche, Karl Marx or Georg Simmel. All of them regard modernity as a move away from early conditions of relatively closed communities—a transition that took place mainly through the spread of commerce and the principles of republicanism.

(6) The cosmopolitan perspective calls into question one of the most important convictions concerning society and politics today: namely, that modern society and modern politics can be organized only in the form of national states. Society is equated with national-territorial society organized in states. When social players subscribe to this belief, I speak of a national perspective; when it defines the perspective of a scientific observer, I speak of methodological nationalism. This distinction between the perspectives of social actors and social scientists is important because the link between the two is not logical but only historical. The rise of sociology coincided with the rise of the national state, nationalism and the system of international politics.[27] This historical connection alone gave rise to the axioms of methodological nationalism, according to which nation, state and society are the natural social and political forms of the modern world.

The whole world that is being shaken to its foundations cannot be grasped, investigated or explained either within the national perspective (of social players) or within the framework of methodological nationalism (the perspective of the scientific observer). The cosmopolitan social science then focuses on the growing contradiction between methodological nationalism and the actual cosmopolitanization of reality. It demonstrates a number of assumptions and errors of methodological nationalism: subsumption of society under the national state; generalization from one society to all others; a territorial conception of culture; a misguided equation of international with cosmopolitan.

(7) Cut-lining a cosmopolitan research program for the social sciences, we have to identify different areas on which the perspective shift from methodological nationalism to *methodological cosmopolitanism* should concentrate. One major example is global risk society: The arenas and conflicts of global public space result from the reactions called forth by the unintended side effects of radical modernization; or, to put it more precisely, the risks of modern society (terrorism, environmental dangers, etc.) are transnational and global in their inner logic, and all attempts to control them throw up global arenas of debate and conflict that do not necessarily lead to global solutions.

As I have argued before, cosmopolitanization usually occurs as a forced and unintended side effect. It is quite another question whether this side-effect then becomes conscious—leading to a cosmopolitan perspective—or even produces a global public space.[28] The theory of world risk society offers a model of interdependence crises that makes it possible to study theoretically and empirically this connection between latent, forced cosmopolitanization and world public awareness of it through the outbreak of scandals.[29] This can be seen from the major risk conflicts of the past twenty years: the nuclear reactor disaster at Chernobyl, the AIDS and BSE (Mad Cow Disease) crises, the controversy over genetically modified Frankenstein foods, and the birth of a global terror risk on September 11, 2001.[30] Here you can study the law of double side effects.[31] It always applies: The self-endangering civilization produces first-grade side effects—less rather than more calculable risks and uncertainties—which in turn generate, as second-grade side effects, cross-border publics and corresponding devaluations of products, everyday practices and bureaucratic routines, new market breakthroughs and allocations of responsibility, and all the related costs, conflicts, commonalities and pressures for action.[32] Both the first-grade and second-grade side effects produce and accelerate cosmopolitanization through interdependence and reflexive globality—indeed, the relationship between the two indicates how latent, forced cosmopolitanization can change into a forced awareness of a globally shared collective future.

A change of focus is necessary to elucidate this perspective. For, unlike in conventional political theory, it is not the decision itself but its unpredictable consequences and risks, which are here the source of the public and the political. In a global public sensitive to risk, the question of power is posed especially in relation to consequences that are experienced as unimaginable and unthinkable. The resulting responsibility beyond frontiers for shared risks is negatively defined in two ways. On the one hand, it is directed towards things that must on no account exist; and it does not involve an integration of values (such as methodological nationalism postulates), but rather an integration of dangers and defenses against danger, whose bonding power grows with the extent of the perceived danger. Instead of national and universal integration of values, then, the global character of dangers reflected in a world public brings with it a new dialectic of conflict and cooperation beyond frontiers. Only in this way, that is on pain of disaster, can the necessary formulas be found and negotiated for a consensus on international action and institutions. It remains an open question, of course, whether this will actually happen.

(8) Thesis eight is about *post*-international politics. The cosmopolitan perspective also makes it possible to go beyond the vision of international relations and to analyze the multiple forms of interdependence not only between states but also between other players at various level of aggregation. A transition is taking place from a politics centered upon national states and international security to a *risk politics* that is *post-international and no longer centered upon national states*. This paradigm shift corresponds to the distinction between first and second modernity. The high-modern period of classical nation-states showed to its best advantage a structural and political logic, which has become clearly distinguishable only as the end of the Cold War brings on its own demise. That logic involved sharply defined boundaries not only between different nations and states but, more generally, among people, things and functional or practical fields; it thus brought about—at least at the level of expectations—clear-cut attributions of responsibility and competence. Today, by contrast, side effects of radical modernization reflected at the level of a global public create an awareness of new global dangers. This globality, together with the fact that the dangers to civilization are known to be incalculable, has been eroding basic distinctions and institutions of the first modernity. Whereas the dangers in the first modernity were limited and easy to pinpoint (imperial, geostrategic, ideological, military and economic interests of powerful national states, in a situation defined by rearmament, arms races, corresponding counter-strategies and calculable diplomacy), what we now see are unlimited risks and uncertainties that are much harder to identify (transnational terrorism, climatic disasters, contested water resources, migration flows, AIDS, genetically modified foods, BSE, computer viruses able to cripple civil and military communications, and so on).[33] Then, conscious knowledge and calculability that presupposed state sovereignty; now, conscious lack of knowledge, or non-conscious lack of knowledge and incalculability, that are canceling state sovereignty. Then, prevention following the logic of deterrence; now, prevention corresponding to the logic of inter-state and post-state cooperation. This entails, however, the beginning of struggles over the

form and content of *institutionalized cosmopolitanism*, in the sense of lasting cooperation among state and post-state players in the global and local space (civil society groups and networks, corporations, international organizations, the UN, churches, etc.).

(9) Denationalized social sciences may further cast light on global inequalities that have previously been concealed by the focus on national inequalities and their legitimation. We are confronted with the paradox that, whereas global inequalities are growing dramatically, they receive only marginal attention if any in methodological nationalism. How is this to be understood? In sociology oriented to national states, the standard justification for social inequalities is in terms of the performance principle. This applies to inequalities within individual countries. But the cosmopolitan perspective takes this a stage further and shows how the nation-state principle functions as a legitimation for global inequalities.[34] The key point here is that, in keeping with the introverted character of the national perspective, the nation-state principle conceals global inequalities from view. Since methodological nationalism focuses on inequalities inside countries, it can neither systematically address nor answer the questions of the legitimation of global inequalities and the transnationalization of social inequalities.

The performance principle enables a positive legitimation of intranational inequalities, whereas the nation-state principle rests upon a 'negative' legitimation of global inequalities. Positive legitimation means that the performance principle functions as a reciprocal and reflexive legitimation of experienced inequality. Performance (however it may be operationalized) is the yardstick that makes it possible, at least in principle, for even those directly affected to distinguish between legitimate and illegitimate distribution of wealth. The nation-state principle, on the other hand, should be conceived as a negative mode of legitimation, because it takes no account of global inequalities. Performance comparison internally is combined with institutional blindness externally. This excludes acceptance of those who are excluded as poor. Upon closer examination, then, the nation-state principle does not legitimate global inequalities. Rather, the introverted character of the national perspective makes invisible, and hence stabilizes, the lack of legitimation.

Which are the principles underlying this institutionalized invisibility of global inequalities? Just as, in the national perspective, world society is fragmented into separate territorially defined and state-organized societies that are inwardly oriented and outwardly closed, so are the realities, conflicts and dynamics of global inequality fragmented into national inequalities that cease even to appear as global in the horizon of national sociologies. In the national perspective, social inequalities are located in the interrelationship between the welfare system and the individual; the responsibility for inequality is attributed partly to the state and partly to individuals. Justice is defined accordingly, and so, too, are social claims on state distributive policy articulated and pursued. This motivates and activates social movements, such as the labor or women's movement, which denounce their respective lack of privileges and demand compensatory payments from the state.

It is commonly suspected that national inequalities may be not nationally but globally determined, that they may be due to global capital flows, crises and upheavals, but this idea is not often thought through and consistently explored. Only in a cosmopolitan perspective—a cosmopolitan way of looking at national as well as global and transnational inequalities—is this caging of thought and investigation both manifest and capable of being overcome; only here do national welfare states cease to be the focus of attention only as guarantors of individual social security. The question then becomes how, and to what extent, national welfare states shift poverty risks on to other states and countries.

(10) Let me return to my question from the beginning: Why do we need a cosmopolitan social sciences and what does that mean? We cannot just use the term globalization or globalizing world because we have to unpack it. There are three reactions to globalization in the social sciences: first, *dismissal*; second, conceptual clarification and empirical-operational *definition*; and third, *epistemological turn*. In a first reaction, the mainstream denied the reality or importance of (economic) globalization and maintained that there was nothing historically new in any of the phenomena coming under the term. This dismissal became less convincing, however, as researchers in all the social sciences got down to the task of conceptualizing the various aspects of globalization and attempted to locate and study them both theoretically and empirically.[35]

In so far as this was successful, an *epistemological turn* has become necessary: that is, it became more widely understood that, if the distinctions and boundaries between internal and external, national and international, local and global, us and others collapse or are being mixed, then the units, issues and basic concepts in each of the social sciences become contingent. Sociology and political science, in particular, but in different ways also ethnography, anthropology, geography and history have usually taken certain units for granted in their theories and research practices, in order then to subject them to systematic study and comparison. But what happens if in reality the premises and boundaries defining those units fall apart and are being mixed? The answer that has been outlined here is that a whole set of concepts associated with the national perspective become disenchanted: that is, deontologized, historicized, stripped of their inner necessity. To be sure, this occurs only within an interpretative framework in which *methodology replaces ontology*, such that methodological cosmopolitanism replaces the nationally centered ontology and imagination dominating thought and action.

RESULTS

What are some of the advantages, what are some of the disadvantages when using the term cosmopolitan for this renewal of the social sciences? Why not use similar terms, like de-national or trans-national or the new metaphors networks, flows, scapes, fluidity, hybridity, creolization, global mélange? We all got the same problem of naming and we all know those problems are as arbitrary as unsolvable. At the same time we all know too that in order to provoke an epistemological shift the Babylonian confusion of languages is not very helpful. Therefore it is necessary that everybody is talking in his or her own language. Trying to explore into some terminological consensus could indeed become quite a challenging test for methodological cosmopolitanism. How far do we acknowledge the otherness of other definitions (or definitions of otherness) in the social sciences? Where are the limits of acceptable disagreements? Who decides upon those? Again, what makes the c-word valuable, usable, attractive, practical, rich, open for a new methodology? It is not a monster word or a word monster like hybridization or creolization. It does have instead a real and long history in philosophy and politics and religion.[36] And these histories are not only related to Europe but go back, for example, to the ancient Islamic mixture of cultures. So the term cosmopolitanism itself has roots and wings.

These roots of cosmopolitanisms (plural!) and cosmopolitan perspectives contain, keep and cover the treasure of a logical also/and model how to handle, live and describe cultural diversity: *affirmation of the other as different but equal*. It rejects the either/or alternative between hierarchical difference and universal sameness. It rejects the either/or alternative between territorial-bounded national and ethnical identities without denying the historical narrative behind them.

Of course, methodological cosmopolitanism presupposes concepts like de-nationalization, transnationalization, network, scapes, interconnectedness, etc. But it has another major advantage: All those concepts are framed in terms of an extension of loyalties, identities, responsibilities across *space*, not across *time* and *history*. They carry a *spatial bias*.[37] They, therefore, can lead to a reification of global social relationships into an abstract global present: into the *metaphysics* of the present. In any case, the historical dimension that cosmopolitanism stands for and opens up, is largely ignored or forgotten. The cosmopolitan social sciences have to come to terms with the past of cosmopolitanization processes that stretch centuries. They have to look towards futures that are already partially determined by the action of the present. They cannot concern merely the well-being of the living but have to realize the responsibilities towards past and future generations, that both effect and are affected by cosmopolitan ideas and practices.[38] The cosmopolitan perspective and methodology stand for this deepening of understanding of political communities in the past and in the future. It involves not restoration of the past but reparation for the wrongs committed in the past which still haunt the present and the future—the consequences of colonialism, the slave system, the holocaust.

Here, at the latest, it is necessary to warn of a possible false conclusion. The basic fact that human experiential space is being subtly changed through an opening to cosmopolitanization should not lead us to assume that we are all becoming cosmopolitans. In fact, it is important to take early action against a cosmopolitan *myth* that life between frontiers or in the diaspora automatically implies greater openness to the world. Cosmopolitan realism says: Cosmopolitanization and anti-cosmopolitanization mesh with each other. But the inner cosmopolitanization of nationally conceived and organized societies also increases the likelihood of a *national* false fabrication of facts and data. The omnipresence of the cultural other dissolves the certainty of universalizing meanings that most of the quantitative research methods depend on. How to conduct research with an other who is at the same time included and excluded is an open and challenging question for cosmopolitan social sciences, as well as a clear indication and justification for the need of methodological cosmopolitanism. The critique of the fabrication of nationally homogenized false facts applies not least to many of the statistics that are worked up and interpreted by nationally oriented mainstream economics and social sciences.[39]

Of course, there are disadvantages, too. I have mentioned some of them already, such as the élitist connotation of cosmopolitanism that sounds so imperialistic in post-colonial ears. One of the differences between cosmopolitan idealism and cosmopolitan realism is that the latter has to pose the question about its own unwanted side effects and dark sides right into the center of attention. Even if this is not intended, the term cosmopolitan can and will be used ideologically, for example, to justify new wars[40] and the growth of the military budgets. Cosmopolitan acknowledgement of diversity can always fall into the shallow differences that constitute the global market place. I am sure those are some of the questions which we have to address and discuss today and tomorrow and maybe even in the days to come long after that tomorrow.

NOTES

1. Breckenridge, Carol A., Sheldon Pollock, Homi K. Bhabha, and Dipesh Chakrabarty, ed. *Cosmopolitanism.* Durham: Duke UP, 2002.
2. Compare Beck, Ulrich. "Toward a New Critical Theory with a Cosmopolitan Intent." *Constellations* 104 (2003): 453–468; Beck, Ulrich. "Beyond Class and Nation: Reframing Social Inequalities in a Globalizing World." *British Journal of Scoiology* 58 (2007): 679–705; Wimmer, Andreas, and Nina Glick Schiller. "Methodological Nationalism and Beyond: Nation-State Building, Migration and the Social Sciences." *Global Networks* 24 (2002): 301–334.
3. See in particular Fine, Robert. "Kant's Theory of Cosmoplitanism and Hegel's Critique." *Philosophy & Social Criticism* 296 (2003): 609–630;

Fine, Robert, and Will Smith. "Jürgen Habermas's Theory of Cosmopolitanism." *Constellations* 104 (2003): 469–487.

4. Beck, Ulrich. *The Cosmopolitan Vision.* Cambridge: Polity Press, 2006.

5. For example, Lohr, Steve. "Offshore Jobs in Technology: Opportunity or a Threat?" *New York Times* 22 Dec. 2003.

6. Beck, Ulrich. *Power in the Global Age: A New Global Political Economy.* Cambridge: Polity Press, 2005.

7. Huntington, Samuel P. *Who Are We? The Challenges to America's National Identity.* New York: Simon & Schuster, 2004.

8. Beck, Ulrich. *What is Globalization?* Cambridge: Polity Press, 2000; Beck, Ulrich, and Natan Sznaider. "Unpacking Cosmopolitanism for the Social Sciences: A Research Agenda." *British Journal of Sociology* 57 (2006): 1–23.

9. Basch, Linda, Nina Glick Schiller, and Cristina Szanton Blanc. *Nations Unbound: Transnational Projects, Postcolonial Predicaments, and Deterritorialized Nation-States.* Langhorne: Gordan and Breach, 1994; Pries, Ludger, ed. *New Transnational Social Spaces: International Migration and Transnational Companies in the Early 21st Century.* London, New York: Routledge 2001; Levitt, Peggy, and Ninna Nyberg-Sorensen. "The Transnational Turn in Migration Studies." *Global Migration Perspectives* 6 (2004): 1–13.

10. Hiebert, Daniel. "Cosmopolitanism at the Local Level: The Development of Transnational Neighborhoods." *Conceiving Cosmopolitanism: Theory, Content, and Practice.* Ed. Steven Vertovec and Robin Cohen. Oxford: Oxford UP, 2002. 209–226.

11. Bhabha, Homi K. ed., *Nation and Narration.* London, New York: Routledge, 1990; Bhabha, Homi K. *The Location of Culture.* London, New York: Routledge, 1994.

12. Beck, Ulrich. "The Terrorist Threat: World Risk Society Revisited." *Theory, Culture & Society* 19 (2002): 39–55; Appadurai, Arjun. *Fear of Small Numbers: An Essay on the Geography of Anger.* Durham: Duke UP, 2006.

13. Sassen, Saskia. *Losing Control? Sovereignty in an Age of Globalization.* New York: Columbia UP 1996; Sassen, Saskia. *Denationalization: Territory, Authority, and Rights in a Global Digital Age.* Princeton: Princeton UP, 2005.

14. Litvak, Robert. *Regime Change: U.S. Strategy Through the Prism of 9/11.* Baltimore: Johns Hopkins UP, 2007.

15. Toulmin, Stephen. *Cosmopolis: The Hidden Agenda of Modernity.* New York: The Free Press, 1990.

16. Castells, Manuel. *The Information Age: Economy, Society, and Culture.* Vol. 1: *The Rise of the Network Society.* Oxford: Blackwell, 1996.

17. Hannerz, Ulf. *Cultural Complexity: Studies in the Sociological Organization of Meaning.* New York: Columbia UP, 1993; Hannerz, Ulf. "Fluxos, fronteiras, híbridos: palavras-chave da antropologia transnacional." *Mana* 3 (1997): 7–35.

18. Appadurai, Arjun. *Modernity at Large: Cultural Dimensions of Globalization.* Minneapolis: Minneapolis UP, 1996.

19. Bhabha. *The Location of Culture*; Nederveen Pieterse, Jan. *Globalization and Culture: Global Mélange.* Boulder: Rowman & Littlefield, 2003.

20. Smith, Norval, and Tonjes Veenstra, ed. *Creolization and Contact.* Amsterdam: John Benjamin's Publishing, 2001; Stewart, Charles, ed. *Creolization. History, Ethnography, Theory.* Walnut Creek: Left Coast Press, 2007.

21. Robertson, Roland. "Glocalization: Time-Space and Homogeneity-Heterogeneity." *Global Modernities.* Ed. Mike Featherstone, Scott Lash, and Roland Robertson. London: Sage, 1995. 25–44.

22. Dirlik, Arif. *The Postcolonial Aura: Third World Criticism in the Age of Global Capitalism.* Boulder: Westview Press, 1997; Young, Robert J. C. *Postcolonialism: A Historical Introduction.* Oxford: Blackwell, 2001.
23. Cohen, Robin. *Migration and its Enemies: Global Capital, Migrant labour and the Nation-state.* Aldershot: Ashgate, 2006.
24. Evans Braziel, Jana, and Anita Mannur, ed. *Theorizing Diaspora.* Oxford: Blackwell, 2003; Sheffer, Gabriel. *Diaspora Politics: At Home Abroad.* Cambridge: Cambridge UP, 2003.
25. Beck, Ulrich, and Christoph Lau. "Second Modernity as a Research Agenda: Theoretical and Empirical Explorations in the Meta-Change of Modern Society." *British Journal of Sociology* 56 (2005): 525–558.
26. Cohen, Robin, and Shirin Rai, ed. *Global Social Movements.* London: Athlone, 2000; Keck, Margaret E., and Kathryn Sikkink. *Activists Beyond Borders: Advocacy Networks in International Politics.* Ithaca: Cornell UP, 1998.
27. Smith, Anthony D. "Nationalism and Classical Social Theory." *British Journal of Sociology* 34 (1983): 19–38.
28. Stichweh, Rudolf. "The Genesis of a Global Public Sphere." *Development* 46 (2003): 26–29.
29. Beck, Ulrich. *World Risk Society.* Cambridge: Polity Press, 1999; see also Beck, Ulrich. *Weltrisikogesellschaft: Auf der Suche nach der verlorenen Sicherheit.* Frankfurt am Main: Suhrkamp, 2007 (within is a completely rewritten version); Adam, Barbara, Ulrich Beck, and Joost van Loon. *Risk Society and Beyond: Critical Issues for Social Theory.* London: Sage, 2000.
30. Wessler, Hartmut. "Can There Be a Global Public Sphere? September 11 in the World's Media." *Mapping the World: New Perspectives in the Humanities and Social Sciences.* Ed. Freia Hardt. Tübingen: Francke, 2004. 179–188; Samhat, Nayef H., and Rodger A. Payne. "American Foreign Policy and the Global Public Sphere." *Peace Review* 18 (2006): 251–259.
31. Woodward, Paul A., ed. *The Doctrine of Double Effect: Philosopher's Debate a Controversial Moral Principle.* Notre Dame: Notre Dame UP, 2001; Bomann-Larsen, Lene, and Oddny Wiggen, ed. *Responsibility in World Business: Managing Harmful Side-Effects of Corporate Activity.* Tokyo: United Nations UP, 2004.
32. Sassen, Saskia. "When National Territory is Home to the Global: Old Borders to Novel Borderings." *New Political Economy* 10 (2005): 523–541.
33. For example Barnett, Tony, and Alan Whiteside. *AIDS in the Twenty-First Century: Disease and Globalization.* New York: Palgrave Macmillan, 2003.
34. Sernau, Scott R. *Worlds Apart: Social Inequalities in a Global Economy.* Thousand Oaks: Pine Forge Press, 2005.
35. Held, David, Anthony McGrew, David Goldblatt, and Jonathan Perraton. *Global Transformations: Politics, Economics, and Culture.* Cambridge: Polity Press, 1999.
36. Heater, Derek. *World Citizenship and Government: Cosmopolitan Ideas in the History of Western Political Thought.* Houndsmill: MacMillan, 1996; Meijer, Roel, ed. *Cosmopolitanism, Identiy, and Authenticity in the Middle East.* London, New York: Routledge, 1999.
37. Massey, Doreen. *For Place.* London: Sage, 2005.
38. Levy, Daniel, and Natan Sznaider. *The Holocaust and Memory in the Global Age.* Philadelphia: Temple UP, 2005.
39. Beck-Gernsheim, Elisabeth. *Wir und die anderen: Vom Blick der Deutschen auf Migranten und Minderheiten.* Frankfurt am Main: Suhrkamp, 2004.
40. Kaldor, Mary. *New and Old Wars: Organised Violence in a Global Era.* Cambridge: Polity Press, 1999.

2 Encounters in the Third Space
Links Between Intercultural Communication Theories and Postcolonial Approaches[1]

Britta Kalscheuer

THE CHALLENGE OF INTERCULTURAL COMMUNICATION

In a globalized world, where intercultural contacts increase significantly because of new communication and information technologies as well as improved transport systems, intercultural communication becomes one of the major challenges. Today, more people than ever are confronted by foreigners, e.g. students, business people and tourists. This development does not only imply great opportunities but it also has potential for conflicts. While the chance to learn from people with divergent cultural backgrounds is quite obvious, a rather problematic aspect, that accompanies the learning process, is not always seen clearly: The fact, that members of all cultures have to cope with people from divergent cultures may contribute to a strengthening of the boundary between oneself and the other—it is a widespread attitude to perceive the foreign as a threat for one's own identity, which therefore needs to be defended. That's why intercultural communication becomes so important and its main task is to make sure that cultural differences do not become a barrier to mutual understanding.

The SIETAR (Society for Intercultural Education, Training, and Research) was established in 1975. Since then, intercultural understanding—which marks the endpoint of the intercultural communication process as such—has become one of the most pressing tasks. To make it happen is just as important today as it was in the 1970s. Correspondingly, one can observe a continuous if not an increasing amount of publications on intercultural topics, especially intercultural communication and intercultural competence, in the course of at least the last four decades.[2] Today, intercultural communication has become a standard topic of research.

In the meantime, many divergent definitions of intercultural communication and related concepts arose in the debate; there is no agreement on one singular definition though. Nevertheless, many of the intercultural approaches use the term intercultural communication in the sense outlined by the anthropologist Edward Twitchell Hall. He is generally perceived as the founder of intercultural communication research. Hall initiated it more than fifty years ago and his interpersonal approach to intercultural communication is still the predominant one in intercultural communication endeavors today. In accordance with Hall's interpersonal approach to intercultural communication, many interculturalists define intercultural communication very broadly as communication between members of different cultures. Samovar and Porter, for example, give the following definition: 'Whenever the parties to a communication act bring with them different experiential backgrounds that reflect a long-standing deposit of group experience, knowledge and values, we have intercultural communication.'[3]

THE RISE OF INTERCULTURAL COMMUNICATION THEORIES IN THE UNITED STATES

The United States was the first to become involved in intercultural communication. As Japan became especially more important in economics, some American researchers began to deal with its cultural specifics, not only in order to find out reasons for the immense economic growth, but also to prepare American business people for their encounters with the Japanese. The interest was mainly a pragmatic one; its intention was to understand cultural differences and thereby ensure that they did not become a barrier to intercultural communication (and in the end to their own economic interests).

Hall had a rather pragmatic interest in intercultural communication. He did not intend to found intercultural communication as a scientific discipline. Nonetheless, today he is seen as having done exactly this. The following brief overview of the history of intercultural communication in the United States follows the system of Chen and Starosta.[4]

After Hall introduced the term intercultural communication in the late 1950s, it took some time to widen the field of intercultural communication and to introduce it as a scientific discipline. But since the 1970s, the debate on intercultural communication has developed quickly. By the end of the decade Asante and Gudykunst edited the *Handbook of International and Intercultural Communication*.[5] Two years before, the first volume of the *International Journal of Intercultural Communication* was published, which until today is one of the most important journals on intercultural communication. Moreover, Samovar and Porter published their first reader on intercultural communication, which has been republished every few years,[6] and Condon and Yousef published their introduction to intercultural communication.[7] Other important works emerged during this period: Prosser's *Intercommunication Among Nations and People* and Dodd's *Perspectives on Cross-Cultural Communication*.[8] These early works on intercultural communication are still today, of great importance. Overall, the 1970s central feature in the intercultural landscape was confusion.

In the 1980's, Condon and Yousef, as well as Samovar and Porter, continued to integrate intercultural communication as a scientific discipline. The debates in the United States were interdisciplinary in nature. Then another prominent representative of intercultural communication theory entered the debate: William B. Gudykunst. He is not only the author of *Intercultural Communication Theory* and co-editor of the volume *Theories in Intercultural Communication*, he is also co-editor of the *Handbook of International and Intercultural Communication*.[9] In the 1980's, Gudykunst was one of the central figures engaged in intercultural communication. Thanks to him, intercultural communication could now be distinguished from cross-cultural, international and mass media communication. Yet, Gudykunst was not the only important person to emerge on the scientific platform. Kincaid published his *Communication Theory: Eastern and Western Perspectives*, which is currently one of the few and very important attempts to combine Western and non-Western concepts.[10] Finally, the most important institution of intercultural communication was founded: the SIETAR (Society for Intercultural Education, Training and Research). Its foundation was an important step towards the institutionalization of intercultural communication. Nowadays, it is acknowledged worldwide as an arena to discuss questions and problems, which emerge in intercultural contexts.

From the 1980s onwards, intercultural communication became self-employed. Many textbooks on intercultural communication and on intercultural training appeared. Besides, the works of some of the most important researchers in the field of intercultural communication are re-edited every few years and in the United States numerous introductions to intercultural communication theory and praxis are published.

Without doubt, the United States was the first to become involved in intercultural communication, but step-by-step the debate spread to other countries. It must not be ignored, that intercultural communication endeavors are embedded in different socio-historical and cultural contexts, which place different value on it. Besides, unlike the interdisciplinary nature of intercultural communication in the U.S., it seems to be a German peculiarity that new intercultural disciplines emerged within the already established ones.

SILENT LANGUAGES AND HIDDEN DIFFERENCES:
THE APPROACH OF EDWARD T. HALL

The origin of the establishment of intercultural communication as a discipline can be traced back to Hall, who is broadly accepted as the founder of all intercultural communication endeavors.[11] As early as in the 1950s—during his work at the Foreign Service Center (FSC)—Hall recognized the importance of cultural differences in cross-cultural situations, where members of different cultures meet. His intention was to describe cultural differences, which affect the communication styles, not to develop a meta-theory of culture. Hall began to publish his ideas on intercultural communication not until he had finished his engagement at the FSC. In 1959, he published the book *Silent Language*, in which he introduced the term intercultural communication. Other books, which summarize his work experiences on cultural differences at the FSC, followed.[12]

Central to Hall's approach to intercultural communication is the assumption that all cultures have an identity of their own, which guarantees that people refer to a common set of values and beliefs. All of these form the material of the *covert culture*. Unlike the *overt culture*, elements of the covert culture are not part of individual awareness and reflection. It was Hall's deepest conviction that cultures hide more than they reveal: 'Each culture has a hidden code of behavior that can rarely be understood without a code breaker. Even though culture is experienced personally [. . .], it is nonetheless a shared system. Members of a common culture not only share information, they share methods of coding, storing, and retrieving that information.'[13]

As long as people are not confronted with members of a different culture, their own culture seems natural and unquestioned. But Hall is quite right to ask, how long one can afford to ignore one's own cultural dimension?[14] Because the members of a specific culture normally are not aware of the constituents of their own unique culture, the primary task is to understand one's own culture, first.[15] According to Hall everyone perceives the world in a specific way:

> The concept that no two people see exactly the same thing when actively using their eyes [. . .] is shocking to some people because it implies that not all men relate to the world around them in the same way. Without recognition of these differences, however, the process of translating from one perceptual world to another cannot take place. The distance between the perceptual worlds of two people of the same culture is certainly less than between two people of different cultures, but it can still present problems.[16]

Correspondingly, the risk that different worldviews lead to misunderstandings is even higher in cross-cultural situations. In general, different worldviews in interactions are held responsible for problems and misunderstandings:

> In the briefest possible sense, the message of this book is that no matter how hard man tries it is impossible for him to divest himself of his own culture, for it has penetrated to the roots of his nervous system and determines how he perceives the world. Most of culture lies hidden and is outside voluntary control, making up the way and weft of human existence. Even when small fragments of culture are elevated

to awareness, they are difficult to change, not only because they are so personally experienced but *because people cannot act or interact at all in any meaningful ways except through the medium of culture.*[17]

As soon as one has learned to think and behave in a specific way, it is very difficult to change this attitude.[18] Paradoxically, in order to be an effective intercultural communicator, it is required to be in a permanent move and change of attitudes. All people tend to consider their own cultural beliefs as universal ones. The risk in intercultural communication lies in the fact that neither side accepts the cultural specifics of other cultures as equally true.

The denial of the (partial) validity of conflicting worldviews represents a great barrier in cross-cultural situations. Some of the problems that arise in intercultural contexts have to do with the fact that little is known about cross-cultural communication. When it becomes apparent that members of different cultures do not understand each other, each side blames the other one. Cultural blindness hinders the acceptance of different cultural identities. Nonetheless, Hall considers diversity as something very positive.[19] The capability to extend ones culture is a necessary one to achieve understanding in intercultural situations.[20]

In agreement with his argument that culture influences the communication styles, Hall searches for standards which allow a comparison (and understanding) of different cultures. In Hall's view, cultural differences not only affect verbal, but also nonverbal communication values, beliefs and worldviews. In cooperation with his colleague Trager he developed a map of culture, which consists of ten primary message systems.[21] Until today, research on cultural dimensions (e.g. the classification of cultures) is a central part of all intercultural endeavors.

One way to approach cultural differences is Hall's proxemic view. Its starting point is that all men structure their space in a unique way. Proxemics serves to learn about the ways different degrees of (spatial) nearness affect behavioral patterns.[22] In this view, space (e.g. distance) is a cultural dimension which influences how people perceive the world. Differences in the distance people need to feel comfortable in an interaction sequence can lead to problems and misunderstandings.

But space is not the only dimension which is culturally specific, another one is time: 'A complicating factor in intercultural relations is that each culture has its own time frames in which patterns are unique. This means that to function effectively abroad it is just as necessary to learn the language of time as it is to learn the spoken language.'[23] His book *The Dance of Life* deals with the question how members of different cultures handle time: 'It deals with the most personal of all experiences: how people are tied together and yet isolated from each other by invisible threads of rhythm and hidden walls of time. Time is treated as a language, as a primary organizer for all activities, a synthesizer and integrator.'[24] According to Hall, each culture has its own rhythm. This leads him to distinguish between monochronic and polychronic cultures, two systems which differ logically and empirically and which do not mix: 'M-time is also tangible; we speak of it as being saved, spent, wasted, lost, made up, crawling, killed and running out. These metaphors must be taken seriously. M-time scheduling is used as a classification system that orders life. The rules apply do everything except birth and death.'[25] On the other hand, polychronic time is less scheduled and more spontaneous; people of polychronic cultures often do several things at once or break the rigid order of the schedule.

Finally, Hall introduces another cultural dimension, which refers to the degree of information transported through the context in the communication process. His starting point is that everything is determined by the degree of contextualization: 'The level of context determines everything about the nature of communication and is the foundation in which all subsequent behavior rests.'[26] Culture selects what is, and what is not perceived by its members:

> One of the functions of culture is to provide a highly selective screen between man and the outside world. In its many forms, culture therefore designates what we pay attention to and what we ignore. This screening function provides structure for the world and protects the nervous system from 'information overload.' Information overload is a technical term applied to information-processing systems. It describes a situation in which the system breaks down when it cannot properly handle the huge volume of information to which it is subjected.[27]

In accordance to the degree, information is verbalized or not, Hall distinguishes between high and low-context cultures: While in low-context cultures almost everything has to be verbalized, high-context cultures transport a great deal of the information by the context, (e.g. non-verbal codes): 'A high-context (HC) communication or message is one in which most of the information is either in the physical context or internalized in the person, while very little is in the coded, explicit, transmitted part of the message. A low-context (LC) communication is just the opposite; i.e. the mass of information is vested in the explicit code.'[28]

The aforementioned cultural dimensions are all etic ones. Etic concepts are concepts which are viewed as universal ones. It is believed that the concepts can be used in order to measure and classify the markedness of the universal in a specific culture. Most of the cultural dimensions presented in the intercultural discourse are etic ones, for example, the dimensions of Hofstede and also the ones of Hampden-Turner and Trompenaars.[29] Etic concepts are criticized for their underlying universalism, which is not regarded as the appropriate way to understand the inner logic of a foreign culture. Therefore, they have been complemented by emic concepts, which have been developed from inside the foreign culture. They are less popular in the intercultural communication discourse but examples for the Chinese culture are the concept of *face* and *guanxi*.[30]

TOWARDS A CRITIQUE OF INTERCULTURAL COMMUNICATION THEORY

It is not the main purpose of this article to give an overview on intercultural communication theories or to formulate a broad critique. Instead, its intention is to hint to several difficulties, which are indicated in intercultural communication theories. The aim is to create a critical consciousness in order to improve further intercultural communication endeavors so that they better fulfil their purpose in the contemporary world, which is more complex than the majority of intercultural communication theory assumes. Many intercultural theories are still formulated in the tradition of the grounding father Edward T. Hall, whose approach has been presented. The interpersonal approach to intercultural communication dominates the field.

As stated before, Hall's starting point is the assumption that all cultures are unique. Whereas communication in the monocultural field is facilitated by a system of common beliefs and values, cultural differences are visible in the intercultural field, when members of divergent cultures meet. No common set of beliefs and values exists to which people from divergent cultures can refer. This is the main reason for the problems, irritations and misunderstandings that emerge in the intercultural context. Intercultural communication is generally regarded as 'problem solver'; its task is to avoid that cultural differences harm the communication process between members of divergent cultures.

Paradoxically, most publications on intercultural communication evoke the impression that cultural differences are unbridgeable; on the surface of the discourse appears a cultural relativism that implies an equality of *all* cultures and *all* members of a culture. However, the relativism, which may be perceived at first glance, is deceptive: Under the cloak of this relativism and equality can be discovered a hidden universalistic tendency based on 'Western' normative concepts like intercultural communication, intercultural understanding, human nature and so on. Most of the approaches are deeply rooted in 'Western' culture and its particularity. European and American ('Western') values are seen as necessary and valid for *all* cultures. Similarly, 'Western' scientific concepts are viewed as valid for *all* cultures, too. Insofar Miike's question, if the intercultural field is truly intercultural is a rhetorical one: 'Are we as intercultural communication scholars really trying to make our work intercultural?' he asks and refers to the topics scientists pursue, the theories they build and the methodologies they employ.[31] He criticizes the 'hegemonic Eurocentrism,' which systematically privileges theorizing and research methods of 'Western' origin. He detects three manifestations of Eurocentrism in intercultural communication studies: '1) theoretical concepts and constructs, 2) research material and methodology, and 3) otherization in theory and research.'[32] Miikes critique implies the imagination of a hidden universalism, that ignores fundamental asymmetries concerning the distribution of power; an argument that can be underlined by the fact that 'non-Western' cultures now have to participate in an intercultural discourse that is entirely dominated by Western concepts. One can interpret this fact as a continuation of Western imperialism. It means that intercultural communication and understanding is already prevented in the very basic foundations of most intercultural approaches.[33]

Many difficulties in the intercultural field already arise from the underlying concept of culture. Hofstede's approach, for example, is very similar to Hall's approach. Both conceptualize culture as something that can be identified in every society and that is relatively stable and homogeneous. Every culture has its uniqueness, so they argue. And Hall as well as Hofstede approach the uniqueness of a foreign culture by using cultural dimensions, which reduce cultural uniqueness to variations of an underlying universal concept—which is normally developed by Western scientists.

Hofstede argues that in each culture, one can identify a few 'mental programs,' that are learned in early childhood and after that fully internalized and hardly to change; in the intercultural field they cause misunderstandings. Mental programs are relatively stable, because once they have been internalized, they become a central component of one's own identity, which cannot be questioned because of the need for certainty. In his extensive analysis of IBM-employees from fifty nations, Hofstede found four dimensions of cultural differences, namely power distance, collectivism vs. individualism, masculinity vs. femininity and uncertainty avoidance.[34] The underlying argument is that all cultures are confronted with a number of common problems, which are solved in a culturally specific way. Among others, Hampden-Turner and Trompenaars as well as Lewis argue similarly.[35]

If cultures are presented as homogeneous and stable in nature, the boundaries between different cultures seem to be very strict and unchangeable; cultural differences seem to be naturally given and unbridgeable. This impression can be traced back to the fact that recently developed concepts of culture, which emphasize the hybrid nature of cultures, are ignored.[36] The consequence is that one fails to consider the reciprocal influences that cultures have on each other and the cultural diversity originating from the increasing mixture of peoples and cultures is neglected. The effect is an essentializing of cultural differences and a strengthening of the boundaries between different cultures. Chuang calls these problems in intercultural communication theories 'the principal shortcomings of logical positivism and essentialized cultural differences.' He finds an 'overwhelmingly binary representation of cultural differences,' which has been achieved by a 'reification of a variety of dualisms.'[37] In addition, he emphasizes that the positivistic approach in intercultural communication hinders the consideration of power and privilege as well as the reflection of the multiplicity of cultural identity.

This is especially evident in approaches to intercultural communication where a 'third culture' is introduced.[38] Santiago-Valles argues that third order research is necessary in the globalized context.[39] In a temporary evolving third culture the own cultural boundedness is loosened: Its general validity is questioned because of the confrontation with divergent cultural patterns. Intercultural communication theorists present this as enrichment: One can escape the prison of his/her own culture and learn from the foreign. The place, where members of different cultures meet, is presented as an in-between space of the original cultures. This space is not fixed—it is temporary and provisional. It is as a place which facilitates cultural encounters: One is open to the expectations and the wishes of the foreign. Tolerance, politeness and flexibility are underlying rules that facilitate the communication process. Thomas uses the term 'transcultural space' for this spatial zone between cultures:

> This transient space can open before one (or under one's feet, so to speak) to suddenly overwhelm one in misrepresentation. It can just as easily close up behind one, or draw away from one's immediate presence, as if nothing significant had taken place, except, perhaps, the inexplicable or accidental catastrophe of one's own injury, or death. To this type of space I have given the name *transcultural space*.[40]

But in the last instance, interculturalists fail to consider the possibility of changes, which they postulate to take place in a temporary evolving in-between space or third culture—their basic theoretical assumptions do not leave any room for a modification or renewal of cultural patterns. The fact that interculturalists ignore the permanent shifting nature of cultures, although they develop models of identity change, which are caused by the confrontation with members of divergent cultures, has to be seen as one of the principal shortcomings of intercultural communication theories. The individual may change,[41] but the widening of its consciousness does not have any consequences with regard to the culture, they belong to. Culture itself remains homogenous and stable. The openness and flexibility of the in-between space or third culture seems to be temporarily restricted to the moment of cultural encounter. Once the members from divergent cultures leave each other, they again identify with the cultural patterns and values of their original culture—this is the impression one gets when studying intercultural theories.

A PLEA FOR THE INTEGRATION OF POSTCOLONIAL INSIGHTS INTO INTERCULTURAL COMMUNICATION THEORIES?

> It is more necessary [. . .] to transform concepts, to displace them, to turn them against their presuppositions, to reinscribe them in other chains, and little by little to modify the terrain of our work and thereby produce new configurations [. . .] Breaks are always, and fatally, reinscribed in an old cloth that must continually, interminably be undone.[42]

In order to overcome the mentioned difficulties in intercultural commu-nication theories, some scholars have demanded to integrate postcolonial insights into intercultural communication theory. As Hibler argues, until today, the majority of intercultural communication theory and research fails to consider postcolonial insights.[43] Collier and Young are exceptions.[44] For this absence of postcolonial reasoning in the intercultural field Hibler offers three reasons: 1) intercultural researchers dominate the field who strive for prediction and effectiveness, 2) intercultural communication researchers focus on micro phenomena, postcolonialists on macro phenomena, and 3) the consideration of postcolonial insights would invalidate nearly all pre-vious research, because it criticizes the Eurocentrism and imperialism of Western discourses. In this perspective, the neglect of postcolonial insights in intercultural communication theories is a defense of the achievements of intercultural communication.

It is true that the combination of postcolonial and intercultural com-munication theory would bring about some problems, one aspect of which has been already mentioned: postcolonialism primarily refers to macro, whereas intercultural communication refers to micro phenomena. The approaches also imply different concepts of culture. While intercultural-ists usually view culture as homogeneous and stable, as something to be attached to a coherent group of symbols and meanings, postcolonial-ists accentuate the fragmented character of culture: culture is a battle-ground, where different people compete for power, where communities of resistance emerge. These different conceptualizations of cultures can-not be easily reconciled. Nonetheless, it remains unquestioned that inter-culturalists could benefit from a more open understanding of culture. If they only would strive less for consistency and accept ambiguities like postcolonialists do, they would be able to become more intercultural in nature. But Hibler is quite right to argue that an integration of postco-lonial insights would invalidate intercultural approaches because most of them use the traditional concept of culture as a starting point for the cultural dimensions they present.

Although it is apparent that the approaches are incompatible, Hibler nonetheless suggests informing intercultural communication by postcolo-nial theory: 'A postcolonial critique of inter/cultural communication would discuss the ways that previous and current intercultural communication research perpetuates imperial domination.'[45] And she quotes Shome, who poses the following question:

> To what extent do our scholarly practices decide whether they be the king issues we explore in our research, the themes around which we organize our teaching syllabi, or the way that we structure our con-ferences and decide who speaks (and does not speak), about what, in the name of intellectual practices—legitimise the hegemony of West-ern power structures?[46]

One of the advantages of a postcolonial informed theory and praxis of intercultural communication would be an increased self-reflexivity, which clarifies the scholars' contribution to the prevalence of hegemony, e.g. imperialism. It would mean to pose questions such as: 'How does my own subject position, in terms of history, economics, race, ethnicity, nationality, citizenship, sexual orientation, religion and occupation affect my research? How might these factors make my research possible? How will they affect my interactions with participants? How do they help me decide what to write and what to keep silent?'[47] This would require putting one's practice to crisis, in the sense Spivak and others have formulated their postcolonial critique.[48] It would mean to force the critical turn in the study of intercultural communication studies, which recently began to develop.[49]

Although a critical turn in the mentioned sense is long overdue in intercultural communication, it is not sure, that it really makes sense to integrate postcolonial insights into intercultural communication theories. Though it is doubtless that interculturalists need to increase their degree of self-reflexivity in order to become more intercultural in nature, it is doubtful that all its problems will be solved in this manner given some problems postcolonial theory still entails.

PROBLEMS WITH POSTCOLONIAL THEORY

The term *postcolonialism* was introduced in the 1970s in order to criticize the power relations, which were established in colonial times. One of the most important representatives in the postcolonial debate is Said, who criticized the practice of Western imperialism. In his work *Occidentalism* he worked out the strategy of *Otherization* that Occidentals used to create an *imaginative geography*. It established a distance between Occidentals and Orientals and implied the imagination of an unequal development. Because Orientals were considered to be backwards, this practice supported the continuation of imperial power.[50]

Central to postcolonialism is an analysis of how power influences the representation and interpretation of the foreign. Postcolonialists stand up for the interests of marignals. Spivak for example asks if the subaltern can speak?[51] Bhabha, too, concentrates on the question of what possibilities do marginals have to build communities of resistance and to be heard.[52]

The 'post' in postcolonialism stands for a critical consciousness. de Toro outlines some characteristics for post-theory in general:

> The *Post* of *Post-Theory* addresses radical epistemological changes, the shifting of traditional disciplinary boundaries, and what is more important, a different organization and delivery of knowledge. What the *Post-theoretical Condition* entails is a radical questioning of how, today, we approach objects of knowledge. In fact, it is this probing of

the *what*, the *where* and the *how* of current 'epistemologies,' that the *post-theoretical* thinking begins, by questioning the *ontological status of knowledge* [. . .] Perhaps the best way to characterize this *epistème* which we have named the *Post-Theoretical Condition*, is by underlining what it introduces to the object and practice of knowledge: (a) the dissolution of disciplinary boundaries; (b) the simultaneous elaboration of theory from conflicting epistemologies, (c) the theoretical production from the margins; and (d) the search for a 'beyond,' a third theoretical space.[53]

In the last years, concepts of in-between spaces (e.g. border zones) have gained prominence. In-between spaces are places of permanent movement; they constantly shift in nature. Thanks to Henri Lefebvre, in-between spaces have been rediscovered.[54] Soja refers to Lefebvre's work in particular. Like Lefebvre, he introduces a third term in order to overcome the dualisms which for a long time dominated in geography: *Thirdspace*. Soja repeatedly accentuates the radical openness and creativity of the third space. If one reads his book *Thirdspace: Journeys to Los Angeles and Other Real-and-Imagined Places*, one gets the impression that he uses the third space as an umbrella term for all new concepts, which imply a going beyond dualistic terms. Soja himself presents thirdspace as 'rooted in just such a recombinational and radically open perspective.' This radical openness is not only constitutive for the 'critical strategy of thirding as othering' but also for the concept of thirdspace itself.[55]

When Soja suggests the term 'critical thirding as othering' he does not only intend to introduce a third dimension, but to permanently strive to complement knowledge. In his opinion, the entrance in a third space enables other positions to emerge—an argument, which is also to be found in Bhabha's argumentation. Soja as well as Bhabha argue that thirdspace as in-between space enables marginals to disorder, deconstruct and reconstitute the dominant definitions of belonging and power relations. They define thirdspace as a place where marginals build a community of resistance in order to be heard by the powerful representatives.

Let us have a closer look at Bhabha's position. As a representative of post-colonialism, Bhabha intends to go beyond colonialism. Differences, which dominated in the colonial period, should loose their validity. Bhabha questions the position of self-appointed authorities who treat culture and its characteristics as something normal and natural. In his opinion the conceptualization of cultures as fixed and homogenous entities is untenable:

> It is only when we understand that all cultural statements and systems are constructed in this contradictory and ambivalent space of enunciation [i.e. the third space, BK], that we begin to understand why historical claims to be inherent originality or 'purity' of cultures are untenable, even before we resort to empirical historical instances that demonstrate their hybridity.[56]

Bhabha repeatedly stresses the hybrid nature of cultures. Even when he does not give a precise definition of hybridity, it is quite clear that he refers to the dynamics of cultures, which even make possible that existing power relations between the colonizer and the colonized can be modified: '[H]ybridity to me,' he states, 'is the "third space" which enables other positions to emerge. This third space displaces the histories that constitute it and sets up new structures of authority new political initiatives, which are inadequately understood through received wisdom.'[57] Hybridity to him is the result of an identification process by others; it is understood as a recombination of elements that are rooted in different traditions and that are creatively combined in the interstitial space between cultures.

Bhabha makes use of the hybridity concept to explain how authority is questioned and thereby disrupted, what resources re-establish authority and eventually where this modification of authority fails. He strives for subverting the dominant discourse and also for putting into practice social justice. For Bhabha, hybridity is a problem of the power discourse of colonial representation. It refers to a constellation of conflicting forces, which is modified, so that the oppressed comes back to the surface and undermines the basis of the colonial authority. It is in the in-between spaces of cultures that the oppressed can come back to the surface and be rearticulated.

But how does it work? To clarify this question, Bhabha gives special attention to the processes that take place in the places between cultures. It is an 'interstitial passage,' which is situated between the fixed identities and their inherent hierarchies. It makes clear that '[t]he very concepts of homogenous national cultures, the consensual or contiguous transmission of historical traditions, or "organic" ethnic communities [. . .] are in a profound process of redefinition.'[58] Central to Bhabha's redefinition of these concepts is his own concept of cultural difference. He pays special attention to the ambiguity of cultural differences; cultural differences are not fixed but negotiated in the moment of enunciation. By focusing on the ambiguity and uncertainty of articulations, he situates cultures in an uncertain, unstable border zone where articulations are negotiated and cultural hierarchies can be judged anew:

> The enunciative process introduces a split in the performative present of cultural identification; a split between the traditional culturalist demand for a model, a tradition, a community, a stable system of reference, and the necessary negation of the certitude in the articulation of new cultural demands, meanings, strategies in the political present, as a practice of domination, or resistance.[59]

For Bhabha this is a very productive space; cultural meanings permanently change.[60]

In this context, hybridity becomes important as an immanent characteristic of cultures; newness enters the world, questions existing structures of authorities and politics thereby establishing the preconditions for a modified relationship between the colonizer and the (oppressed) colonized. Bhabha conceptualizes the third space as a place, where marginals can alter identity and power relations. These are not fixed, but the result of negotiations. In this manner, he argues, it is made possible to go beyond the power relations, which have been established by the colonizers. In Bhabha's opinion, which is compatible with Soja's view, this crossing of colonialism is to be viewed as the most innovative aspect:

> What is theoretically innovative, and politically crucial, is the need to think beyond narratives of originary and initial subjectivities and to focus on those moments or processes that are produced in the articulation of cultural differences. These 'in-between' spaces provide the terrain for elaborating strategies of selfhood—singular or communal that initiate new signs of identity, and innovative sides of collaboration, and contestation, in the act of defining the idea of society itself.[61]

It remains unquestioned, that Bhabha's approach has the potential to criticize the grounding for hegemony and to change the relation between colonizer and colonized. However, when Bhabha states, that '"people" always exist as a multiple form of identification, waiting to be created and constructed' and thereby stresses interventions and the agency of marginals, perhaps he is too idealistic. Do marginals *really* have the chance to 'set up new structures of authority'?[62] Or did Bhabha forget the question that Spivak raised in 1998, namely: Can the subaltern speak? Enthusiastically, he searched for possibilities and ways for marginals to get heard; yet he forgot to prove if marginals, once they enter the third space, have a chance to be heard or not. The precondition would be that they have equal chances to articulate their interests as do the powerful representatives. Here lies the problem: although Bhabha aims to point out ways, which allow marginals to become more powerful, he paradoxically fails to consider aspects of power. Marginals do not have the same chances to articulate their interests and the powerful representatives surely have an interest to keep their powerful position. It is to be expected that they do everything to break down the resistance of the marginals who would then remain ineffective. Like interculturalists, Bhabha (and other postcolonialists, too) does not pay enough attention to aspects of power and the unequally distributed chances of articulating ones very own interests.

THE CONCEPT OF TRANSDIFFERENCE— A WAY OUT OF THE DILEMMA?

An alternative approach that takes aspects of power into consideration and therefore could inform intercultural theories is transdifference, which was formulated by Breinig and Lösch. Starting from their own dissatisfaction with those concepts that either underestimate the importance of cultural differences by deconstructing them or overestimate cultural differences by formulating a new synthesis, they define transdifference as follows:

> Transdifference, as we define it, denotes all that which resists the con-
> struction of meaning based on an exclusionary and conclusional binary
> model. While there can be no transdifference without difference—
> transdifference does not mean indifference—, the term refers to what-
> ever runs 'through' the line of demarcation drawn by binary difference.
> It does not do away with the originary binary inscription of difference,
> but rather causes it to oscillate. Thus, the concept of transdifference
> interrogates the validity of binary constructions of difference without
> completely deconstructing them. This means that difference is simulta-
> neously bracketed and yet retained as a point of reference. The term of
> transdifference refers to such areas of language, thought, and experi-
> ence that are excluded by the either/or while retaining difference both
> in its logical and experiential aspects.[63]

Breinig and Lösch place transdifference on three levels: the intrasystemic, the intersystemic, and finally the individual level. A closer examination of all three levels reveals different aspects of power. On the *intrasytemic level*, Breinig and Lösch focus on the question of how everything is oppressed that threatens the order and how alternative possibilities to fix meaning are exorcised. By referring to Luhman's systems theory, and especially the underlying definition of the term meaning, they argue that a reduction of world complexity is necessary to function within a given society or culture. Nonetheless, they point to opposing forces that can function to question the validity of the given order and its implication and that can be taken as a starting point for initiating resistance and for abolishing the distribution of power. In order to describe this process in more detail they use the palimpsest metaphor.

> From a diachronic perspective, systems of meaning can therefore be
> aptly described as palimpsests: what has been excluded can never be
> erased, but only overwritten by what has been selected. The traced of
> the repressed are therefore present and the repressed alternatives can
> be recovered. Expanding the metaphor of the palimpsest in dynamic
> terms, we propose to call the reproduction of systems of meaning a
> palimpsestic *process*: in the cycles of reproduction the excluded has to
> be re-inscribed and overwritten again and again in order to neutralize
> its destabilizing threat. One could argue that this iterative moment pro-
> duces transdifference, since it reintroduces world complexity by neces-
> sarily referring to other possibilities to validate its selection.[64]

What follows from this is that transdifference can never be completely controlled; a permanent work on transdifference has to take place in order to

guarantee the maintenance of the given order. On the intrasystemic level, transdifference has to be exorcised in order to prevent anomic tendencies.

On the *intersystemic level*, which refers to the permanent negotiation of identities in the cross-cultural context, aspects of power also can be tackled. When members of different cultures meet, they are inevitably confronted with conflicting worldviews, values and behavioral patters. This not only facilitates that they begin to question the universal validity of their own cultural material, but also hints at the necessity to negotiate identity in a neutral third space. In this process, boundaries become fluent and modes of inclusion and exclusion are confronted with conflicting ones. Therefore, identity has to be negotiated. In this process of negotiation transdifference is experienced:

> Transdifference thus refers to moments of contradiction, tension and indecidability that run counter to the logic of inclusion/exclusion. All processes of constructing and marking difference necessarily produce transdifference insofar as they, on the one hand, highlight individual aspects of the self/other relation at the expense of others and, on the other hand, stand in contradiction to various other differences along alternative lines of inclusion/exclusion.[65]

At first glance, the argumentation is similar to the one of interculturalists: they also argue that people are confronted with divergent worldviews and therefore have to negotiate meanings in an in-between space. But interculturalists refer to a homogenous and stable concept of culture, whereas Breinig and Lösch built their concept of transdifference on Clifford's understanding of culture, which is more open and leaves room for effective modifications of culture. Similarly, important differences can also be traced with regard to transdifference and Bhabha's concept of third space. Breinig and Lösch make out at least four differences: 1) Bhabha's concept of third space is an emancipatory project and it implies normative judgements, whereas transdifferecne does not; 2) Bhabha's concept relies on deconstruction and rejects any fixed meanings and notions of self-presence, transdifference does not; 3) because transdifference is not located in poststructuralist thinking, it can be combined with actor-oriented social science theories with their consideration of agency, and 4) while Bhabha's approach is restricted to a specific historical and political context (postcolonialism), transdifference is not.[66]

The third level, on which transdifference can be identified, is the *level of the individual*:

> As to the level of individual identity construction, transdifference denotes the mutual overlapping of contradictory aspects of belonging that arise from simultaneously being (or aspiring to be) a member of different groups, that is from situations, in which the individual is subject to at least two semantics of inclusion/exclusion. Multiple cultural

affiliations, mutually exclusive ascriptions of membership, incompatible loyalty claims by those groups and the individual's participation in different formations of social interaction employing different semantic registers produce moments of transdifference.[67]

To experience transdifference means to be confronted with at least two divergent systems of belongings that cannot be reconciled. The construction of a relatively stable identity is impossible. In every situation, the individual has to reflect and to choose its position—something which can be a painful experience, but which implies potentials for emancipation, too.

The advantage of the concept of transdifference is that it considers aspects of power: on the intrasystemic level, it is described, how alternative constructions of meaning are ignored in order to continue the existing order. Though potentials for resistance are mentioned, it is obvious that these are hardly being heard because they threaten the existing order. On the intersystemic level, power aspects influence which mechanisms of inclusion and exclusion are effective. Finally, on the individual level, power aspects influence the positioning of the individual: when the individual is confronted with divergent mechanisms of inclusions and exclusions, in every situation it is forced to position itself. This is not only a free choice, but also a constraint.

Because in the concept of transdifference, difference is not deconstructed and transdifference introduced as its complement, it is possible to take into consideration that on the one side, people are confronted with ascribed identities (accentuation of difference), but also—this is the other side of the medal—that they can question these ascriptions and modify them (introduction of transdifference). At the same time, it is not overseen that it is not the individual's free choice to position themselves, but also a societal constraint that they are confronted with. This fact hints to the limits of emancipation. Individuals do not exist in a power free space, in-between spaces, where aspects of power become secondary, are only temporary ones, which are supplemented very soon by spatial modes, which require fixed positions.

In my opinion, this concept could inform intercultural theories better than postcolonialism can. It hints at the potential but also the limits of intercultural communication. However, in agreement with Thurlow, I would prefer the term *trans*cultural communication, for it better fits the 'moving through and across cultural systems,'[68] which is to be observed everywhere—even if it is influenced by existing power relations, which do not lose their relevance.

NOTES

1. I would like to thank Lars Allolio-Näcke for many fruitful discussions about intercultural communication and transdifference in the last five years. Parts

of this paper have been presented at international congresses together with him. See also: Kalscheuer, Britta, and Lars Allolio-Näcke. "Why does the Debate on Interculturality Prevent the Development of Intercultural Competencies? A Critical Note on the Interculturality Discourse." http://sietarcongress.wu-wien.ac.at/docs/T6_Kalscheuer.pdf (2002).

2. Asante, Molefi Kete, Yoshitaka Miike, and Jing Yin. *The Global Intercultural Communication Reader*. London: Routledge, 2007; Brislin, Richard W., and Tomoko Yoshida. *Intercultural Communication Training: An Introduction*. Thousand Oaks, London, New Delhi: Sage, 1994; Chen, Guo-Ming. *Foundations in Intercultural Communication*. Lanham: America UP, 2005; Gudykunst, William B., and Bella Mody, ed. *Handbook of International and Intercultural Communication*. Second Edition. Thousand Oaks, London, New Delhi: Sage, 2002; Gudykunst, William B. *Cross-Cultural and Intercultural Communication*. Thousand Oaks, London, New Delhi: Sage, 2003; Hampden-Turner, Charles, and Fons Trompenaars. *Building Cross-Cultural Competencies: How to Create Wealth from Conflicting Values*. New York: John Wiley & Sons, 2000; Jandt, Fred E. *An Introduction to Intercultural Communication: Identities in a Global Community*. Thousand Oaks, London, New Delhi: Sage, 2006; Kim, Young Yun. *Becoming Intercultural: An Integrative Theory of Communication and Cross-Cultural Adaptation*. Thousand Oaks, London, New Delhi: Sage, 2000; Landis, Dan, and Rabi S. Bhagat, ed. *Handbook of Intercultural Training*. Second Edition. London, New Delhi: Sage, 1996; Martin, Judith N., Thomas K. Nakayama, and Lisa A. Flores, ed. *Readings in Intercultural Communication: Experiences and Contexts*. New Delhi: McGraw-Hill Humanities, 2001; Martin, Judith N., and Thomas K. Nakayama. *Experiencing Intercultural Communication: An Introduction*. New Delhi: McGraw-Hill Humanities, 2007; Samovar, Larry A., and Richard E. Porter. *Communication between Cultures*. Belmont: Wadsworth, 2003; Ting-Toomey, Stella, and John G. Oetzel. *Managing Intercultural Conflict Effectively*. Thousand Oaks, London, New Delhi: Sage, 2001.

3. Thurlow, Crispin (2000). "Transcultural Communication: A Treatise on Trans." http://faculty.washington.edu/thurlow/research/transculturalcommunication.html. *Inter*cultural communication has to be carefully distinguished from *intra*cultural communication; the difference lies in the degree of experienced heterogeneity. Related terms for intercultural communications are cross-cultural, multicultural, transcultural communication and others. They differ in the underlying concept of culture and the context in which they are applied.

4. Chen, Guo-Ming, and William J. Starosta. *Foundations of Intercultural Communication*. Boston: Allyn and Bacon, 1998.

5. Asante, Molefi Kete, and William B. Gudykunst, ed. *Handbook of International and Intercultural Communication*. Newbury Park, London & New Delhi: Sage, 1989.

6. Latest edition: Samovar, Larry A., Richard E. Porter, and Edwin R. McDaniel, ed. *Intercultural Communication: A Reader*. Belmont: Wadsworth, 2005.

7. Condon, John C., and Fathi S. Yousef. *An Introduction to Intercultural Communication*. New York: Macmillan, 1975.

8. Prosser, Michael H. *Intercommunication Among Nations and Peoples*. New York: Harper & Row, 1972; Dodd, Carley H. *Perspectives on Cross-Cultural Communication*. Dubuque: Kendall and Hunt, 1977.

9. Gudykunst, William B. *Intercultural Communication Theory: Current Perspectives*. Thousand Oaks, London & New Delhi: Sage, 1983; Kim, Young Yun, and William B. Gudykunst, ed. *Theories in Intercultural Communication*.

Thousand Oaks, London, New Delhi: Sage: 1988; Gudykunst and Mody, ed. *Handbook of International and Intercultural Communication.*

10. Kincaid, D. Lawrence, ed. *Communication Theory: Eastern and Western Perspectives.* Human Communication Research Series. San Diego: Academic Press, 1987.

11. Rogers, Everett M., and William B. Hart. "The Histories of Intercultural, International, and Development Communication." *Handbook of International and Intercultural Communication.* Ed. William B. Gudykunst and Bella Mody. Thousand Oaks, London, New Delhi: Sage, 2002. 1–18.

12. Hall, Edward T. *The Silent Language.* New York: Anchor Books, 1990; Hall, Edward T. *The Hidden Dimension.* New York: Anchor Books, 1990; Hall, Edward T. *Beyond Culture.* New York: Anchor Books, 1989; Hall, Edward T. *The Dance of Life: The Other Dimension of Time.* New York: Anchor Books, 1989.

13. Hall, Edward T., and Mildred Reed Hall. *Hidden Differences: Doing Business With the Japanese.* New York: Anchor Books, 1990, XVII.

14. Hall. *The Hidden Dimension.* 189.

15. Hall. *The Silent Language.* 29.

16. Hall. *The Hidden Dimension.* 65.

17. Ibid. 188.

18. Hall. *The Silent Language.* 47.

19. Hall. *Beyond Culture.*

20. Hall. *The Dance of Life.*

21. Hall. *The Silent Language.* 190–191.

22. Hall, Edward T. "Proxemics." *Current Anthropology* 9 (1968): 83–108.

23. Hall. *The Dance of Life.* 3.

24. Ibid. 3.

25. Ibid. 49.

26. Hall. *Beyond Culture.* 92.

27. Ibid. 85.

28. Hall, Edward T. "Context and Meaning." *Intercultural Communication: A Reader.* Ed. Larry A. Samovar and Richard E. Porter. Belmont: Wadsworth, 2000. 34–43. 36.

29. Hofstede, Geert. *Lokales Denken, globales Handeln: Kulturen, Zusammenarbeit und Management.* München: Beck, 1997; Hofstede, Geert. *Culture's Consequences: Comparing Values, Behaviors, Institutions and Organizations Across Nations.* Thousand Oaks, London & New Delhi: Sage, 2003; Hampden-Turner and Trompenaars. *Building Cross-Cultural Competencies.*

30. Ho, David Yau-fai. "On the concept of face." *American Journal of Sociology* 91 (1975): 867–884; Hu, Hsien Chin. "The Chinese Concept of 'Face.'" *American Anthropologist* 46 (1944): 45–64; Hwang, Kwang-Kuo. "Face and Favor: The Chinese Power Game." *American Journal of Sociology* 92 (1987): 944–74; Ting-Toomey, Stella, ed. *The Challenge of Facework: Cross-Cultural and Interpersonal Issues.* Albany: State University of New York Press, 1994; Bell, Duran. "Guanxi: A Nesting of Groups." *Current Anthropology* 41 (2000): 132–138; King, Ambrose Y. C. "Kuanshi and Network Building: A Sociological Interpretation." *Daedalus* 120 (1991), 63–84; Lin, Nan. "Guanxi: A Conceptual Analysis." *Contributions in Sociology* 133 (2001): 153–166; Yang, Zhong Fang. *Gifts, Favours and Banquets: The Art of Social Relationships in China.* Ithaca, London: Cornell UP, 1994.

31. Miike, Yoshitaka. "Beyond Eurocentrism in the Intercultural Field: Searching for an Asiacentric Paradigm." *Ferment in the Intercultural Field: Axiology, Value, Praxis (International and Intercultural Communication Annual*

Vol. 26). Ed. William J. Starosta and Guo-Ming Chen. Thousand Oaks, London, New Delhi: Sage, 2003. 243–276. 243–244.

32. Ibid.

33. This is an argument, I presented at several congresses in the last few years. The analogy between colonialism and intercultural communication refers to some common features. But of course, it is to be understood as a metaphor; the aims of colonialism and intercultural communication are quite distinct. See Kalscheuer, Britta, and Lars Allolio-Näcke. "Intercultural Research. A New Colonial Strategy?" 15ᵗʰ World Congress of Sociology: The Social World in the 21ˢᵗ Century: Ambivalent Legacies and Rising Challenges. Brisbane (Australia), 2002.

34. Hofstede, *Lokales Denken, globales Handeln*; Hofstede. *Culture's Consequences*. *Power distance* refers to the extent to which the unequal distribution of power is accepted by the less powerless members of a culture; *individualism vs. collectivism* refers to the extent people identify with the belonging to a group, e.g. strive for individualisation; *masculinity vs. femininity* refers to the value placed on traditionally male or female values, and finally *uncertainty avoidance* reflects the extent to which members of a society attempt to cope with anxiety by minimizing uncertainty.

35. Hampden-Turner and Trompenaars. *Building Cross-Cultural Competencies*; Lewis, Richard D. *When Cultures Collide: Managing Successfully Across Cultures*. London: Nicolas Brealey, 2000.

36. Bhabha, Homi K. *The Location of Culture*. London, New York: Routledge, 1994; Hannerz, Ulf. "The World in Creolization." *Africa* 57 (1987): 546–559.

37. Chuang, R. (2003). "A Postmodern Critique of Cross-Cultural and Intercultural Communication Research: Contesting Essentialism, Positivist Dualism, and Eurocentricity." *Ferment in the Intercultural Field: Axiology, Value, Praxis (International and Intercultural Communication Annual, Vol. 26)*. Ed. William J. Starosta and Guo-Ming Chen. Thousand Oaks, London, New Delhi: Sage, 2003. 24–53. 25.

38. Casmir, Fred L. "Third-Culture-Building: A Paradigm-Shift for International and Intercultural Communication." *Communication Yearbook* 16 (1992): 407–428.

39. Santiago-Valles, William F. (2003). "Intercultural Communication as a Social Problem in a Globalized Context: Ethics of Praxis Research Techniques." *Ferment in the Intercultural Field: Axiology, Value, Praxis (International and Intercultural Communication Annual, Vol. 26)*. Ed. William J. Starosta and Guo-Ming Chen. Thousand Oaks, London, New Delhi: Sage, 2003. 57–90. 66.

40. Thomas, David. *Transcultural Space and Transcultural Beings*. Oxford: Westview Press, 1996. 1.

41. Bennett, Milton J. "Overcoming the Golden Rule: Sympathy and Empathy." *Basic Concepts of Intercultural Communication: Selected Readings*. Ed. Milton J. Bennett. Yarmouth: Intercultural Press, 1998. 191–214.

42. Derrida, Jacques. *Positions*. London: Athlone Press, 1981. 24.

43. Hibler, Kristen. "Inter/cultural Communication and the Challenge of Postcolonial theory." *The Edge: The E-Journal of Intercultural Relations*. (1998) www.hart-li.com/biz/theedge.

44. Collier, Mary Jane. *Constituting Cultural Difference Through Discourse (International and Intercultural Communication Annual, Vol. 23)*. Thousand Oaks, London, New Delhi: Sage, 2000; Collier, Mary Jane. *Transforming Communication about Culture: Critical New Directions (International and Intercultural Communication Annual, Vol. 24)*. Thousand Oaks, London,

New Delhi: Sage, 2002; Young, Robert. *Intercultural Communication: Pragmatics, Genealogy, Deconstruction.* Clevedon, Philadelphia, Adelaide: Multilingual Matters, 1996.

45. Hibler. "Inter/cultural Communication and the Challenge of Postcolonial Theory."
46. Ibid.
47. Ibid.
48. Spivak, Gayatri Chakravorty "Can the Subaltern speak?" *Marxism and the Interpretation of Culture.* Ed. Cary Nelson and Lawrence Grossberg. London: Macmillan,1988. 271–313; Spivak, Gayatri Chakravorty. *The Postcolonial Critic.* London: Routledge, 1990.
49. Starosta, William J., and Guo-Ming Chen, ed. *Ferment in the Intercultural Field: Axiology, Value, Praxis (International and Intercultural Communication Annual,* Vol. 26). Thousand Oaks, London, New Delhi: Sage, 2003. 3.
50. Said, Edward. *Orientalism.* New York: Vintage Books, 1979.
51. Spivak. "Can the Subaltern speak?"
52. Bhabha. *The Location of Culture.*
53. Toro, Fernando de, ed. *Explorations on Post-Theory: Toward a Third Space.* Frankfurt am Main: Verwuert, 1999. 7.
54. Lefebvre, Henri. *The Production of Space.* Oxford: Basil Blackwell, 1991.
55. Soja, Edward W. *Thirdspace: Journeys to Los Angeles and Other Real-and-Imagined Places.* Cambridge: Blackwell Publishers, 1996. 5.
56. Bhabha. *The Location of Culture.* 37.
57. Bhabha, Homi K. "The Third Space: Interview with Homi Bhabha." In: *Identity: Community, Culture, Difference.* Ed. Jonathan Rutherford. London: Lawrence and Wishart, 1990. 207–221. 211.
58. Bhabha. *The Location of Culture.* 5.
59. Ibid. 35.
60. Bhabha. "The Third Space." 209.
61. Bhabha. *The Location of Culture.* 1–2.
62. Bhabha. "The Third Space." 220.
63. Breinig, Helmbrecht, and Klaus Lösch. "Introduction: Difference and Transdifference." *Multiculturalism in Contemporary Societies: Perspectives on Difference and Transdifference.* Ed. Helmbrecht Breinig, Jürgen Gebhardt, and Klaus Lösch. *Erlanger Forschungen. Reihe A: Geisteswissenschaften.* Erlangen: Universitäts-Bund Erlangen-Nürnberg, 2002. 11–36. 23.
64. Ibid. 24–25.
65. Ibid. 25.
66. Breinig, Helmbrecht, and Klaus Lösch. "Transdifference." *Journal for the Study of British Cultures* 13 (2006): 105–122. 114.
67. Ibid. 116.
68. Thurlow. "Transcultural Communication."

Part II
The Spatial Turn

3 Thirdspace

Toward a New Consciousness of Space and Spatiality[1]

Edward W. Soja

THE SPATIAL TURN AND THE CONCEPT OF THIRDSPACE

The spatial dimension of our lives has never been of greater practical and political relevance than it is today. Whether we are attempting to deal with the increasing intervention of electronic media in our daily routines; seeking ways to act politically to deal with the growing problems of poverty, racism, sexual discrimination, and environmental degradation; or trying to understand the multiplying geopolitical conflicts around the globe, we are becoming increasingly aware that we are, and always have been, intrinsically spatial beings, active participants in the social construction of our embracing spatialities. Perhaps more than ever before, a strategic awareness of this collectively created spatiality and its social consequences has become a vital part of making both theoretical and practical sense of our contemporary lifeworlds at all scales, from the most intimate to the most global.

Indeed, one of the most important intellectual renewals of the 20th century is this spatial turn, which can be observed in all human and social sciences. At the same time, it becomes obvious that creative spatial thinking needs to be open to new concepts and ideas. Space and spatiality have long been muddled and misconstrued either by the baggage of tradition, by older definitions that no longer fit the changing contexts of the contemporary moment, or by faddish buzzwords that substitute apparently current relevance for deeper understanding. It thus becomes more urgent than ever to keep our contemporary consciousness of spatiality—our critical geographical imagination—creatively open to redefinition and expansion in new directions; and to resist any attempt to narrow or confine its scope.

Until today, numerous geographical perspectives are built on dualistic terms. This binary logic results in polarizations, e.g. objectivity vs. subjectivity, material world vs. mental world, real world vs. imagined world, and so on. In order to widen the geographical view it is necessary to deconstruct these dualisms and to work out new conceptualizations. This has already been achieved for the historical and social dimension of the world. As far as the spatial dimension is concerned, dualisms still prevail. However, the concept of Thirdspace provides a different kind of thinking about the meaning and significance of space and those related concepts that compose and comprise the inherent spatiality of human life: place, location, locality, landscape, environment, home, city, region, territory, and geography.[2] First of all, Thirdspace is a metaphor for the necessity to keep the consciousness *of* and the theorizing *on* spatiality radically open. It is used most broadly to highlight what are considered to be the most interesting new ways of thinking about space and spatiality. In its broadest sense, it is a purposefully tentative and flexible term that attempts to capture what is actually a constantly shifting and changing milieu of ideas, events, appearances, and meanings.

Central to the understanding of Thirdspace is the insight that there is not just one single definition of space and spatiality but rather a multitude of approaches and perspectives; all of them with new insights on the geographical imagination and the potentials and limits to extend the scope of a critical geography. Therefore Thirdspace is not to be understood as an alternative concept to the already existing approaches. It rather urges spatial thinkers to set aside the demands to make an either/or choice and contemplate instead the possibility of a both/and also logic, one that not only permits but encourages a creative combination of postmodernist and modernist perspectives, even when a specific form of postmodernism is being highlighted. Singling out a radical postmodern perspective for particular attention is not meant to establish its exclusive privilege in exploring and understanding Thirdspace. It is instead an invitation to enter a space of extraordinary openness, a place of critical exchange where the geographical imagination can be expanded to encompass a multiplicity of perspectives that have heretofore been considered by the epistemological referees to be incompatible, uncombinable.

Thirdspace is a space where issues of race, class, and gender can be addressed simultaneously without privileging one over the other; where one can be Marxist and post-Marxist, materialist and idealist, structuralist and humanist, disciplined and transdisciplinary at the same time. Thirdspace is rooted in just such a recombinational and radically open perspective. If one would like to invent a different term for this perspective, one should go ahead and do so. It is only asked that the radical challenge to think differently, to expand the geographical imagination beyond its current limits, is retained and not recast to pour old wine into new barrels, no matter how tasty the vintage has been in the past.

HENRI LEFEBVRE'S CONTRIBUTION TO THE EXTENDED SCOPE OF GEOGRAPHY

The concept of Thirdspace was inspired by Henri Lefebvre, especially by his study *The Production of Space* in which the term Thirdspace appears.[3] Lefebvre was one of the first to theorize difference and otherness in explicitly spatial terms and he linked this spatial theorization directly to his meta-Marxist critique of the representations of power and the power of representations. He did so by insisting that difference be contextualized in social and political practices that are linked to 'spatio-analysis', the analysis, or better, the knowledge of the (social) production of (social) space.[4]

Lefebvre argued for a need to struggle on a wider terrain, for the right to be different against the increasing forces of homogenization, fragmentation, and hierarchically organized power that defined the specific geography of capitalism. He located these struggles for the right to be different at many levels, beginning significantly with the body and sexuality and extending through built forms and architectural design to the spatiality of the household and monumental building, the urban neighborhood, the city, the cultural region, and national liberation movements, to more global responses to geographically uneven development and underdevelopment. He embedded these multi-tiered struggles for the right to difference in the contextualized dialectics of centers and peripheries, the conceived and the lived, the material and the metaphorical; and from these concatenated dialectics of uneven development and differentiation he opened up a new domain, a space of collective resistance, a *Thirdspace of political choice* that is also a meeting place for all peripherized or marginalized subjects wherever they may be located.

In this politically charged space a radically new and different form of citizenship can be defined and realized. One important step in this direction was his critique of the prevailing dualisms in geography, especially the Firstspace—Secondspace dualism, which is held responsible for geography's difficulties to respond adequately to the new developments.[5] Lefebvre used the terms 'perceived space' and 'conceived space' instead.[6] Firstspace includes all forms of direct spatial experiences, which can be empirically measured and also presented in cartographies. Unlike Firstspace, Secondspace refers to the spatial representations, cognitive processes as well as modes of construction, which give rise to the birth of geographical imaginations. Whereas Firstspace epistemologies are used to describe spatial dimensions, which can be perceived, Secondspace epistemologies rather deal with symbolic worlds, which are conceived. For a long time, geographical thinking was defined by this dualism. Lefebvre's project, which remained almost invisible until the 1990s, was to inject a third dimension to the dually privileged dynamics of historicality and sociality: an encompassing and problematic spatiality that demanded at least equivalent attention in critical theory and praxis.[7] In his critique of discourse theory and other comments on alternative critical theoretical perspectives, Lefebvre appears to be harshly dismissive. His aim, however, is not to reject but to spatialize, to make sure that a *spatial problematic* is recognized whatever the theoretical emphasis employed, and to show how such spatialization works against theoretical closure and reductionism whatever interpretive pathway is chosen. For Lefebvre, spatial knowledge is a source and stimulus for radical openness and creativity.

In Lefebvre's view, perceived, conceived and lived space refer to spatial practice, the representations of space and representational spaces. In his own words:

(1) *Spatial practice* [. . .] embraces production and reproduction, and the particular locations and spatial sets characteristic of each social formation. Spatial practice ensures continuity and some degree of cohesion. In terms of social space, and of each member of a given society's relationship to that space, this cohesion implies a guaranteed level of *competence* and a specific level of *performance*.

(2) *Representations of space* [. . .] are tied to the relations of production and to the 'order' which those relations impose, and hence to knowledge, to signs, to codes, and to 'frontal' relations.

(3) *Representational spaces* [embody] complex symbolisms, sometimes coded, sometimes not, linked to the clandestine or underground side of social life, as also to art (which may come eventually to be defined less as a code of space than as a code of representational spaces).[8]

By introducing a third dimension, Lefebvre made it possible to escape the prison of the Firstspace—Secondspace dualism. This dimension, a third possibility or moment that partakes of the original pairing, is not just a single combination or an 'in-between' position along some all-inclusive continuum but can be understood as critical thirding-as-Othering. It is the first and most important step in transforming the categorical and closed logic of either/or to the dialectically open logic of both/and also. Two terms are never enough: *Il y a toujours l'Autre*. There is always the Other, a third term that disrupts, disorders, and begins to reconstitute the conventional binary opposition into an-Other that comprehends but is more than just the sum of two parts. This observation is also true for the Firstspace—Secondspace dualism.

Lefebvre begins with a critique of the opposition of (objective) physical and (subjective) mental space, which—according to him—is insufficient to come to terms with all dimensions of life. He then proceeds to fuse (objective) physical and (subjective) mental space into social space through a critique of what he calls a 'double illusion'—the 'illusion of transparency' and the 'realistic illusion'—'each side of which refers back to the other, reinforces the other, and hides behind the other.'[9] This powerful attack on reductionism in spatial thinking is a vital part of the thirding process, working to break down the rigid object–subject binarism that has defined and confined the spatial imagination for centuries, while simultaneously maintaining the useful knowledges of space derived from both of these binary fields. In this first round of thirding, *social space* takes on two different qualities. It serves both as a separable field, distinguishable from physical and mental space, *also/and* as an approximation for an all-encompassing mode of spatial thinking. Lefebvre continues to use social space in both ways. Thirdspace retains the multiple meanings Lefebvre persistently ascribed to social space. It is both a space that is distinguishable from other spaces (physical and mental, or first and second) and a transcending composite of all spaces.

By criticizing the double illusion, which had captured geographers for a long time, Lefebvre paves the way for a 'trialectics of spatiality',[10] always insisting that each mode of thinking about space, each 'field' of human spatiality—the *'physical'*, the *'mental'*, the *'social'*[11]—be seen as simultaneously real and imagined, concrete and abstract, material and metaphorical. No one mode of spatial thinking is inherently privileged or intrinsically better than the others as long as each remains open to the recombinations and simultaneities of the real-and-imagined. This rebalanced and non-illusive trialectics of spatiality, however, is for Lefebvre more an anticipated and desired state than an achieved one. For the present moment, a temporary strategic privileging is necessary to break the hammerlock of binarist logic and to prevent any form of reductionism from constraining the free play of the creative spatial imagination. Lefebvre thus begins his critical thirding-as-Othering by devoting his attention to 'social space',[12] firstly, as a distinctively different way of thinking about space that has long been obscured by exclusive fixations on illusive materialist and/or idealist interpretations; and secondly, as an all-inclusive and radically open mode of defining the limitlessly expandable scope of the spatial imagination: the envisioning of social space as 'Aleph'.[13] In this manner, space at least is radically open in two ways: through the 'sociospatial dialectic' ('Spatiality–sociality') and through the problematic interplay between space and time, the making of historical geographies or geohistories ('Spatiality–historicality').[14] Lefebvre established the basis for trialectical thinking that considers not only the social and historical dimensions of life but also the spatial one.

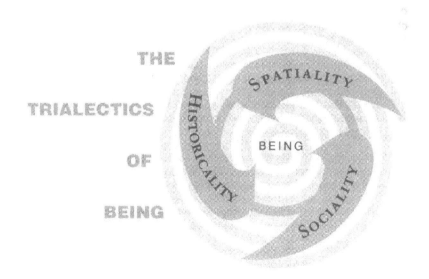

Figure 1 The Trialectics of Being.

Although primarily an ontological assertion, the trialectics of spatiality, historicality, and sociality (summary terms for the social production of space, time, and being-in-the-world) apply at all levels of knowledge formation, from ontology to epistemology, theory building, empirical analysis, and social practice. At all these levels, however, there has been a persistent tendency during at least the course of the past century to over-privilege, in another double illusion, the dynamic relations between the making of historicality and the constitution of social practices or sociality. Built into the arguments of *The Production of Space* is a critical vision of a thirding-as-Othering that involves the reassertion of spatiality against this pronounced tendency in Western philosophy, science, historiography, and social theory (including its most critical variants) to bifocalize on the interactive historicality and sociality of being.

With the introduction of trialectical thinking, Lefebvre succeeded in creating a Thirdspace as a limitless composition of lifeworlds that are radically open and openly radicalizable; that are all-inclusive and transdisciplinary in scope, yet politically focused and susceptible to strategic choice; that are never completely knowable but whose knowledge nevertheless guides our search for emancipatory change and freedom from domination. Trialectical thinking is difficult, for it challenges all conventional modes of thought and taken-for-granted epistemologies. It is disorderly, unruly, constantly evolving, unfixed, never presentable in permanent constructions.

It is important to keep in mind that the three moments of the ontologic trialectics contain each other; they cannot successfully be understood in isolation or epistemologically privileged separately, although they are all too frequently studied and conceptualized this way, in compartmentalized disciplines and discourses. Here again, however, the third term, spatiality, obtains a strategic positioning to defend against any form of binary reductionism or totalization.

It is in this sense, then, that Lefebvre's *The Production of Space* inspired the concept of Thirdspace. The latter denotes a space where, like Borges's Aleph, all places are capable of being seen form every angle, each standing clear; but also a secret and conjectured object, filled with illusions and allusions, a space that is common to all of us yet never able to be completely seen and understood, an 'unimaginable universe', or as Lefebvre would put it, 'the most general of products'.[15] *Everything* comes together in Thirdspace: subjectivity and objectivity, the abstract and the concrete, the real and the imagined, the knowable and the unimaginable, the repetitive and the differential, structure and agency, mind and body, consciousness and the unconscious, the disciplined and the transdiciplinary, everyday life and unending history. Anything which fragments third space into separate specialized knowledges or exclusive domains— even on the pretext of handling its infinite complexity—destroys its meaning and openness.

Thirdspace is characterized by a number of extraordinary simultaneities. And this thirding-as-Othering is much more than a dialectical synthesis *à la* Hegel or Marx, which is too predicated on the completeness and temporal sequencing of thesis/antithesis/synthesis. Thirding introduces a critical other-than choice that speaks and critiques through its otherness. That is to say, it does not derive simply from an additive combination of its binary antecedents but rather from a disordering, deconstruction, and tentative reconstitution of their presumed totalization producing an open alternative that is both similar and strikingly different. Thirding recomposes the dialectic through an intrusive disruption that explicitly spatializes dialectical reasoning along the lines of Lefebvre's theory. The spatialized dialectic 'no longer clings to historicity and historical time, or to a temporal mechanism such as thesis-antithesis-synthesis or affirmation-negation-negation of the negation'. Thirding produces what might best be called a cumulative *'trialectics'* that is radically open to additional otherness, to a continuing expansion of spatial knowledge.[16] The following diagram/triagram elaborates further the multiple meanings of third space.

Here the emphasis shifts from an existential ontology (statements about what the world must be like in order for us to exist as social beings) to a more specific discussion of the epistemology of space (how we can obtain accurate and practicable knowledge of our existential spatiality). Again, for at least the past century, there has been a 'double illusion' bracketing the accumulation of spatial knowledge within the oscillation between two contrasting epistemes, two distinctive modes of producing spatial knowledge.[17] Lefebvre's trialectics helps us to break down this

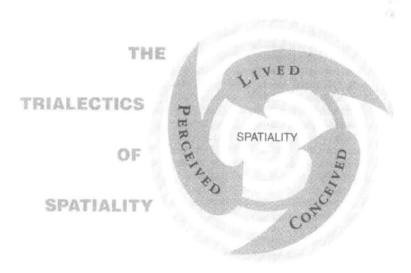

Figure 2 The Trialectics of Spatiality.

dualism to a third alternative, to other ways of making practical sense of the spatiality of social life.

To sum it up: Thirdspace epistemologies can now be briefly re-described as arising from the sympathetic deconstruction and heuristic reconstitution of the Firstspace—Secondspace duality, another example of what is called 'thirding-as-Othering'.[18] Such thirding is designed not just to critique Firstspace and Secondspace modes of thought but also to reinvigorate their approaches to spatial knowledge with new possibilities heretofore unthought of inside the traditional spatial disciplines. Thirdspace becomes not only the limitless Aleph but also what Lefebvre once called the city, a 'possibilities machine'; or, recasting Proust, a madeleine for a *recherche des espaces perdus*, a remembrance-rethinking-recovery of spaces lost . . . or never sighted at all.[19]

Thirdspace is contradictory and ambiguous. It has restricting as well as liberating aspects. It arouses a space of radical openness, a space of resistance and permanent struggle, a space of various representations, which can be analyzed in binary terms but where there is always a third additional dimension, an other space as Foucault called it in his heterotopology, which also has to be studied. Thirdspace is a meeting point, a hybrid place, where one can move beyond the existing borders. It is also a place of the marginal women and men, where old connections can be disturbed and new ones emerge. A Thirdspace consciousness is the precondition to building a community of resistance to all forms of hegemonic power.

THE MULTIPLICITY OF THIRDSPACE PERSPECTIVES AND HOMI K. BHABHA'S *THE LOCATION OF CULTURE*

Thirdspace thinking implies a new view on the world and the production of knowledge. It implies a new spatial awareness which, emerges as a product of a thirding of the spatial imagination, the creation of another mode of thinking about space that draws upon the material and mental spaces of the traditional dualism but extends well beyond them in scope, substance, and meaning. Simultaneously real and imagined and more (both and also . . .), the exploration of Thirdspace can be described and inscribed in journeys to 'real-and-imagined' (or perhaps 'realandimagined'?) places.[20]

I use the term critical thirding-as-Othering to break open the prison of the Firstspace—Secondspace dualism. According to this critical thirding thinking follows not a linear but a lateral or spatial logic. Thirding does not only mean adding a third dimension but also creating new possibilities to expand the scope and reach of our knowledge. Its precondition is a radical openness, which allows us to move beyond the already known and to analyze new aspects of space and spatiality. In this sense, Thirdspace is (1) a way to understand the spatial dimension of human life; (2) an integral part of the often neglected trialectics of spatiality; (3) an all encompassing spatial perspective, which has the same potential as historical and sociological views; (4) a mutual political strategy against all forms of oppression; and (5) a starting point for many new approaches.

As I have mentioned earlier, the concept of Thirdspace is not to be understood as a substitute for existing approaches that have been formulated recently; rather it is understood as complementary. Similar intentions have been formulated by Michel Foucault, Homi K. Bhabha, bell hooks, Cornell West and some other feminist and postcolonial critics. As black intellectuals, hooks and West have been marginalized in multiple ways and made peripheral to the mainstreams of American politics, intellectual, and everyday life; but they have also consciously chosen to envelop and develop this *marginality*, as hooks puts it, as a space of radical openness, a context from which to build communities of resistance and renewal that cross the boundaries and double-cross the boundaries of race, gender, class, and all oppressively Othering categories.[21]

All are engaged in a new cultural politics of difference, distinctive features of which are to trash the monolithic and homogeneous in the name of diversity, multiplicity, and heterogeneity; to reject the abstract, general, and universal in light of the concrete, specific, and particular; and to spatialize, historicize, and pluralize by highlighting the contingent, provisional, variable, tentative, shifting, and changing. An important aim behind these radical postmodernisms of resistance and redirection is to deconstruct (not to destroy) the ebbing tide of modernist radical politics, to renew its strengths and shed its weaknesses, and to reconstitute an explicitly postmodern radical politics, a new cultural politics of difference and identity that moves toward empowering a multiplicity of resistances rather than searching for that one 'great refusal', the singular transformation that somehow must precede and guide all others.[22]

Bhabha's approach, which he develops in his book *The Location of Culture*, is an excellent example for the understanding of 'third space' as a mutual political strategy against all forms of oppression, e.g. in a broader sense to engage with the aforementioned new cultural politics of difference as well as with what I called critical thirding-as-Othering.[23] Bhahbha explores the nature of cultural difference of what he tellingly calls the location of culture. He locates his particular postcolonial project in the following way: 'With the notion of cultural difference, I try to place myself in that position of liminality, in that productive space of the construction of culture as difference, in the spirit of alterity or otherness.'[24] This place is a productive one, which differs from liberal relativist perspectives on 'cultural diversity' and 'multiculturalism', which form another discursive space. In that space 'Western connoisseurship' locates cultures 'in a kind of *musée imaginaire*,' in a grid of its own choosing, wherein the urge to universalize and historicize readily acknowledges the social and historical diversity of cultures but at the same time transcends them and renders them transparent, illusive. Speaking in particular of Great Britain, Bhabha describes the liberal 'entertainment and encouragement of cultural diversity' as a form of control and 'containment': 'A transparent norm is constituted, a norm given by the host society or dominant culture, which says that "these other cultures are fine, but we must be able to locate them within our own grid". This is what I mean by a *creation* of cultural diversity and a *containment* of cultural difference.'[25]

For Bhabha, the difference of cultures cannot be contained within the universalist frameworks of liberal democracy or Marxist-historicism, for these different cultures are often *incommensurable*, not neatly categorized, a triggering observation for identifying a 'third space' of alternative enunciation.

This argument connects to his critique of colonial discourse and Orientalism, whose 'predominant function is the creation of a space for a "subject peoples" through the production of knowledges in terms of which surveillance is exercised and a complex form of pleasure/unpleasure is incited.'[26] Against this 'containment of cultural difference', Bhabha introduces the notion of *hybriditiy* and locates it in another example of trialectical thirding-as-Othering. Denying the essentialism that comes from either the genealogical tracing of cultural origins or the representation act of cultural 'translation' (a term he borrows from Walter Benjamin), he posits a third space that echoes the chosen marginality of bell hooks and does, similar to Gayatri Chakravorty Spivak's and Edward Said's endeavors, explicitly challenge hegemonic historiography:

> all forms of culture are continually in a process of hybridity. But for me the importance of hybridity is not to be able to trace two original moments from which the third emerges, rather hybridity to me is the 'third space' which enables other positions to emerge. This third space displaces the histories that constitute it, and sets up new structures of authority, new political initiatives, which are inadequately understood through received wisdom. [. . .] The process of cultural hybridity gives rise to something different, something new and unrecognisable, a new area of negotiation of meaning and representation.[27]

Inspired by his deep involvement with the Third Cinema,[28] Bhabha locates the third space in the margins, and 'it is from the affective experience of social marginality that we must conceive a political strategy of empowerment and articulation.'[29] He also firmly roots the third space in the experience of postcoloniality:

> It is significant that the productive capacities of this Third Space have a colonial or postcolonial provenance. For a willingness to descend into that alien territory [. . .] may reveal that the theoretical recognition of the split-space of enunciation may open the way to conceptualizing

an *inter*national culture, based not on the exoticism of multicultural-ism or the *diversity* of cultures, but on the inscription and articulation of culture's *hybridity*. To that end we should remember that it is the 'inter'—the cutting edge of translation and negotiation, the in*between* space—that carries the burden of the meaning of culture. [. . .] And by exploring this Third Space, we may elude the politics of polarity and emerge as the others of ourselves.[30]

Along with other key figures such as Stuart Hall and Paul Gilroy, Bhabha adds his voice to a particularly Black British tradition of postcolonial debate that connects with, yet is distinct from, the North Amercian tradition exemplified by hooks, West, Said, Spivak, Anzaldúa, Gómez-Peña, and most of the postmodern spatial feminists. Setting these differences aside, the project that is shared across the Black Atlantic (the latter is also the title of one of Gilroy's insightful books) is the exploration of new identities that build alternatives to a double illusion created, on the one hand by a cultural essentialism that promotes such polarizing exclusivities as black nationalism; and on the other hand by an unlimited cultural relativism that dissolves black subjectivity in an universalist melting pot or a pluralist jumble of equals.

The third space of Bhabha is occasionally on the edge of being a spatially ungrounded literary trope, a floating metaphor for a critical *historical* con-sciousness that inadvertently masks a continued privileging of temporality over spatiality. Nevertheless, in his *The Location of Culture*, Bhabha effec-tively consolidates a strategic envisioning of the cultural politics of third space that helps to dislodge its entrapment in hegemonic historiography and historicism:

> The social articulation of difference, from the minority perspective, is a complex, on-going negotiation that seeks to authorize cultural hybridities that emerge in moments of historical transformation. The 'right' to signify from the periphery of authorized power and privilege does not depend on the persistence of tradition; it is resourced by the power of tradition to be reinscribed through the conditions of contin-gency and contradictoriness that attend upon the lives of those who are 'in the minority'.[31]

Bhabha also elaborates on the notion of going beyond, which means that interventions can modify the existing power relations, if only a Third Space emerges; the entering into a Third Space is the precondition for possible interventions:

> Being in the 'beyond', then, is to inhabit an intervening space, as any dictionary will tell you. But to dwell 'in the beyond' is also [. . .] to be part of a revisionary time, a return to the present to redescribe our

cultural contemporaneity; to reinscribe our human, historic commonality; *to touch the future on its hither side.* In that sense, then, the
intervening space 'beyond' becomes a space of intervention in the here
and now.[32]

This is another instance where Bhabha's Third Space comes close to my own
conceptualization of Thirdspace, especially to what I call critical thirding-
as-Othering. Both concepts contribute to broadening the knowledge and
let new (critical) positions emerge. Both exemplify a new consciousness of
space and spatiality.

NOTES

1. This chapter consists of selected passages from Soja, Edward W. *Thirdspace:
   Journeys to Los Angeles and Other Real-and Imagined Places.* Malden,
   MA, Oxford: Blackwell, 1996, supplemented by additional material. My
   thanks to the editors for preparing this re-composition.
2. Soja. *Thirdspace.*
3. Lefebvre, Henri. *The Production of Space.* Trans. Donald Nicholson-Smith.
   Cambridge, MA, Oxford: Blackwell, 1991. 188.
4. Ibid. 356–357, 404–405.
5. Soja. *Thirdspace.* 78, 120–122.
6. Lefebvre. *The Production of Space.* 38–41.
7. Ibid. 38–41.
8. Ibid. 33.
9. Ibid. 27–30, 27.
10. Soja. *Thirdspace.* 8–12, 45, 48–49.
11. Lefebvre. *The Production of Space.* 11.
12. Ibid. 68–168.
13. Soja. *Thirdspace.* 53–60.
14. Ibid. 72.
15. Ibid. 56.
16. Ibid. 61.
17. Ibid. 73–74.
18. Ibid. 81.
19. Ibid. 81.
20. Ibid. 11.
21. Ibid. 84.
22. Ibid. 92–93.
23. Bhabha, Homi K. *The Location of Culture.* London, New York: Routledge,
    1994.
24. Bhabha, Homi K. "The Third Space." *Identity, Community, Culture, Dif-
    ference.* Ed. Jonathan Rutherford. London: Lawrence and Wishart, 1990.
    207–221. 209.
25. Ibid. 208.
26. Bhabha, Homi K. "The Other Question: Difference, Discrimination and the
    Discourse of Colonialism." *Out There: Marginalization and Contemporary
    Cultures.* Ed. Russell Ferguson et al. Cambridge, MA, New York: MIT Press
    and New Museum of Contemporary Art 1, 1990. 71–88. 75.
27. Bhabha. "The Third Space." 211.

28. Pines, Jim, and Paul Willamen, ed. *Questions of Third Cinema*. London: British Film Institute, 1989.
29. Bhabha, Homi K. "Postcolonial Authority and Postmodern Guilt." *Cultural Studies*. Ed. Lawrence Grossberg, Cary Nelson, and Paula Treichler. New York, London: Routledge, 1992, 56–68. 56.
30. Bhabha. *The Location of Culture*. 38–39.
31. Ibid. 2.
32. Ibid. 7.

4   Pitfalls of (Third) Space
Rethinking the Ambivalent Logic of Spatial Semantics

Julia Lossau

INTRODUCTION

At present many scholars are engaged in the broader intellectual movement which has been called the spatial turn of social and cultural theory. While it is difficult to make out the origin of the term, let alone of the movement indicated by it, the spatial turn arguably became popular in the discussions around books written by David Harvey and Edward W. Soja.[1] In *Third-space*, to name but one, Soja explores what he calls 'the contemporary reassertion of a critical spatial perspective and geographical imagination throughout all of the human sciences': 'As we approach the *fin de siècle*, there is a growing awareness of the simultaneity and the interwoven complexity of the social, the historical, and the spatial, their inseparability, and interdependence.'[2]

Amongst Soja's witnesses are many voices from feminist and postcolonial critique.[3] Engaging in the present discussions of cultural politics, difference and identity, both fields aim at questioning and disturbing the images of power and authority by 'pushing against oppressive boundaries set by race, sex and class domination'.[4] In doing so, they are infused with a thoroughly spatial rhetoric. As many feminist and postcolonial writings reveal, the subjects of critical identity discourse live between margin and center; in intercultural or in-between spaces, thereby traveling and eventually crossing, if not transforming, borders, gaps and (different sorts of) oppositional spheres. The African American cultural critic bell hooks, for instance, has conceptualized the margin as 'a space of radical openness [. . .]—a profound edge',[5] which 'gives us a new location from which to articulate our sense of the world'.[6] In a similar vein, Homi K. Bhabha is interested in the position of marginality—or liminality, as he sometimes calls it: 'With the notion of cultural difference, I try to place myself in that position of liminality, in that productive space of the construction of culture as difference, in the spirit of alterity or otherness.'[7] Inspired by post-structuralist authors such as Jacques Lacan and Michel Foucault, Bhabha connects his concept of liminal space to the notion of hybridity. To him, 'the importance of hybridity is not to be able to trace two original moments from which the third emerges, rather hybridity [. . .] is the "third space" which enables other positions to emerge'.[8]

Due to the popularity of his writings, notably of his book on *The Location of Culture*,[9] Bhabha's concept of third space has become a talisman of the current academic endeavors to reconceptualize difference by means of spatial thinking. In some fields, especially in those occupied with literary criticism rather than with material practices, it is even more popular now than Soja's concept of Thirdspace, which, in turn, emanates from a re-reading of Lefebvre's *The Production of Space*.[10] While it would be of some interest to investigate the differences (and similarities) of Bhabha's and Soja's concepts from a spatial, or indeed topological, perspective, it is another aspect of the debate that stands at the heart of this paper. At first sight, the close link between difference, on the one hand, and space, on the other hand, which is conveyed in concepts like third space seems to be self-evident. Ten years after the publication of Soja's *Thirdspace*, twelve years after Bhabha's *The Location of Culture*, and after almost fifty years of poststructuralist reasoning we seem to have become used to a new division of labor between time and space which has put an end to the traditional predominance of time and history. While time is nowadays frequently found guilty of conveying linear order and teleological succession, space and spatial language are hailed for opening up ways of seeing and communicating, which keep together that which is different.

Although the apparent proliferation of spatial thinking is to be welcomed from the viewpoint of geography as a discipline, I have to admit that, as a geographer, I am of two minds regarding the pivotal status that space seems to enjoy in contemporary social and cultural theory. On one hand, I appreciate the deployment of space as a concept, or at least a buzzword, which allows for the coexistence of different things—be it narratives, cultures, knowledge or identities—at the same time.[11] On the other hand, though, it seems to me that spatial semantics are not only about difference and differentiation. Apart from representing a tool of differentiation, space can be seen to function as a means of identification, which generates reifications and tends to render fluidity into spatial fixations. Metaphors of intended difference, like third space or margin, are not an exception in this regard. Although the spatial language of hooks, Bhabha, Soja and many others attempts to dispense with the belief in essential, authentic and pure entities, their writings run the risk of leading into a 'territorial trap' of identity and homogeneity, thus repeating the very reductionism they set out to overcome.[12] This danger, I would like to suggest, is—at least in part—a result of the ambivalent logic of spatial language, which does not only allow for difference but also for the fixation of difference by locating identities.

Against such a background, my paper aims at critically rethinking the complex relations of identity, difference and space. Taking Bhabha's concept of third space as a case study, it proceeds in four steps. The following section rehearses the main arguments of Bhabha's preoccupation with space in general and third space in particular, highlighting that the latter is aimed at overcoming the reductionist power of cultural and political fixations. In the third section it is argued, however, that third space as a concept is hardly capable of avoiding certain shortcomings of the more traditional conceptualizations of identity and difference. The concept's pitfalls can be traced back to the ambivalent logic of space, which will be sketched out by means of system theoretic arguments. The fourth section then considers ways to reach beyond the pitfalls of third space. If spatial semantics pose a threat to difference, is there still space (sic) for alternative and truly different approaches to reality and its spatial dimensions? It is by trying to answer this question that this paper comes to its conclusions.

DISLOCATING IDENTITIES

Who is keen to sit on the fence? In different Western languages, the metaphor of sitting on the fence and its equivalents are associated with coercion and conflict, relating to the necessity to make a difficult choice between two mutually exclusive options.[13] In the context of German domestic politics, the metaphor is popular for describing the particular situation of *Ausländer*.[14] More precisely, it often denotes the special place that the offspring of the first and second generation of immigrants—or *Gastarbeiter*—inhabit in German society. Especially young German Turks whose parents and grandparents came to Germany to work as Turkish guest workers are often regarded as sitting on the fence between Turkey and Germany. What is signaled by the metaphor is that immigrants and their families have a problem—the problem of being at home neither in Germany nor in Turkey, that is, the problem of living as 'hybrids' between two worlds.[15] Although there are less problematic and more 'enriching' representations of Turkish immigrants in German public discourse, the stereotype of the 'hybrid and thus problematic *Ausländer*' enjoys hegemonic status and is frequently reproduced in media as different as newspapers, academic articles or schoolbooks.[16]

It is precisely this exclusionary vision of hybridity—hybridity as the ambigious, problematic and hence non-desirable middle ground that lies between two fixed and authentic realms—which Bhabha's concept of third space seeks to disturb and reconceptualize. To achieve this aim, cultural fixity itself is called into question and disclosed as a means of constructing supposedly homogenous communities by arranging them in a stereotypical framework of otherness based on repetition:

> Fixity, as the sign of cultural/historical/racial difference in the discourse of colonialism, is a paradoxical mode of representation: it connotes rigidity and an unchanging order as well as disorder, degeneracy and daemonic repetition. Likewise the stereotype, which is its major

discursive strategy, is a form of knowledge and identification that vacillates between what is always in place, already known, and something that must be anxiously repeated.[17]

Deeply critical of the urge to put identities 'in place', as Bhabha puts it, postcolonial authors are keen to open up ways of thinking that can lead to a politics of displacement.[18] Not least against the background of the time-space compressing processes of globalization, new and more complex perspectives of location and relocation are called for. Deconstructing the belief in cultural totality and ethnic essence, the postcolonial critique focuses on a different form of cultural politics which relies on the negotiation of incommensurable meanings and judgements: 'The non-synchronous temporality of global and national cultures opens up a cultural space [. . .] where negotiation of incommensurable differences creates a tension peculiar to borderline existences.'[19]

Borderline existences, in turn, are linked to concepts of multiple identities which depict subjects as able to partake in different cultures at the same time.[20] Accordingly, the protagonists of postcolonial texts—be it novels, poems, films, music or performances—refuse to be located either here or there; they insist on being related to many different places and communities, avoiding to be part of either us or them. Due to their unstable positionalities, these subjects dissolve the boundaries between cultures and nations that have gone unquestioned for a long time. In their practices of traveling and border crossing, a new space is opened up that 'innovates and interrupts the performance of the present',[21] becoming 'a space of intervention in the here and now'.[22] Located in-between, beyond or *abseits* stable cultural entities, this is a space at cultural margins, on their borderlines, at the crossroads between cultures: 'It is that third space, though unrepresentable in itself, which constitutes the discursive sites or conditions that ensure that the meanings and symbols of culture have no primordial unity or fixity; that even the same signs can be appropriated, translated, and historicised anew.'[23]

Closely related to the concept of third space is a form of difference as a powerful category, which stands right at the heart of the social construction of reality. In one of the chapters of *The Location of Culture*, for instance, Bhabha describes the production of the nation as a process in which multiple differences are expressed in contradictory ways both between and within nations:

The boundary that marks the nation's selfhood interrupts the self-generating time of national production and disrupts the signification of the people as homogenous. The problem is not simply the 'selfhood' of the nation as opposed to the otherness of other nations. We are confronted with the nation split within itself, articulating the heterogeneity of its population. The barred Nation *It/Self*, alienated from its eternal self-generation, becomes a liminal signifying space that is *internally* marked by the discourses of minorities, the heterogeneous histories of contending peoples, antagonistic authorities and tense locations of cultural difference.[24]

In the realm of third space, difference is thus conceptualized as contra-dictory and 'irregular', taking place decidedly outside the dualistic system of thinking that characterizes Western understandings of culture and dis-courses of modernity more broadly.[25] Accordingly, Bhabha's notion of dif-ference aims at liberating itself from artificial dichotomies as well as related binary hierarchies and antagonisms. It is related to a political agenda of hybridity as a place 'from which to speak both of, and as, the minority, the exilic, the marginal and the emergent'.[26]

Entailing temporal and spatial contradictions which, as Donna Har-away might put it, 'do not resolve into larger wholes' but have to be held in tension,[27] hybridity in Bhabha's terms poses a constant threat to sta-bility, unity and homogeneity. As such, it is very different from what is conveyed by the term in the German discourse on domestic policies, immi-gration and cultural integration. While in the latter, hybridity is depicted as an uncomfortable position on the fence (or rather between two chairs), postcolonial understandings of hybridity represent a condition that puts into question the very metaphor of the fence—or the image of two chairs or spaces with a gap between them.[28] Put differently, Bhabha's concept of hybridity stands in contrast to unambiguous forms of cultural in-betweenness which rely on the geographical imagination of supposedly homogenous containers, i.e. a vision of the world divided up into distinct and bounded parcels, a vision where cultures can be put 'in their proper places, located either here or there. Instead of trying to put 'them' back 'in place' and, thereby, redraw the demarcation lines between 'us' and 'them', postcolonial hybridity both presupposes and conveys a different form of cultural politics that works 'contingently, disjunctively, in the inscription of signs of cultural memory and sites of political agency'.[29] Criticizing the homogenizing, objectifying and exoticizing impetus of traditional identity politics, the related endeavors

> may open the way to conceptualizing an international culture, based not on the exoticism of multiculturalism or the *diversity* of cultures, but on the inscription and articulation of culture's *hybridity*. To that end we should remember that it is the 'inter'—the cutting edge of translation and nego-tiation, the in-between space—that carries the burden of the meaning of culture. It makes it possible to begin envisaging national, anti-national histories of the 'people'. And by exploring this third space, we may elude that politics of polarity and emerge as the other of our selves.[30]

SPATIALIZING DIFFERENCE—(RE-)LOCATING IDENTITIES

Intellectual projects inspired by poststructuralism defy easy definition. While the same is true for Bhabha's writings, the concept of third space can be said to rely on (at least) two rationales. First, third space is focused on difference in decidedly non-dualistic terms. Instead of denoting the incommensurability between antagonistic groups, third space can be described as the result of myriad circulations across boundaries, aiming at disintegrating fixed entities by unpredictable movements between center and periphery. Secondly, third space testifies to a deep interest in spaces and positions of enunciation which, in turn, mirror non-equivalent—and yet ambivalent—sites of representation, i.e. of histories of discrimination, misrepresentation and unequal power relations. By critically analyzing the narratives of domination and suppression within the story of modernity, the subaltern other is made visible and relocated from the periphery to the center of knowledge production.

What comes with both rationales is a deeply spatialized language. Striving at articulating and capturing his preoccupation with difference and ambivalence as well as his sensitivity to unequal power relations, Bhabha employs in his writings a variety of spatial expressions like 'place', 'in-between space' and, last but not least, 'third space'.[31] The latter can stand as a prime example of how scholars from various disciplines currently deploy spatial metaphors in order to adequately address the differential, even disjunctive, moments of culture and society. According to geographer Doreen Massey, for instance, a spatialized perspective holds open the possibility of the existence of alternatives in that the spatial is 'the sphere of juxtaposition, or co-existence, of distinct narratives, [...] the product of power-filled social relations':

> Within that context, 'places' may be imagined as particular articulations of these social relations, including local relations 'within' the place and those many connections which stretch way beyond it. And all of these embedded in complex, layered, histories. This is place as open, porous, hybrid—this is place as *meeting place* [...]. This is a notion of place where specificity [...] derives not from some mythical internal roots nor from a history of relative isolation—now to be disrupted by globalization—but precisely from the absolute particularity of the mixture of influences found together there.[32]

While Massey seems to refer to Foucault's notion of space as a mode of juxtaposition,[33] there are other facets of the endeavor to think (about) difference by means of spatial terms. Amongst the most popular is the decidedly spatial 'system' developed by Gilles Deleuze und Félix Guattari. With the 'rhizome', as it is named, they aim at reaching beyond simplistic either/or choices, contemplating instead the possibility of a both/and logic: 'All we talk about are multiplicities, lines, strata and segmentarities, lines of flight and intensities, machinic assemblages and their various types, bodies without organs and their construction and selection.'[34] A third element of the deployment of spatial terminology—apart from juxtaposition and multiplicity—is the idea of concreteness and context. From a system theoretic perspective, Elena Esposito has noted that reference to space always implicates the vision of a specific context.[35] In her view, spatial thinking underlines the 'situatedness' of all knowledge and tends to reject universalist understandings.[36] Referring to Gotthard Günther's notion of 'polycontexturality', she pleads for the acceptance of a plurality of situated approaches (or forms of thinking) which all depend on their specific contexts without sharing the idea of a common, overarching and all-encompassing horizon.[37]

The assumption that space can stand as a symbol of radical difference, indicating the incommensurability of different narratives and the multiplicity of enunciative positions, is thus well rehearsed not only in different disciplines but in different theoretical quarters too. From a variety of theoretic perspectives—be they postcolonial, poststructuralist or system theoretic—the differentiality of space (and particularly of third space) is often taken for granted. It can be argued, however, that space does not necessarily represent a symbol of difference and heterogeneity. From a system theoretic perspective, for instance, it is equally possible to think of space as a fundamental ordering scheme which, in a transcendental sense, allows for the basic process of identification and differentiation, thus representing the very condition of the possibility to identity and sameness.[38] According to Niklas Luhmann, 'space is a mode of thinking that is both constituted and applied if two different things cannot occupy the same position in space at the same time'.[39] Space, in other words, serves as a fundamental category which is helpful whenever inconsistencies need to be negotiated. The reason this is the case is the capacity of spatial thinking to put things in order either by arranging them between two extremes according to 'closer' and 'further' or by drawing a clear line that places 'everything on one side or the other with noting on both sides at once'.[40] Space can, therefore, be conceptualized as a pre-requisite for distinction insofar as the process of distinguishing is not conceivable without distance, without a gap, without (at least) two sides/sites, a 'here' and a 'there'.[41]

In this sense, the imagery of space represents a cognitive grid in which different things are located at different places. While difference is, therefore, always bound to spatial imaginations,[42] it can only be realized by means of a hidden reification as the essential by-product of distinction. As sociologist Peter Fuchs argues, the process of distinguishing, i.e. of drawing distinctions (in space), conveys some hidden or rather underhand form of reification. In the process of distinguishing, both sides of the distinction are turned into spatial units which seem to be arranged, 'side by side', in space.[43] By virtue of the 'quasi-ontology of the spatial metaphor',[44] both sides of a distinction, say us and them, can be handled as isolated objects and treated as separate units. As a consequence, we and they are both identified and containerized, i.e. we (in our space) and they (in their space) appear like entities occupying different places while containing, in each case, homogenous contents. Against such a background, it can be argued that, from a system theoretic perspective, space is not exclusively a symbol of difference and heterogeneity. In contrast to what is attributed to space by many authors engaging in the ongoing discussions of the spatial turn— i.e. space as a marker of difference–, space can be regarded as an ordering tool which enables us to locate identities by spatializing difference and vice versa.

BEYOND THIRD SPACE?

All this is not to say that postcolonial theory is not sensitive to the ambivalent workings of spatial language. The identifying and objectifying power of space has been critically analyzed by postcolonial theory, too, albeit not so much with reference to Luhmann's theory of observation as indication and distinction but rather with regards to the French structuralist school. Edward Said, for instance, in his book *Orientalism*, refers to Claude Lévi-Strauss and what the latter termed the science of the concrete in order to describe the workings of space as a mode of assignation.[45] Unveiling the spatial strategies standing at the heart of Western forms of knowledge regarding the (subaltern) other, *Orientalism* can be read as a critical analysis of how the supposedly essentialist categories of the 'Orient' came into being as a sort of 'surrogate self' of European culture:

> My contention is that without examining Orientalism as a discourse one cannot possibly understand the enormously systematic discipline by which European culture was able to manage—and even produce—the Orient politically, sociologically, militarily, ideologically, scientifically, and imaginatively during the post-Enlightenment period. [...] How this happens is what this book tries to demonstrate. It also tries to show that European culture gained in strength and identity by setting itself off against the Orient as a sort of surrogate and even underground self.[46]

Accordingly, the writings of Said can be—and have been—interpreted as poignant critiques of the ascribing and fixating logic of space.[47] More generally speaking, it can even be argued that it is precisely the fixating logic of the spatial metaphor and its homogenising effects that represents one of the main targets of postcolonial critique. It is in this respect, after all, that third space has become an epitome for a different sort of spatial thinking, one that deconstructs the objectifying logic of spatial language and allows instead for difference in the sense of both/and.

Taking into consideration the system theoretic point of view sketched out in the previous section, however, third space, like ordinary spatial metaphors, is nevertheless always in danger of being misconstrued as a spatial unit—and thus precisely not as a marker of difference. From such a perspective, it is extremely difficult, if not impossible, not to reify third space, i.e. not to think of and use third space in terms of a classical container or at least in terms of some bounded space which is located next to or between other spaces. In what Fuchs has called 'a quasi Euclidian prolongation',[48] the use of spatial language is always problematic if space 'is released from the Cartesian pincers and if, in doing so, the interest is shifted to difference, i.e. towards un-jects (sic) which do not fill or occupy a space in any classical (container-analogous) understanding'.[49] The problem is that the classical understanding is present and is necessarily reproduced, even if a notion, a term or a concept is intended to overcome precisely the imagination of the container. According to Fuchs, notions and concepts of 'intended differ-ence', i.e. concepts which are supposed to work beyond Cartesian thinking, cannot be used without invoking 'something' which is supposed to be dis-carded by the very use of the notion.[50] From such a perspective, third space cannot help but invoke the idea of something fixed instead of referring to cultural hybridity. Third space seems, in other words, to '"check out" of the realm of liquidity and flow, and check back into the realm of [. . .] fixed being'.[51] The danger inherent in the metaphor of third space is thus that 'something' could be at stake 'there', that this 'something' could be miscon-strued as palpable, manifest phenomenon—and not as atopia.[52]

It can be argued, of course, that Bhabha is fully aware of the objectifying character of spatial language not only with regards to classical or first-order metaphors but also with regards to his own use of spatial notions. When he writes of third space as 'unrepresentable in itself', for instance, Bhabha seems to hint at the problem that third space is deprived of its potential power as soon as it is represented, or in system theory diction, as soon as it is thought of as an element of a series of discrete and bounded spatial units which have 'condensed' alongside distinctions.[53] Despite such precaution, Bhabha has difficulties in preventing third space from eventually becom-ing such a unit itself. A review of the respective literature reveals that the *différance* third space makes is surreptitiously transformed into 'simple' spatial differences invoking the imagination of an area or a territory which is located between two (internally homogenous) spaces. In some cases, the idea of third space as binary in-between space has even been applied to material, geographical spaces and places (like cities, streets, plazas etc.).[54] One does not need to work, like Soja does,[55] with a more materialist account of third space, however, in order to run the risk of transforming social dis-tinctions into spatial differences, thereby reducing the disruptive power of third space to an interstitial position on the fence. On an abstract level, too, third space tends to be transformed into a bounded space which is located next to (or, more precisely) in-between other bounded spaces, like a piece of a jigsaw puzzle.

What makes the pitfalls of third space even more problematic is that the homogenizing productiveness and the objectifying consequences of spatial terminology often seem to go unnoticed even in critical social and cultural theory. By not being reflexive of the reifying power of the spatial metaphors deployed in their own writings, however, scholars of third space tend to endow their concepts with ontological credentials, transforming contingent realities (once again) into essential truths. Against the temptation eventually and tacitly to mistake one's account of reality with an objective reality existing independently of the way it is observed and framed, it is important to keep in mind that reality, to us, only exists as an object of our observation and analysis.[56] If we are interested in a truly different understanding of reality and its spatial aspects, we have to take into consideration the possibility of our own deconstruction, developing a relationship to our own contingency in which 'circularity is no longer excluded'.[57] By paying greater attention to the workings of spatial language in our own writings, I would like to suggest, we would be able to critically analyze the theoretical lenses of our own observations in order to clarify what our objects of study owe to the fact that they are observed, framed and thereby constituted in a particular way. What I find crucial, therefore, is a more rigorous stance towards the politics of location within our own writings—a stance, which continuously reflects the degree to which critical concepts like third space, margin or borderland are involved in the production and objectification of our objects.

While the pitfalls of third space hence cannot be avoided, the identifying, reifying and objectifying effects of spatial language can be coped with if the productive power of spatial metaphors is systematically reflected upon. The way to come to terms with the ambivalent logic of spatial semantics thus consists of a much more careful, self-reflexive and circumspect way of representing and locating our objects (and subjects) of study. If the invention and the placement of objects and identities is linked to particular theoretical and practical interests at particular times and in particular places, it is important not only to carefully analyze the spatial language of traditional discourses but also to acknowledge the objectifying power of the spatial metaphors which play a crucial role in both postcolonial theory and practice.

CONCLUSIONS

Discontented with binary opposites and essentialisms, postcolonial scholars have been at work for some time attempting to reconceptualize difference. Traditional imaginations of culture as stable and self-sufficient containers are said to be outdated in globalized times and replaced by more fluid understandings of cultural identification. Despite its critical attitude, however, the concept of third space cannot help but repeat the very repetition—the normalization and objectification of the other—it started out to interrupt. Put differently, the postcolonial project necessarily seems to convey some form of (quasi-)ontology opposite to its anti-foundationalist impetus which, in turn, aims to dissolve supposedly fixed entities. In this paper, it has been argued that the pitfalls of third space follow from postcolonialism's preoccupation with spatial language. In much of the literature of the spatial turn, space is associated with difference in that it supposedly allows for the existence of different narratives. Not denying the differentiating power of spatial semantics, it has been suggested, however, that spatial language quietly conveys sameness and identity.[58] Due to what Fuchs has called the 'quasi-ontology of the spatial metaphor', spatial language leads into the very 'territorial trap' of identity and homogeneity which is tried to be avoided by the scholars of the spatial turn.[59]

Against this background, it seems to be somewhat paradoxical to deploy spatial terminology in order to convey radical difference and multiplicity. Yet at the same time, it is impossible to avoid the deployment of spatial language because it is by space that we deal with inconsistencies, that we identify things, that we set things right. There is no meaningful way of speaking which does not rely upon at least some very basic spatial concepts like close and remote, above and below or fore and aft. There is no way of speaking which is not spatial and, therefore, objectifying the phenomena which are located in the symbolic space of language. There is, in short, 'no language of the before of time and space'.[60] While there is hence no way to avoid the pitfalls of third space, the effects of spatial semantics, i.e. the reification and objectification of identities, can be minimized. What is crucial thereby is to critically and resolutely reflect on the workings of the spatial metaphors which are deployed in order to observe and frame reality. Confining the deconstructionist endeavor to the spatial concepts and metaphors of the traditional discourses of traditional identity politics—like sitting on the fence, for instance—seems insufficient to me. If postcolonial theory fails to take into account the constructed character and the contingency of its own categories, it runs 'considerable risk to take the observation for the object, the category for the item, and semantics for reality'.[61]

That this is not a problem of quaint academic interest can be demonstrated by returning to the example of the Turkish immigrants in Germany. If third space is not taken as a concept but misconstrued as spatial reality, it can turn into a semantic prison-house whose inhabitants—often thought of as subaltern and marginalized by traditional identity politics—are further objectified and represented as both internally homogenous and different from their surroundings. If third space is not thought of as a category of observation but transformed into a spatial unit, it is converted from a marker of difference to an element of traditional identity politics. It appears, in other words, as some kind of third space on the fence, which reifies identities rather than disturbs taken-for-granted fixations and assignations. Inhabiting third space can then become as homogenizing and even stigmatizing as sitting between two chairs. By locating the Turkish community between Germany and Turkey—that is between two chairs—, the demarcation line between us (*Inländer*) and them (*Ausländer*) is once again actualized; 'its political function being to incorporate and regulate "us" or "the same" by distinguishing "us" from "them", the same from the "other".[62] It is against the background of fixations of the either/or kind that the constructedness of the respective categories should be reflected upon. Highlighting the invented character of the categories is not to deny their reality, their real effects for those who are categorized. On the contrary, the categories are to be thought of as real and effective precisely because they are constructed and made real in spatial language. *Ausländer*, however, do not make up a coherent group or *Gemeinschaft*; there are innumerable differences between them which, cannot be reduced to the traditional identity of an imagined community. The same applies to *Inländer*.

ACKNOWLEDGMENTS

I would like to thank Nicola Burns, Michael Flitner, Matthew Hannah, Roland Lippuner and Wolfgang Zierhofer for helpful comments on earlier drafts of this chapter.

NOTES

1. Harvey, David. *The Condition of Postmodernity: An Inquiry into the Origins of Cultural Change.* Cambridge, MA, Oxford: Blackwell, 1990; Soja, Edward W. *Postmodern Geographies: The Reassertion of Space in Critical Social Theory.* London, New York: Verso, 1989; Soja, Edward W. *Thirdspace: Journeys to Los Angeles and other Real-and-Imagined Places.* Oxford, Cambridge, MA: Blackwell, 1996.
2. Soja. *Thirdspace*. 163, 3. For his argument of the apparent growing significance of spatial thinking, Soja turns to a paper by Michel Foucault in which the latter sets space against time: 'The great obsession of the 19th century was, as we know, history: with its themes of development and of suspension, of crisis and cycle, themes of the ever-accumulating past [...]. [...] The present epoch will perhaps be above all the epoch of space. We are in the epoch of simultaneity: we are in the epoch of juxtaposition, the epoch of near and far, of the side-by-side, of the dispersed.' Foucault, Michel. "Of other Spaces." *Diacritics* 16 (1986): 22–27. 23.
3. E.g., Bhabha, Homi K. *The Location of Culture.* London, New York: Routledge, 1994; hooks, bell. *Yearning.* Boston: South End Press, 1990; Rose, Gillian. *Feminism and Geography.* Cambridge: Polity Press, 1993; Hooper, Barbara. "Split at the Roots: A Critique of the Philosophical and Political Sources of Modern Planning Doctrine." *Frontiers* 13 (1992): 45–80; Spivak, Gayatri Chakravorty. *In other Worlds.* London, New York: Routledge, 1988; Anzaldúa, Gloria. *Borderlands/La Frontera.* San Francisco: Aunt Lute Press, 1999; Said, Edward. *Orientalism.* New York: Vintage, 1979.
4. hooks. *Yearning*. 149.
5. Ibid. 149.
6. Ibid. 153.
7. Bhabha, Homi K. "The Third Space." *Identity, Community, Culture, Difference.* Ed. Jonathan Rutherford. London: Lawrence and Wishart, 1990. 207–221. 209.
8. Ibid. 211.

9. Bhabha. *The Location of Culture.*
10. Soja. *Thirdspace.* 54; Lefebvre, Henri. *The Production of Space.* Oxford, Cambridge, MA: Blackwell, 1991.
11. In much of my own work, I refer to postcolonial texts and notably to Bhabha's writings in order to elaborate what I have termed 'a different geography of the world'; see Lossau, Julia. *Die Politik der Verortung: Eine postkoloniale Reise zu einer anderen Geographie der Welt.* Bielefeld: transcript, 2002; Lossau, Julia. "Anders denken. Postkolonialismus, Geopolitik und Politische Geographie." *Erdkunde* 54 (2000): 157–168.
12. For the idea of a 'territorial trap', see Agnew, John. "The Territorial Trap: The Geographical Assumptions of International Relations Theory." *Review of International Political Economy* 1 (1994): 53–80. 'Territorial', in this chapter, does not necessarily refer to a geographical area in the physical-material sense of the word. Although my academic background is in human geography, I am equally interested in the manifold reifications that occur in the symbolic space of language, leaving this space fragmented, i.e. structured by countless boundaries between supposedly homogenous fields or areas. For a brief exploration into the field of 'unspatial' spatialisations, see Lossau, Julia, and Roland Lippuner. "Geographie und Spatial Turn." *Erdkunde* 58 (2004): 201–211. 208.
13. In German, 'sitting on the fence' translates into 'sitting between two chairs'. The French also tend to 'sit between two chairs' rather than 'on the fence'. Perhaps more so than 'sitting on the fence', however, 'sitting between two chairs' relates to a miserable situation that stems from the misfortune of not being in a proper, self-sufficient and thus comfortable place.
14. While '*Ausländer*' usually is translated as 'foreigner' or 'immigrant', there is an edge of meaning which is not captured adequately by either of the two options. '*Ausländer*' is the antonym of '*Inländer*', literally translating into somebody who is (from) 'outside of' but not 'inside of' the respective country.
15. In the last decade, the German debate on domestic politics and immigration has increasingly been haunted by scenarios of so-called parallel worlds developing amongst 'non-integrated' foreigners who live not only 'on the fence' but according to their own rules of law and order. See, e.g., Ramm, Christoph. "Head on: Hybridity as Fascination and Irritation in Constructing the Turkish Community in Germany." *New Hybridities: Societies and Cultures in Transition.* Ed. Heidemann, Frank, and Alfonso de Toro. Hildesheim, Zürich, New York: Georg Olms, 2006. 197–206.
16. See, e.g., Lossau, Julia. "Zu Besuch in Ereğli. Kulturelle Grenzen im Schulbuch 'grenzenlos'." *Berichte zur deutschen Landeskunde* 79 (2005): 241–251.
17. Bhabha. *The Location of Culture.* 66.
18. Ibid. See also Hall, Stuart. "New Ethnicities." *'Race', Culture and Difference.* Ed. Donald, James, and Ali Rattansi. London, Newbury Park, New Delhi: Sage, 1992. 252–259.
19. Bhabha. *The Location of Culture.* 218.
20. Borderline identities have sometimes been celebrated, conceptually and empirically, as morally superior and bestowed with some utopian power. Instead of romanticising postcolonial identities, however, in-between-ness should rather be thought of as a more everyday condition which is, *per se*, neither good nor bad, but necessarily produced in any cultural transaction: 'It is only when we understand that all cultural statements and systems are constructed in [the] contradictory and ambivalent space of enunciation that we begin to understand why hierarchical claims to the inherent originality or "purity" of cultures are untenable, even before we resort to empirical historical instances that demonstrate their hybridity.' Ibid. 37.

21. Ibid. 7.
22. Ibid.
23. Ibid. 37.
24. Ibid. 148, original emphasis.
25. In his critique of the 'discourse of modernity', Bhabha is far from reducing 'a complex and diverse historical moment, with varied national genealogies and different institutional practices, into a singular shibboleth—be it the "idea" of Reason, Historicism, Progress—for the critical convenience of postmodern literary theory. My interest in the question of modernity resides in the influential discussion generated by the work of Habermas, Foucault, Lyotard and Lefort, amongst many others, that has generated a critical discourse around historical modernity as an epistemological structure.' Ibid. 239.
26. Ibid. 149.
27. Haraway, Donna. "A Cyborg Manifesto. Science, Technology, and Socialist-Feminism in the Late Twentieth Century." *Simians, Cyborgs and Women: The Reinvention of Nature*. Ed. Donna Haraway. London, New York: Routledge, 1991. 149–181, 149.
28. Needless to say, there is a variety of postcolonial perspectives pursuing different accounts of hybridity. Whereas, according to Bhabha, *The Location of Culture*. 113, hybridity involves 'a disturbing questioning of the images and presences of authority', Robert J.C. Young seems to be more critical about any progressive and liberating reformulation of hybridity. Young, Robert J.C. *Colonial Desire*. London, New York: Routledge, 1995; see also Hall, Stuart. "When was the Postcolonial? Thinking at the Limit." *The Post-Colonial Question: Common Skies, Divided Horizons*. Ed. Iain Chambers and Linda Curtis. London, New York: Routledge, 1996. 242–260.
29. Bhabha. *The Location of Culture*. 7.
30. Ibid. 38–39.
31. To highlight the importance of the spatial dimension is not to deny the relevance of time in Bhabha's writings. On the contrary, Bhabha's ideas very much revolve around temporal categories, too. At critical moments throughout his texts, it even seems as if his overall motivation was directed at the development of a specific temporality (and not spatiality)—a temporality beyond the '"progressive" myth of modernity': '[...] to dwell "in the beyond" is also [...] to be part of a revisionary time, a return to the present to redescribe our cultural contemporaneity; to reinscribe our human, historic commonality; to touch the future on its hither side.' Ibid. 240, 7. Against this background, Soja has noted that Bhabha's concept of third space 'is occasionally teasingly on the edge of being a spatially ungrounded literary trope, a floating metaphor for a critical *historical* conscience that inadvertently masks a continued privileging of temporality over spatiality'. Soja. *Thirdspace*. 141–142, original emphasis.
32. Massey, Doreen. *Power-Geometries and the Politics of Space-Time*. Heidelberg: Department of Geography, University of Heidelberg, 1999. 21, 21–22.
33. Foucault. "Of other Spaces." See footnote 2.
34. Deleuze, Gilles, and Felix Guattari. *A Thousand Plateaus. Capitalism and Schizophrenia*. Trans. Brian Massumi. Minneapolis: Minnesota UP, 1987. 4. In their search for multiplicity, Deleuze and Guattari differentiate between tracing and map, thus employing a pivotal metaphor in the realm of spatial imagery: 'The rhizome is altogether different, *a map and not a tracing*. Make a map, not a tracing. [...] The map is open to and connectable in all of its dimensions; it is detachable, reversible, susceptible to constant modification. It can be torn, reversed, adapted to any kind of mounting, reworked by an individual, group, or social formation.' Ibid. 12, original emphasis.

35. Esposito, Elena. "Geheimnis im Raum, Geheimnis in der Zeit." *Räumliches Denken.* Ed. Dagmar Reichert. Zürich: Verlag der Fachvereine, 1996. 303–330. 319.

36. Ibid. 317.

37. Ibid. 319. For the notion of polycontexturality, see, e.g., Fuchs, Peter. *Die Erreichbarkeit der Gesellschaft: Zur Konstruktion und Imagination gesellschaftlicher Einheit.* Frankfurt am Main: Suhrkamp 1992. 43–58, and, rather critical, Wagner, Gerhard. "Der Kampf der Kontexturen im Superorganismus Gesellschaft." *Die Logik der Systeme: Zur Kritik der systemtheoretischen Soziologie Niklas Luhmanns.* Ed. Peter-Ulrich Merz-Benz and Gerhard Wagner. Konstanz: UVK, 2000. 199–223.

38. By speaking of space as an ordering scheme or grid, I do not only think of the modernist project of the 'world as exhibition' where objects and identities are assigned to particular spaces and places, arranged on the earth's surface as something to be observed. See Gregory, Derek. *Geographical Imaginations.* Cambridge, MA, Oxford: Blackwell, 1994. 15–69; Mitchell, Timothy. "The World as Exhibition." *Comparative Studies in Society and History* 31 (1989): 217–236. While the reifying power of geographical and cartographical technologies of depicting the world from above/nowhere have been criticized from various perspectives; see, e.g. Harley, J.B. "Deconstructing the Map." *Cartographica* 26 (1989): 1–20; the system theoretic argument deployed in this paper is related to a more abstract level of reasoning.

39. Luhmann, Niklas. *Social Systems.* Stanford, CA: Stanford UP, 1995. 385. Not widely read in the realm of English (and French) speaking social and cultural theory, Luhmann is one of the most popular authors in the field of social theory in German-speaking countries. Having been a scholar of Talcott Parsons, he developed a general theory of observation deriving, in turn, from George Spencer Brown's operative logic. See Spencer Brown, George. *Laws of Form.* London: Allen & Unwin, 1969. Following Spencer Brown's directive 'draw a distinction', observation Luhmann is defined as indication based upon a distinction. Put differently, both distinguishing and indicating are components of one single operation—the operation of observation. An introduction into Luhmann's work from a spatial perspective can be found in the work of Wolfgang Zierhofer who made an effort to introduce the 'geographical arguments' of Luhmann's system theory to an English-speaking audience. See Zierhofer, Wolfgang. "State, Power and Space." *Social Geography* 1 (2005): 29–36; Gren Martin, and Wolfgang Zierhofer. "The Unity of Difference: A Critical Appraisal of Niklas Luhmann's Theory of Social Systems in the Context of Corporeality and Spatiality." *Environment and Planning A* 35 (2003): 615–630.

40. Luhmann. *Social Systems.* 595.

41. See Fuchs, Peter. "Vom Unbeobachtbaren." *Beobachtungen des Unbeobachtbaren.* Ed. Oliver Jahraus and Nina Ort. Weilerswist: Velbrück, 2000). 39–71. 44. See also Lippuner, Roland. *Raum, Systeme, Praktiken: Zum Verhältnis von Alltag, Wissenschaft und Geographie.* Stuttgart: Steiner, 2005. 135–149.

42. Ibid. 44.

43. While the respective units can be observed, the distinctions itself becomes invisible. See Fuchs, Peter. *Die Metapher des Systems: Studien zu der allgemein leitenden Frage, wie sich der Tänzer vom Tanz unterscheiden lasse.* Weilerswist: Velbrück, 2001. 145.

44. Fuchs, Peter. "Das psychische System und die Funktion des Bewusstseins." *Theorie—Prozess—Selbstreferenz: Systemtheorie und transdisziplinäre Theoriebildung.* Ed. Oliver Jahraus and Nina Ort. Konstanz: UVK, 2003. 27.

45. Said. *Orientalism*. 53; Lévi-Strauss, Claude. *The Savage Mind*. Chicago: Chicago UP, 1967.
46. Said. *Orientalism*. 3.
47. According to British geographer Felix Driver, for instance, Said's work can be read as an argument against 'geographical essentialism'. See Driver, Felix. "Geography's Empire: Histories of Geographical Knowledge." *Environment and Planning D. Society and Space* 10 (1992): 23–40.
48. Fuchs. *Die Metapher des Systems*. 134.
49. Ibid., trans. ('Raum ist schließlich immer problematisch, wenn er aus der cartesischen Zange entlassen und wenn dabei umgestellt wird auf Differenz, also auf Un-jekte, die keinen Raum in einem klassischen (behälteranalogen) Verständnis füllen oder besetzen.').
50. Ibid. 120.
51. Hannah, Matthew G. "Sceptical Realism: From either/or to both-and." *Environment and Planning D: Society and Space* 17 (1999): 17–34. 23.
52. Fuchs. *Die Metapher des Systems*. 120.
53. Bhabha. *The Location of Culture*. 37.
54. A typical example of the 'materialization' of third space can be found in a paper on 'the shopping mall as a teenage hangout'. Referring to Bhabha's concept of third space, the authors conceptualize young people as 'the hybrid', 'a group in-between', 'neither One [adult] nor the Other [child], but something else besides'. Matthews, Hugh et al. "The Unacceptable Flaneur: The Shopping Mall as a Teenage Hangout." *Childhood* 7 (2000): 279–294. 282. The places where the young people hang out and negotiate their identity, i.e. 'roads, cul-de-sacs, alleyways, walkways, shopping areas, car parks, vacant plots and derelict sites' (ibid. 281)—in short: 'the street'—, is then described as the young people's third space: 'From this perspective the street becomes a "third space", a dynamic zone of tension and discontinuity where the newness of the hybrid identities can be articulated' (ibid. 282). See also Matthews, Hugh, Melanie Limb, and Mark Taylor. "The 'Street as Third-space'." *Children's Geographies: Playing, Living, Learning*. Ed. Sarah Holloway and Gill Valentine. London, New York: Routledge, 2000. 63–79.
55. Soja. *Thirdspace*.
56. See Luhmann, Niklas. *Die Gesellschaft der Gesellschaft*. Frankfurt am Main: Suhrkamp, 1997. 1128–1142; Luhmann, Niklas. "'Was ist der Fall?' und 'Was steckt dahinter?'" *Zeitschrift für Soziologie* 22 (1993): 245–260. Another scholar who has reminded us of the 'epistemological break' dissociating academic research from its objects in the social world is French sociologist Pierre Bourdieu. In his *Outline of a Theory of Practice*, Bourdieu states that knowledge 'does not merely depend, as an elementary relativism teaches, on the particular standpoint an observer "situated in space and time" takes up on the object. The "knowing subject", as the idealist tradition rightly calls him (sic), inflicts on practice a much more fundamental and pernicious alteration which, being a constituent condition of the cognitive operation, is bound to pass unnoticed: in taking up a point of view on the action, withdrawing from it in order to observe it from above and from a distance, he constitutes practical activity as an *object of observation and analysis, a representation*.' Bourdieu, Pierre. *Outline of a Theory of Practice*. Trans. Richard Nice. Cambridge, New York: Cambridge UP, 1977. 2, original emphasis. For an account of Bourdieu's approach from a geographical perspective, see Lippuner. *Raum, Systeme, Praktiken*. 157–180.
57. Luhmann, Niklas. "Kontingenz als Eigenwert der modernen Gesellschaft." *Beobachtungen der Moderne*. Opladen: Westdeutscher Verlag, 1992. 93–128. 95.

58. Maybe this is the reason why Bhabha seems to privilege temporality over spatiality, as argued by Soja (see footnote 31). At any rate, the rhetoric of time (e.g. the deployment of temporal terminology like 'iteration', 'synchronicity' or 'reinscription') is closer to the vocabulary of an author Bhabha is drawing heavily upon. It is Jacques Derrida's concept of 'différance' which epitomizes the fundamental delay or 'deferral' in the movement of signification which cannot be signified itself without delay. See Derrida, Jacques. "Différance." *Margins of Philosophy*. Trans. Alan Bass. Chicago: Chicago UP, 1982. 3–27. Différance allows for signification while it cannot be represented itself. 'In' the delay, however, a space is opened up in which identity and difference occupy different places. In this sense, spatialization is closely connected to temporalization and vice versa. See Fuchs, *Die Metapher des Systems*. 122.
59. Fuchs. "Das psychische System und die Funktion des Bewusstseins." 27.
60. Fuchs. "Vom Unbeobachtbaren." 45. While space involves hidden forms of identification and objectification opposite to the postcolonial project, there are, however, more positive, liberating and deliberate aspects of the spatial metaphor, too. It can be argued that a more deliberate reason for the postcolonial preoccupation with—and devotion for—space is their commitment to what can be described as a 'marginal' or 'subaltern' form of identity 'on the margin'. See, e.g., Bhabha, Homi K. "Interrogating Identity: The Real Me." *Identity: The Real Me.* Ed. Lisa Appignanesi. London: ICA Documents 6, 1987. 5–11; Hall, Stuart. "Old and New Identities, Old and New Ethnicities." *Culture, Globalisation and the World System: Contemporary Conditions for the Representation of Identity.* Ed. A.D. King. Minneapolis: Minnesota UP, 1991. 41–68.
61. Zierhofer. "State. Power and Space." 31.
62. Dalby, Simon. "Critical Geopolitics. Discourse, Difference, and Dissent." *Environment and Planning D: Society and Space* 9 (1991): 261–283. 274.

Part III
Theorizing the Third Space

5   The Void of Misgiving

Robert J.C. Young

The 'third space' of the third man of postcolonial theory is not a space as such. Not a space at all in fact, if by space we mean architectural space, or physical space, or even those of the sort of twilight zones that Harry Lime or Ramon Miguel Vargas moved around in. It's not just another, off-Broadway kind of alternative space either. You will never find yourself walking by mistake into the third space, even though you may at times find that you are already there, stumbling and stuttering right in the thick of it without knowing it. And though Bhabha developed his concept of 'third space' as a counterspace of modernity most fully in response to Jameson's theory of postmodern space, nor can it be simply constituted in that historical sequence where it corresponds to the third stage of capitalism.[1] By the same token, the third space is not a third space in the sense that the third world is a different territorial domain from the first or the second worlds, nor is it even an alternative space for minorities within a dominant culture, in the sense of being a place of their own, a place to congregate, worship or perform. Bhabha's third space begins to seem something of a tease. It winks at us and draws us in; but as soon as we try to grasp it or to map it, like the real itself, it begins to elude us. Though among the most influential and widely invoked of his concepts, it is, perhaps for this reason, rarely analyzed, discussed or defined in theoretical terms. In his section on Bhabha's 'third space' in his *Thirdspace*, a discussion that could hardly be avoided, Edward Soja is reduced to quoting large passages of Bhabha's prose, from which he moves on virtually without comment, speechless.[2] David Huddart, in his recent book on Bhabha, mentions the concept only once.[3] What, where then is the third space? Is it invisible? Or is its visibility so obvious that it goes without saying? Why is it the concept that is most invoked but at the same time the one that cannot be found, located, or spoken?

The third space is not a space, nor is it a place. If anything, it is a site, but even then it is not a site in the sense of a building site, somewhere bounded and fixed that can be located with the right coordinates with your Satnav/ GPS on a map. It doesn't have a postcode or a zip code. If anything, it is more like a shifting caravan site, a place where people come unobserved and where they go without trace, the place which determines their lives for the moment they pitch their tents there, a place which is not a space because it is the site of an event, gone in a moment of time. It is the non-place of the no-fixed-abode, the NFA people, migrants, those torn from their homes, cultures, literatures, a multitude always on the move across shifting sites riven with the lapsed times in between one pitching and another, the movement from one location to another, the place where you find yourself momentarily *in situ*, a literal lieutenant, standing in, holding the place while something else happens—which is why, therefore, it is in a sense no more place than space.

The third space is also a site in the sense of a situation, and, for the subject, a site's other sense too, that is, of care or sorrow, grief and trouble: to make site is to lament or mourn. For the third space is above all a site of production, the production of anxiety, an untimely place of loss, of fading, of appearance and disappearance.

ENUNCIATION: L'HOMME DANS LA LANGUE

In the first place the third space is not a place because it is an instance of production in time—the moment of speech. The third space, above all, is the site of enunciation, the instance of every utterance, and, at the point of the tongue, the fall into language. Its theoretical origins begin from Emile Benveniste, whose *Course on General Linguistics* represents the hidden, forgotten site from which much poststructuralism was constructed.[4] The interest in linguistics focussed on the parts where it addressed the role of the subject in speech: the act whereby the individual fuses *langue* and *parole* in the momentary event when he or she opens his or her mouth and says 'I'. Among the poststructuralist brigade, there was a general agreement to restrict subjectivity to this single function.[5]

Benveniste was fascinated by the linguistic anomaly of the operation of the pronoun in speech:

> these pronouns are distinguished from all the other designations a language articulates in that *they do not refer to a concept or to an individual*.[6]

Neither a word nor a concept, the shifting designation of I, you, he, she, and it, made the pronoun unlike any other kind of word: for Benveniste the pronoun had become a third space. Pronouns are not merely part of syntax; the 'I' and the 'you' also form what he calls 'instances of discourse',[7] that is, discrete and each time unique acts by means of which language is actualized in speech by a speaker—comparable to what Otto Jespersen had already called 'shifters', words that have no meaning without a context. Until the moment of speech, the pronoun remains empty: a void (*vide*), into which the speaker or addressee find themselves dropping into but an emptiness which at the same times enables the articulation and assertion of their own subjectivity. It is only in the event of speech that it becomes actualised, full—every I has its own singular reference, momentarily. Moreover, each act of speech also involves the production of a third term, the other:

> immediately, as soon as he declares himself a speaker and assumes language, he implants the other opposite him, whatever maybe the degree of presence that he attributes to this other. All enunciation is, explicitly or implicitly, an address, and posits an addressee.[8]

Speech draws the other into being, like a genie from its bottle. By saying 'I', you cannot help yourself constructing another. And then, as soon as your interlocutor responds, you become othered yourself.

The psyche, at this point, becomes a storm of floating signifiers of I and you, of he and she and it, disorientateurs all. Your identity fractures into any and every one of these. How can we deal with them all, reposition ourselves to take account of their constant shifty shiftings? Benveniste's perspective means, as is always said, that here the subject far from being the author or origin becomes an effect of language, of the moment of speech. But then so do all other subjects. In the exchange of pronouns, the resituating of the demands of the I, it becomes a space of production and loss, of contestation and of negotiation. From the moment we say 'I', we set up the circulation of the positions of I, you, he or she, splitting narration from description, subjectivity into objectivity. The position of the I is not fixed: in any conversation, the I and the you reverse each other at each moment of speech. The I becomes a place that you occupy, but a place that you immediately lose, until you interrupt, and assert yourself as the I again: 'Enough of you. Let's talk about me'. Or: 'I love you'. Yet even at the moment of the declaration of love, or the performative assent of the marriage ceremony, 'I do', you never wholly occupy the I, you can never fully bring language to match its I to your own ego, your own observing, thinking I, the real me. For this reason, said Benveniste, good Hegelian that he was, at the moment of utterance, of enunciation, the speaker experiences a form of splitting, a division between the I or the subject who speaks the sentence, and the I which he or she voices in the declarative sentence, which never fully subsumes or becomes wholly identified with the speaker. Paradoxically therefore, the exercise of the term 'I' in speech, the singular, produces a doubling and turns you into a plural: *I* is also the 'person who is uttering the present instance of the discourse containing *I*'.[9] As Jean Michel Rabaté puts it, 'the speaking subject will be made and unmade in this linguistic hole through which he or she emerges at the time of a statement before fading away'.[10] Knowledge can only become absolute at the moment the philosopher leaps from the particularity of the 'I speak' to the 'it speaks', where the fragmentary subjective is transformed into the totality of the objective. Even here, though, the unconscious remains dormantly, mordantly at work: *ça parle*. It speaks; and what though, its shadowy voice whispers, if Benveniste was wrong? That the subject isn't split by speaking, that it's just a bit of neo-Hegelian linguistics? That we manage very well . . . ?

'Tu vas y arriver?' Not always. Even so, it is when you speak, at all events, that you are constituted as human, as a person. 'It is in and through language that man constitutes himself as a *subject* [. . .]'.[11] But the split that this introduces between the I that speaks and the I of the sentence means that you are never quite one or the other, left in a third space, a limbo land between them which at the same time does not exist. It is nowhere. The speaker, whether subaltern or not, becomes once again a literal lieutenant, a mere stand-in, undecidably 'left' or 'loo'.

Benveniste argues that this unsituatable third space of the moment of speech is really a place of time. The domain of time is always constructed away from the present, and the only criterion for the present, the time in which one is, is that of the time in which one speaks, the moment of presence:

> This is the eternally 'present' moment, although it never relates to the same events of an 'objective' chronology because it is determined for each speaker by each of the instances of discourse related to it. Linguistic time is *self-referential*. Ultimately, human temporality with all its linguistic apparatus reveals the subjectivity inherent in the very using of language.[12]

So the act of discourse that founds the subject also produces the foundation of temporality, the act from which all other moments become arraigned into pasts and futures. 'I think therefore I am'. And yet this moment of the present is itself fractured, so that it is not a pure moment of being, of presence, but an interrupted moment, in which the two 'I's produced in the act of enunciation are fractured by a third which is not part of language itself, not the you from which the spoken I implicitly distinguishes itself, but an other, a space of alterity which intervenes between the two, a fractured sliver of time between the two 'I's, neither of which is wholly 'I', separated into different times by the temporal void between them, leaving the subject 'out of balance, caught between one temporality and another'.[13] This alterity, this spliced space of being and non-being, of speaking and of not speaking, which Bhabha describes as the 'spiral' of *différance*, is the third space, the space which is a non-space, hooked into the fractured moments of the event of splitting which happens instantaneously upon speaking, and which, though it divides up the two forms of subjectivity, the linguistic from the subjectivity of the ego, meaning from being, becomes in some sense the non-place of the subject itself, a place which is no place, a space

through which you spiral downwards, down into the depths of the void
... a vast, bubble-shaped empty space, *Śūnyatā*, into 'an emptiness more
extreme and exploratory than mere vacant or "negative" space can ever
accommodate'.[14]

THE LUNULA

Benveniste identified a split in consciousness through language—a linguistics of Hegel, so to speak, that produces psychic alienation. His account was
magic to Lacan's ears. For here was an account of alienation through the subject's assumption into language. In order to become human you must use language: but to use language is to enter a domain, a space, in which you are an
outsider and which you do not control. In Lacan's terms, you move from the
imaginary to the symbolic, except that you never entirely leave the imaginary
behind you, while the symbolic henceforth ruptures the imaginary with its
impersonal charge. Psychic life is a constant to-ing and fro-ing among the two
realms. Benveniste's distinction between the 'I' who makes the statement and
the 'I' that is the grammatical subject of the statement itself, between being
and meaning, is less threatening when it comes down to it, for it suggests only
that there is a split between the speaker and his or her statement—the statement moves off into circulation, while the subject remains behind, still coherent and unified, even if separated from his or her own wayward speech act.
Lacan pushes this much further, arguing that subjectivity itself is an effect of
the fact that in entering language, the subject takes up signifying positions for
others which become the subject itself: 'the subject', he says, 'is inserted in a
function whose exercise grasps it'.[15] You are captured in language, snapped in
a photograph, except that in language the camera is snapping all the time, and
that snapping is you. As in Hegel, it is only in the recognition of the other—as
the lens of the observing camera—that the subject comes to be, that is to know
him or herself. Moreover, since the subject is an effect of the signifier, its experience of subjectivity is one of 'suturing', that is, of a constant displacement
along the signifying chain. Think of this as if you are the person watching a
film: as spectator, the I who observes is constantly refashioned, reconstructed,
stitched together, from shot to shot. It is the spluttering between frames, the
visible invisible. Bhabha draws on Stephen Heath's account of Lacan's evoca-
tion of that moment in the production of language, the imaginary space of
signification which produces the suturing of the subject:

> the unconscious is the breaking edge, a constant flickering of the sub-
> ject, flickering in eclipses [...]. The subject is thus nothing other than
> that which 'slides in a chain of signifiers', its cause is the effect of lan-
> guage: 'by this effect, it is not cause of itself; it carries in it the worm of
> the cause of its splitting'. The unconscious is the fact of the constitution-
> division of the subject in language; an emphasis which can even lead

Lacan to propose replacing the notion of the unconscious with that of the subject in language; 'it is a vicious circle to say that we are speaking beings; we are *speakings*, a word that can be advantageously substituted for the unconscious'.[16]

In Lacan, what for Benveniste was an invisible, flickering moment of time, is also spatialized, into a breaking edge. The linguistic moment of splitting becomes the division, the constitutive alienation of the subject: 'there where I think, I am not, and here, where I am, I do not think'. 'Alienation consists in this *vel*, which [. . .] condemns the subject to appearing only in that division', the division between meaning and being:

> if I have spoken to you of the unconscious as of something that opens and closes, it is because its essence is to mark that time by which, from the fact of being born with the signifier, the subject is born divided. The subject is this emergence which, just before, as subject, was nothing, but which, scarcely having appeared, solidifies into a signifier.[17]

The interstitial site of enunciation, of splitting and a hurried stapling together, where the subject comes into being only as a signifier in the field of the Other, marks nothing less than the emerging unconscious itself, the edgy moment of psychic anxiety in which the stuttering subject is faced with incommensurable demands, faced with the prospect of having been hijacked between being and meaning for all futurity.

'The very place of identification', Bhabha writes, 'caught in the tension of demand and desire, is a space of splitting'.[18] Lacan illustrates this with the logic of set theory, through the form of the *vel*, the either/or. There are different logics of the 'or'. In fact, says Lacan, there are three kinds of *vel*. The first is the simplest, where you choose between one thing and another: would you like to eat Italian or Japanese tonight? If you choose Italian, then you will not be eating sushi. If you choose Japanese, you will not be eating saltimbocca. The second *vel* comes when you don't have to choose, or when one is as good as the other. 'What's the best way to Cambridge from London?' 'You can take the A1 or the M11'. You will get to Cambridge either way, whatever you decide, it makes no difference. This is almost the undecidable form of Archie Bunker's laces, the de Manian form of deconstruction, in which two incompatible meanings indifferent to each other are lodged in the same verbal sequence. 'What's the difference?' There is no difference—you will get to Cambridge either way—but at the same time there is a difference because if you take the A1, then you can leave the unbearably busy ring-road round London earlier. Then there is what Lacan calls a 'third' *vel*, which is that of a certain kind of symbolic logic in set theory, where two different sets are joined together, so that some parts overlap and belong to both sets, by which token they will also belong fully to neither.

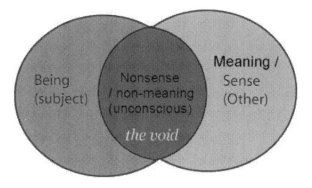

Figure 1: Lacan's *vel*: the splitting of alienation

The elliptical space in the middle is not simply a space because it is at the same time constituted by both the other elements and yet not fully one or the other. It is both a doubling and a lack: 'Of this was neither and was both at once', as Wordsworth put it. Lacan comments: 'The *vel* of alienation is defined by a choice whose properties depend on this, that there is, in the joining, one element that, whatever the choice operating may be, has as its consequence a *neither one, nor the other*'.[19] This undecidable element in-between, of the neither the one nor the other, of the white but not quite, is the realm of the third space. Lacan continues:

> Let us illustrate the *vel* by what concerns us here, namely, the being of the subject, the subject which is there beneath the meaning. If we choose being, the subject disappears, escapes us, falls into non-meaning and non-sense. If we choose meaning, or sense, then meaning only survives deprived of the part of non-sense which is, strictly speaking, what constitutes, in the realization of the subject, the unconscious.[20]

Lacan famously illustrates this with the highwayman's demand, which finds an uncanny echo with every psychoanalyst's demand for payment: 'Your money or your life!' If you choose 'money', then you lose both. But even if you choose 'life', you only have life deprived of something, namely your money. The logic of the *vel* is that you are always left with something that is partial, something that is lacking, a metonymic structure in which you find yourself with only the part instead of the whole. Lacan compares this 'alienating *vel*' to the structure of the dialectic of master and slave in Hegel: '*Your freedom or your life!*' If the slave chooses freedom, he loses both, but if he chooses life, he only has his life deprived of something, namely freedom. The only lesson of colonial rule is that whatever it claims to offer you, it also leaves you with something missing.

The essence of 'the alienating *vel*', which Lacan calls 'the lethal factor', is that the subject is both created, and left, in the space between, with something that is not really either. Lacan names this lacuna the 'lunula', a term which in geometry designates 'a plain terminated by the circumferences of two circles, which touch one another on the inside',[21] making the crescent shape of the moon in its moments of partial eclipse, which is why lunula also comes to be used as the word for the white, crescent shaped mark at the base of the fingernail.

> Examining the bedsheet was one thing. Looking at his fingernails was the other. They were invariably bitten down; but sometimes he saw a thin white rim on one nail, and thought these rims never lasted, he took their appearance to mean that release was near.[22]

The geometrical lunula is the space of the third *vel*: it is within the logic of its conflicting sectors that we find the unlocatable, partial moment of the third space. The lunula is where the subject remains in a state of partial eclipse, where meaning is always lacking something, never full: taking up a residency in colonial crescent, an address permanently marked by lack and desire.

While Benveniste argued that the phenomenological and psychoanalytical models of subjectivity amount only to the emergence within the individual of a fundamental property of language, Lacan responded by incorporating the split between the two levels of enunciation into a psychoanalytical account of the speaking subject, where the entry into language is also the entry into the symbolic, social space, the space of the other through which the subject is both produced and eclipsed. So Lacan displaces the anxiety from space (which for Freud was itself a displacement from unconscious fantasy) to language, which now becomes originary. Bhabha too relocates consciousness within the interstices of the split, at the point of the opening and closing of the unconscious. This then becomes a shadowy third space, taking on spatial as well as imaginary dimensions. Imaginary and symbolic: how much more resonant are these incompatible realms in the colonial situation, where the alien symbolic realm of language may not be your own mother-tongue at all, but that of the conquerors, to whose occupation you are forced to assent every time you speak and enter their alien cultural domain, at once doubling you and splitting you in two in an alienation that is repeated twice. For Bhabha, enunciation always remains foundational. In his writing he repeatedly emphasizes the significance of enunciation and the splitting of the subject that occurs at the moment of speech, according to Benveniste's model. Indeed, Bhabha's whole work could be summarized in his own phrase as 'the implication of this enunciative split for cultural analysis'.[23] In the form of Bhabha's architectonics, enunciation operates both as the necessary form of speech, in the Benvenistian formulation, and as the production of the subject and the unconscious as in Lacan, but also becomes the larger condition of modernity and the performativity of its cultures, no longer necessarily spoken as such.

In Benveniste, *énonciation* is the act of making a statement, located in a particular context, while the statement itself, the *énoncé*, remains independent. Following Foucault in the *Archaeology of Knowledge* (1969), Bhabha argues that every speech act, every statement, is also an *event*, an intervention that takes place within the markings of historical time and in a specific setting and circumstance. Texts and statements, do not just circulate: they are riven with their own forms of historicity in the necessary location of culture. So enunciation both (de)constitutes the speaker and situates him or her, while the act of enunciation embodies and positions speech in time and space so that it becomes a 'diagonal' event that slices through to become at once 'a meeting place of modes and meanings, and a site of the contentious struggles of perspective and interpretation'.[24]

Bhabha puts this Foucault with Lacan. Each 'discursive instance' of enunciation will undergo a form of splitting, a moment of anxiety, ambivalence. Not only the speaking subject, but the discourse itself, is marked, Bhabha argues, by the dynamics of the 'enunciatory space, where the work of signification *voids* the act of meaning in articulating a split-response'.[25] In developing the implications of the enunciative split for cultural analysis, Bhabha, like Benveniste, especially emphasizes its 'temporal dimension'. The split always involves a form of temporality:

> It transforms that 'imperceptible' moment in the 'sign' which permits the narrative of history to begin, to inscribe a present. This is the proximate margin between the caesura of 'time-lag'—a form of temporality—that turns into the disjunctive present of a modernity that is now marginalised, a space for minorities and the postcolonial.[26]

The third space of the caesura in the moment of enunciation here becomes also the disjunctive moment of modernity, the non-place of its time-lag that opens between modernity's different temporalities. The time-lag, Bhabha argues, marks 'the historical construction of a specific position of historical enunciation and address'.[27] The third space becomes a measure of time, of temporalities, the form of subjectivity, a space of intersubjective negotiation, a difficult dialogue conducted in different tongues. It is, above all, a *caesura*, the pause in between, the stop, the cut, *caedere*; the event of the subject, wounded at the moment of the fall (*cadere*) into language.

That moment of a wounding occurs in a flash: however miniscule its interstitial split-second, it opens up a gap, a lacuna that is not emptiness, into which the subject is dropped, evacuated. In his earliest discussion of the 'third space', Bhabha cites Wilson Harris on the necessity of that fall into the void:

> And if indeed therefore any real sense is to be made of material change it can only occur with an acceptance of a concurrent void and with a willingness to descend into that void [. . .].[28]

Bhabha comments: 'This meditation by the great Guyanan writer Wilson Harris on the void of misgiving in the textuality of colonial history reveals the cultural and historical dimension of that Third Space of enunciations which I have made the precondition for the articulation of cultural difference'. In *Tradition, The Writer, and Society*, Wilson Harris observes that there is 'a certain "void" or misgiving attending every assimilation of contraries'.[29] The colony is inexorably marked by its contradictory history: 'I dreamt I had been robbed of my native roots and heritage. I suffered from a void of memory, I belonged to peoples of the Void [. . .]'.[30] It is the void, above all, that situates 'the cultural and historical dimension of that Third Space of enunciations'.

> Whatever the wounds inflicted on the body of the Caribbean, that body secretes in itself [. . .] a paradoxical and creative spirit. We are aware of this, I think, but its significance lies in a void.[31]

The colonial 'void of misgiving' constitutes at once the 'precondition for the articulation of cultural difference' and postcolonial creativity.

PLATZANGST IN THE LUNULA

This splitting, nugatory non-space where the unconscious opens and closes, winking like a seeping wound, engendering the subject in that moment of splicing as it passes through the needle's eye of lack, is also, unsurprisingly, for the subject who experiences it, a seat of anxiety, even of paranoia. It hardly sounds like a pleasant experience. And to make things worse, as we fall into the void, we glimpse out there that other, alien social dimension opened up by the entry into the domain of language in the act of enunciation.

While for Lacan, the enunciative split marks the irruption of the unconscious, Bhabha's third space is more like the unconscious writ large, as in Freud, into the phobias and anxieties of social space: *Platzangst*. If the symbolic is the realm of the social, it is also social space, says Freud, which allows us to articulate the forms of our anxiety; social space enables a productive staging of trouble down in the unconscious. This relation was always a reciprocal one. It was the development of open spaces in the city in the 19th century, of plazas bordered by the clean lines of a rationalized architecture, that in turn produced in the city dwellers who lived in them a whole new arena of neuroses, neurasthenia and agoraphobia: fear of open spaces, fear of the place of assembly, and, beyond that, of the need to negotiate the symbolic architectural space of that imagined community, the nation—that 'vast agora, or assembly of the whole community' created by 'the telegraph and the printing-press', as W.T. Stead put it in 1886, anticipating Benedict Anderson by almost a century.[32]

The vast imaginary space of the nation itself reduces the vulnerable psyche to fear and trembling. Antony Vidler has pointed to the links between space and anxiety that developed in the 19ᵗʰ century out of the lassitude of neurasthenia: *agoraphobia, Platzangst*.[33] This space, both physical and psychic at once, constitutes, as Vidler names it, the *warped space* of modernity. Neither open or empty, it is warped: twisted, Moebian, distorted by a damp invisibility, unknowable because ambivalent, simultaneously a real space that can be mapped out and walked through anxiously, and a psychic space that frames anxiety and desire, highlighting the 'active role of objects and spaces in anxiety and phobia' which are then translated into a geography of fear and dread of outer voids.[34]

In many ways, though he grounds his work on the Benvenistian/Lacanian model, Bhabha is closer to the anxiety of the *Platzangst* of Freud than the rest of Lacan's trajectory of the subject towards the *jouissance* of desire. Bhabha's warped space is the surreal location of anxiety, averse to the open, rationalized spaces of modernism that open up far away from the jumble of the crowded, unplanned city, of moving from Old Delhi to New Delhi, from Chandhi Chowk to the Rajpath, from Peshawar to Chandigarh, from the narrow lanes of the seething markets to the anxieties of modernity that erupt in the widely spaced guarded buildings full of emptiness between. This third space is space that is both physical and psychic at once, where the subject, who has been split, is beset by the angst of the vast caesura of modernity, of his or her drop into the void of misgiving, into a well-tried tired thirdness, neither the one nor the other, that is, neither I nor you—the moment when you face the loss of subjectivity altogether to become an alien, displaced third person. With the forms of modernity, the unwitting subject begins to *faire la fenêtre*: perched on the windowsill of desire, resting on the invisible cut between inside and outside through which she or he moves without realizing which side she will find herself on. The subject of modernity moves along the *lignes de refend*, the grooves on the partition between the imaginary and the symbolic which ought to be signs of a clear-cut division but which in practice become intermixed and reversible, so that it is impossible to know whether you are on the inside or the outside. *Platzangst* is when the outside becomes the inside, as in Pascal's famous void that habitually opened up beside him on his left-hand side and into which he feared he would plunge, like his coach horses into the Seine, into the horror of the vacuum, turning being into nothingness.[35]

So the split space of the speaking subject, the void of anxiety and desire, is figured in social and architectural space in psychoanalysis as agoraphobia and neurasthenia, the trauma of anxiety, just as the third space marks the unquiet site of negotiation for minorities in a majoritarian society. At the same time, split between the imaginary and symbolic, it equally goes inwards, into psychic space, engendering apprehension and indeterminacy. It can go outwards or inwards, or rather both, always doubled. Like Pascal, we all live with this void which equally seems to be outside and inside at the same time. What's always presented as a choice is in fact both, the *vel*, in which what we are offered is neither and both at once.

And insofar as that thirdness, that warped moment of splicing, requires gendering, then further anxiety ensues.

QUEER SPACE

In the irresolvable third *vel* the subject undergoes its identificatory processes through a swithering sexuality confused in terms of normative models, masculinity or femininity—faced with the impasse of the neither nor, the both and, the queer and wait—straight?, the uncertain vacillating realm in which the modes of sexuality are transferred to the field of the Other. Gayatri Gopinath cites Bhabha's father's demand 'Are you a man or a mouse?', and his response—'"Do I have to choose?" I remember thinking, in anxious awkwardness, caught impossibly, ambivalently, in between "two different creeds and two different outlooks on life"'.[36] Sexuality gets formed at the edge of a void of misgiving. How can you take up a subject position, a gender, in that moment of anxiety, that nonplussed realm of nothingness? Charged in the space of the third *vel*, you are neither the one nor the other. Gopinath comments that 'for Bhabha, his father's question speaks to the ambivalent and oscillating nature of masculinity itself, in its need to compulsively interrogate itself and act out its power and powerlessness'.[37] At the same time she intuits a link between his father's masculist demand and Bhabha's own early interest in V.S. Naipaul's *A House for Mr Biswas* (1961), the subject of his earliest writings. Mr Biswas who is born with an extra finger, which falls off in a moment of phallic dismemberment long before he inadvertently kills his own father who drowns in the deep void of the pond looking for him, as the boy in hiding awkwardly looks on. For Mr Biswas, like Oedipus himself, the Oedipus complex is no dream, just as when he escapes his abject poverty by marrying into the Tulsi family he finds that in marrying his wife he has married into a family who casts him out to hover becalmed at the edge of an unending sea of unmanning, leaving him faced with the prospect of nothing more than being stranded forever in a state of faded nothingness deprived of both being and meaning.

The third space becomes a space of gendering, of emasculation but also of reorientation and multiplicity, just as for Gopinath, house and home become 'a space that is ruptured and imaginatively transformed by queer diasporic subjects even as they remain within its confines'.[38] It becomes the place where you and I, male or female, no longer seem locked into such a rigid binarism in which each individual is caught within a particular fixed identity. Here sexuality becomes as fluid as the pronouns themselves. We are both I, you, she, he, it. Despite our dissimilarities, we are both the same. Sexuality, no more than pronouns, is not riven on differences which are embodied and fixed. It too is a field of positions, of shifting voids waiting to be embodied, of deviations which touch one another on the inside, not the outside. The other is already within, disturbing, queering the erotics of intimacy.

The moment of splitting is also the instance of separation, and hence, of engendering the subject through a process of suture, joining the lips of a wound, a sewing together into sameness. The suturing of the subject may take place through the production of difference, but these differences are those of the inside, not the outside. The lunula is 'a plain terminated by the circumferences of two circles, which touch one another on the inside'. In Lacan's lectures the moon-like lunula is soon morphed into the lamella, which in turn anamorphises its tertiary space into a fluid oval membrane: the anxious site of splitting and the ever-present threat of a descent into the lacuna of the lunula are transformed into the lamella's unrecognisable rim which 'inserts itself into the erogenous zone'.[39] Its shifting amoeba-like Mobean form opens up modes of queer desire, rimming, bristling with an erotics of touch when you enter 'that third-space—"that transitional space, an in-between space"—where the man-made and the self-made, the material and the non-material gather together and tangentially touch in the fevered movement—hither and thither, back and forth—of doubt' across the surfaces of the body.[40]

'The void slips sideways from the grasp of frame and figure'.[41] With *A House for Mr Biswas*, all these ungraspable factors are brought together in Naipaul's mundane exuberant narrative of the back traces of rural Trinidad, where Mr Biswas' psychic abjection, his emasculated and anxious masculinity, his petty desires for status and self-improvement, to make a mark on the faded nothingness of his colonial milieu, all descend into a engulfing fear of a tenantless futurity:

> And always the thought, the fear about the future. The future wasn't the next day or the next week or even the next year, times within his comprehension and therefore without dread. The future he feared could not be thought in terms of time. It was a blankness, a void like those in dreams, into which, past tomorrow and next week and next year, he was falling [. . .]. He sank into despair as into the void which, in his imagining, had always stood for the life he had yet to live.[42]

Yet at the same time, Mr Biswas' willingness to descend into this null and void of misgiving simultaneously marks also, as for Harris and Bhabha, a space of creativity and possibility, a subjecthood always symbolized for Mr Biswas by his house: 'But bigger than them all was the house, his house. How terrible it would have been, at this time, to be without it [. . .] to have lived and died as one had been born, unnecessary and unaccommodated'.[43] Such subaltern lives comprise what Alain Badiou would call the multiplicity at the edge of the void, the nothings and nobodies that the controlling state fails to enumerate or represent amongst the dull banalities of the everyday situation, but whose invisible third space outside the structures of power hosts a site from which the ungraspable, unrecognizable event of a transformative postcoloniality erupts, 'a space that is ruptured and imaginatively transformed', turning wound and fracture into the emergence of being, anxieties of enunciatory ambivalence into inventive productivity, vacuity and emptiness into a plenitude of rich particularities.[44]

NOTES

1. Bhabha, Homi K. *The Location of Culture*. London, New York: Routledge, 1994. 217–218, discussing Jameson, Fredric. *Postmodernism, or the Cultural Logic of Late Capitalism*. London: Verso, 1991. 410–413. Bhabha's earliest elaboration of the concept of the third space, developed in the context of Third World Cinema, can be found in Bhabha. *The Location of Culture*. 36–39. His other major statement comes in Bhabha, Homi K. "The Third Space: Interview with Homi K. Bhabha." *Identity: Community, Culture, Difference*. Ed. Jonathan Rutherford. London: Lawrence & Wishart, 1990. 207–221.

2. Soja, Edward W. *Thirdspace: Journeys to Los Angeles and Other Real-and-Imagined Places*. Oxford: Blackwell, 1996. 13–18.

3. Huddart, David. *Homi K. Bhabha*. London, New York: Routledge, 2006. 126.

4. Benveniste, Emile. *Problèmes de linguistique générale*. Vol. 1. Paris: Gallimard, 1966; Benveniste, Emile. *Problèmes de linguistique générale*. Vol. 2. Paris: Gallimard, 1974. Quotations from volume 1 are cited from the English translation, Benveniste, Emile. *Problems in General Linguistics*. Trans. Mary Elizabeth Meek. Coral Gables: Miami Press UP, 1971. For volume 1, page references will be to the English translation, followed by the French original. All emphases are Benveniste's own.

5. Rabaté, Jean-Michel. *The Future of Theory*. Oxford: Blackwell, 2002. 42.

6. Benveniste. *Problems in General Linguistics*. 226 (fr. Vol. 1: 261).

7. Ibid. 217 (fr. Vol. 1: 251).

8. Benveniste. *Problèmes de linguistique générale*. Vol. 2: 82.

9. Benveniste. *Problems in General Linguistics*. 218 (fr. Vol. 1: 252).

10. Rabaté. *The Future of Theory*. 42.

11. Benveniste. *Problems in General Linguistics*. 224 (fr. Vol. 1: 259).

12. Ibid. 227 (fr. Vol. 1: 262–263).

13. Bhabha, Homi K. "Anish Kapoor: Making Emptiness." *Anish Kapoor* with essays by Homi K. Bhabha and Pier Luigi Tazzi. London: Hayward Gallery, 1998. 11–41. 39.

14. Ibid. 24.

15. Lacan, Jacques. *The Four Fundamental Concepts of Psycho-Analysis*. Trans. Alan Sheridan. London: Hogarth Press, 1977. 100.

16. Heath, Stephen. "Notes on Suture." *Screen* 18 (1977/8): 48–76. 50.

17. Lacan. *The Four Fundamental Concepts of Psycho-Analysis*. 210. 199.

18. Bhabha. *The Location of Culture*. 44.

19. Lacan. *The Four Fundamental Concepts of Psycho-Analysis*. 211.

20. Ibid. 211. Translation modified.

21. Ozanam, Jacques. *Cursus Mathematicus: or, A Compleat Course of the Mathematicks*. Trans. John T. Desaguliers. London: Printed for John Nicholson at the Queen's-Arms in Little-Britain, and sold by John Morphew near Stationers-Hall, 1712. 123, cited in *Oxford English Dictionary*, on-line edition, entry 'lunula'. 1(b).

22. V.S. Naipaul, *A House for Mr Biswas* (London: Picador, 2003), 282.
23. Bhabha. *The Location of Culture*. 36. For Bhabha's commentary on enunciation in Lacan and Benveniste, see in particular pages 132 and 134.
24. Bhabha. "Anish Kapoor." 31.
25. Bhabha. *The Location of Culture*. 132.
26. Ibid. 36.
27. Ibid. 243.
28. Ibid. 38.
29. Harris, Wilson. *Tradition, The Writer, and Society*. London: New Beacon Books, 1967. 62.
30. Harris, Wilson. *Selected Essays*. London, New York: Routledge, 1999. 50.
31. Ibid. 223.
32. Stead, W.T. 'Government by Journalism', *Contemporary Review* 49 (1886). 654; Anderson, Benedict. *Imaginary Communities. Reflections on the Origin and Spread of Nationalism*. London: Verso, 1983.
33. Vidler, Antony. *Warped Space. Art, Architecture, and Anxiety in Modern Culture*. Cambridge, Mass.: MIT Press, 2000.
34. Ibid. v.
35. Ibid. 17–24.
36. Gopinath, Gayatri. *Impossible Desires. Queer Diasporas and South Asian Public Cultures*. Durham: Duke UP, 2005. 83, citing Bhabha, Homi K. 'Are You a Man or a Mouse.' *Constructing Masculinity*. Ed. Berger, Maurice, Brian Wallis and Simon Watson. London, New York: Routledge, 1995. 57–65.
37. Gopinath. *Impossible Desires*. 81.
38. Ibid. 79.
39. Lacan. *The Four Fundamental Concepts of Psycho-Analysis*. 200.
40. Bhabha. "Anish Kapoor." 39.
41. Ibid. 13–14.
42. Naipaul. *A House for Mr Biswas*. 197. 523.
43. Ibid. 8.
44. Badiou, Alain. *L'être et l'événement*. Paris: Editions du Seuil, 1988; Badiou, Alain. *Abrégé de métapolitique*. Paris: Editions du Seuil, 1998.

6 Postcolonial Subjectivity and the Transclassical Logic of the Third

Karin Ikas and Gerhard Wagner

Anyone who has closely read Homi K. Bhabha's works will know that there is no single, precise definition of the term third space to be found there. Maybe it is exactly this vagueness, which explains the term's attractiveness. It enables Bhabha, as well as his readers, to read almost anything into it and apply it in their own ways for their very own purposes. However big the heuristic gain might be in all this, such a proceeding is rather detrimental to scientific analysis. The following essay aims to prepare the ground to change this. Setting out to contribute to the clarification of the term, it first takes a closer look at the two connotations Bhabha associates with the term as such and then proceeds by connecting them systematically with each other. What is at stake here is the problem of the thirdness of third space on the one hand and the issue of postcolonial subjectivity on the other hand. The two issues are related insofar as the emerging of the third space as a space of enunciation comes along with a new—namely postcolonial—positioning of the speaking subject. That's why the problem of newness in terms of a third is the focal point of Bhabha's theory as well.

Postcolonial critic Bhabha understands the relation of the first space (the indigenous) to the second space (the colonial) as an opposition that corresponds to the asymmetrical power relations in the colonies. In the case of simple difference (such as between master and mouse) neither the One nor the Other actually have something to do with each other; thus both moments of difference fall indifferently apart as G.W.F. Hegel once put it. The two moments of an opposition (such as between master and slave), however, are determined either-way through negation resp. through reciprocal negation. The slave is the not-master and the master is the not-slave. Here the Other is not any Other but the Other of the One, i.e. its Other or the Other of itself. Hegel calls this 'negativity' and he means by this 'the negation of otherness', which is '*self-reference*'.[1] This, of course, is only valid if both moments are discussed in a particular way: in this case with face view of the power relation. Both moments have to be 'different in *one* identity.'[2] One moment is only identical with the negation of another moment if it is the definition of something in relation towards which the other moment acts as an exclusively antagonistic definition. In other words, two values have to be identical in a certain way in order to appear as antagonistic values. In view of power relations, the two moments colonial and indigenous are, beyond doubt, in opposition to each other.

Yet Bhabha distances himself from Hegel's classic dialectical logic, which amounts to a reconciliation of the opposition. For Hegel, the Other is always the Other of the One, which designates it as the Other of itself to define itself. This is achieved as soon as it reconciles the opposition between Itself and its Other again: 'this movement, designating oneself as the Other of oneself and reconciling this very Other, declaring it to a mere appearance and by doing so returning to oneself'.[3] Bhabha, however, points out that what he has in mind is rather 'to articulate antagonistic and oppositional elements without the redemptive rationality of sublation or transcendence'.[4] He thinks of 'a dialectic without the emergence of a teleological or transcendent'.[5] As a postcolonial theorist he is apparently not interested in a reconciliatory assignation of the indigenous in reference to the colonial as the Other of itself: 'The language of critique is effective not because it keeps forever separate the terms of the master and the slave [. . .] but to the extent to which it overcomes the given grounds of opposition and opens up a space of translation: a place of hybridity [. . .] that is new, *neither the one nor the other*'.[6] The new—the third space and with it postcolonial subjectivity—is not supposed to come into existence by reconciling the opposition between the indigenous and the colonial: 'the transformational value of change lies in the rearticulation, or translation, of elements that are *neither the One* [. . .] *nor the Other* [. . .] *but something else besides*, which contests the terms and territories of both'.[7]

It is lamentable, though, that Bhabha fails to make clear what he exactly means by that. His hints—modelled after Derrida's concept of 'différance'—that iterations and translations cause deferrals of meaning are not sufficient to explain the emergence of something truly new that transgresses the original opposition so much as to even 'question it.'[8] His reference to Rodolpho Gasché's concept of an impure heterology does not meet the demand for clarification either.[9] It is thus legitimate to call on a different theory in our endeavor to substantiate Bhabha's concept and his concerns theoretically. The theory of transclassical logic by Gotthard Günther, a German-American philosopher, seems most suitable for that purpose.

Günther aims at finding an answer to 'the question of the essence of subjectivity and its ontological anchorage in the universe'.[10] For him, this question points at an age-old and yet to be solved problem that has puzzled thinkers ever since ancient times. Classical logic is an example of the fact that the subject has no noteworthy, nameable position in a world whose understanding has been determined by Aristotle: 'A basic philosophical requirement of classical logic is the condition that the ontological basics of the world are representable as pure objective structures. The subject as such is something further that remains outside of any logical analysis.'[11] Not even modern philosophers like René Descartes or Immanuel Kant were able to change this. Of course, this very question about the essence of subjectivity has been raised all the time; yet, to answer it has always turned out to be a counterproductive venture or a rather wild-goose chase so far. This is because it has been common practice to explain the subject in a transcendental-metaphysical way thus substantiating it even more explicitly as something further.

Günther asks for a revision of Aristotle's worldview assuming 'that the whole world—as long as one abstracts in it from all subjectivity and sees it as a pure objective context—is strictly two-valued. For the object totally removed from the subject the two-valued logic is completely sufficient for all descriptive purposes.'[12] Yet, if one wants to take account of subjectivity, the classical logic has to be expanded by at least one value. It needs a transclassical logic with three or more values in order to free the thinking from the chains of classical logic with its law of the excluded third.

In the German Idealism of Schelling and Hegel, Günther discovers some preliminary approaches for a transition of the classical logic to the transclassical logic. The triplicate structure of the dialectical logic holds out the prospect of posting a place to the subject. Hegel's concept of becoming is of particular interest in that regard: 'The unity with its inseparable moments of existence and non-existence is also different from these two moments, actually a third against them, which is in its idiosyncratic form a becoming.'[13] Günther is not interested in the specific opposition of existence and non-existence here. Rather, in a more general mode, he is concerned with the opposition emerging between two opposite moments on the one hand and a third on the other. Unlike Hegel, he is not interested in reconciling the opposition that exists between the two moments. Quoting a verse from the Gospel of John, he illustrates that he is rather interested in rejection: 'My kingdom is not of this world.'[14] For Günther '*subjectivity* can only be conceived as a function in which the total two-valency of the objective [. . .] and hence the whole world in its existence is rejected.'[15] From this, he concludes that the rejection has to appear as a function in the transclassical logic. In the classical logic 'even in those instances were a choice is possible at all, a value has to be accepted out of the offer'.[16] This can be verified by a look at the classical logic with its values 'true' ('t') and 'false' ('f').[17] If one takes the single-digit connection (p) of the negation (not), the following table of truth arises:

p	not-p
t	f
f	t

If one takes the two-digit connection (p, q) of the conjunction (and), this then results in the following table of truth:

p	q	p and q
t	t	t
t	f	f
f	t	f
f	f	f

Even if a choice exists, that is if p is true and q false, or conversely, if p is false and q true, one of the two values—in this case 'false'—has to be accepted, too. The same, for instance, is also true for the two-digit connection (p, q) of the alternation (or) where the value 'true' has to be accepted:

q	q	p or q
t	t	t
t	f	t
f	t	t
f	f	f

Compared with this, the transclassical logic should give the opportunity 'to reject a value alternative as a whole'.[18] This demands the implementation of a third value, 'which does not belong to the given two-valued system'.[19] Unlike classical logic that has just two values of acceptance at its disposal—namely 'true' and 'false'—, transclassical logic needs an additional value of rejection: *'the value of rejection is the index of subjectivity in a transclassical calculation'*.[20] Subjectivity is manifested in the rejection of a value alternative. Consequently, Günther, introduces the rejection (R) as an additional two-digit connection (p, q) to the classical logic thereby transforming it into a transclassical three-value logic:

p	q	p and q	p or q	p R q
t	t	t	t	t
t	f	f	t	3
f	t	f	t	3
f	f	f	f	f

As values of acceptance and values of rejection appear in such a transclassical calculation, making the later thus 'a mixture of objectivity and subjectivity', Günther thus believes to have solved the basic problem of occidental thinking. He concedes, though, that the solution he offers by seeing the essence of subjectivity in rejection is rather 'poor'.[21] Notwithstanding, he gives himself credit for designating subjectivity not in a metaphysical way—as transcendental philosophy does it—but rather as a fact of the empirical world, that is to say as a specific form of human action embedded in an ontologically plausible way. To specify transclassical calculations more closely, Günther introduces the term 'contexture'.[22] A contexture is a two-valued structure area—for example: 'true/false'. If the value of rejection of this contexture—for example: '3'—turns out to be capable of designating insofar as it refers to a value oppositional to itself—for example '4'—, a second contexture emerges—namely '3/4'—and the transclassical calculation becomes 'poly-contextural'.[23]

Günther is not only interested in a specification of Hegel's logic but also in his dialectical philosophy of history. In his essay "The Historical Category of the New" he takes up the distinction between nature and history that originates from Hegel's *Lectures on the Philosophy of History*.[24] According to Hegel, changes in nature happen in a circular way. Under the sun nothing new happens because there is no opposition in nature. This is different in history where the spirit defines itself by negating the other of itself. That's why something new can rise in history. Günther is in agreement with Hegel here, yet, surely enough, he then interprets Hegel's idea of a dialectical movement in history through his own transclassical logic:

> The opposition Hegel refers to when talking about the category of the new and which he contrasts with the so-called natural changes is the 'total' opposition of sub-contextural principles and connections that exclude each other qua contexture. Compared to this, and while the structural principle remains constant, intra-contextural, that is material resp. contingent differences, shrink to a state that rather lacks any opposition. The new thing in history, which, according to Hegel, arises from the spirit's 'involuntary work' at its opposition is thus not the product of contesting determinations of contents within a given contexture. Rather, it results from the opposition of two contextures. This conclusion is unavoidable! Given that what we call spirit in a mythological way is pure contexture, the spirit can *only* oppose itself as a contexture and not as an isolated content of a contexture.[25]

It is negligible though if Günther interprets Hegel correctly in this context or not. Günther is not interested in Hegel's metaphysical spirit of the world but in the empirical fact of the human spirit that does not want to accept value alternatives but rather rejects them. There, it is significant that for Günther the new can only arise from the rejection of a contexture as such and not from the negativity of the two values of a contexture. Indeed, the rejection of a contexture refers to a third value that confronts the given contexture as the new. Even if the kingdom or realm shall not be of this world, a realm is mentioned after all. Bhabha comes pretty close to Günther's line of reasoning when arguing that the third is *neither the One nor the Other but something else besides* that contests the terms and territories of both. The wording 'which contests the terms and territories of both' is, by all means, comprehensible as a rejection of a contexture that refers to a third value—*something else besides*. Thus, for instance, the rejection of the value alternative colonial/indigenous refers to a third value that is called 'postcolonial'.

Here, sure enough, a basic problem is discernible that is already manifested by the empty name postcolonial. The expression postindigenous might as well have been applied here. A positive designation of the third value does voice neither the first nor the other formulation. The new does not take any specific shape. In the formal calculation of the transclassical logic this may be overlooked. Yet, in the cultural area, one would have more knowledge about the specifics of the third value at one's disposal. How is it determined in a positive way? Bhabha, at least, reaches not far enough, once he replaces the connection of *'negation'* by the one of *'negotiation'*[26] because thereby he only replaces the negativity of both values of the contexture by another concept. While in the course of *negotiations* deferrals of meaning with regard to both values arise due to iterations and translations, the contexture as such is accepted and not rejected. Contradicting Bhabha's very own intention, this solution eventually only implies a kind of synthesis for which Bhabha finds the expression 'hybridity'.[27] There are plenty of examples available for these kinds of syntheses:

> I'm just a red nigger who love the sea,
> I had a sound colonial education,
> I have Dutch, nigger, and English in me,
> And either I'm a nobody, or I'm a nation.[28]

One could indeed argue that Derek Walcott, the West Indies' author of the poem, generates a third space of enunciation: 'I'm just a red nigger who love the sea'. On the one hand, he applies English language, which forms a first space. On the other hand, he makes up a second space in as far as he does not use the correct English expression 'who loves' but rather the semi-grammatical Patois of the Caribbean (that is, the inflected verb form instead of the infinitive) 'who love'. Thereby a third space emerges that is *neither the One* (colonial English) *nor the Other* (indigenous Patois) but, in its hybridity, is rather *something else besides*. If, however, the third contests the terms and territories of both is indeed questionable within its own rights. It is not something truly new but rather only an additional Other.

The latter, however, does remind oneself even more so of the fact that English and Patois are on their parts hybridizations and not pure languages.

The same is true for postcolonial subjectivity. Bhabha, it is true, follows Derrida's insight, namely that there is 'disjuncture between the subject of a proposition (*énoncé*) and the subject of enunciation'.[29] Actually, that the subject uttering a proposition is never identical with the subject of that proposition completely is therefore also valid for a subject by the name Walcott, who expresses himself poetically, as well as for the subject—the 'I'—of his poetic expression. In spite of this disjuncture, however, one can proceed from the assumption that the originating of a third space of enunciation goes along with a new positioning of the subject of this enunciation. What it says about itself corresponds, at all events, with the hybridity of its enunciation; in fact, it even outdoes it: 'I have Dutch, nigger, and English in me, / And either I'm a nobody, or I'm a nation'. The subject reveals itself as a postcolonial one insofar as in it both, the colonial and the indigenous, mix. As this subject had 'a sound colonial education', it is no longer only 'just a red nigger'. Then again, it applies the incorrectness of the wording 'who love the sea' to cleave to a remainder of ineducability in order to overcome its status as 'object' of a colonial 'pedagogy'[30] and to position itself as subject thereafter. Thereby it does not become something truly new, nonetheless. What emerges, though, is only another 'marginal man',[31] the kind who has arisen in history quite a million times in the course of the development and breaking-up of Empires.

In this light, the emergence of the new, it seems, is not explicable without the rejection of a value-alternative. How this double-negation itself can result in a positive designation is explicable once we take a glance at the Hegel critique of another German philosopher. It is true, neither Gasché nor any other postmodern critic did invent heterology. Rather, the latter originates from Heinrich Rickert's[32] critical assessment of Hegel at the beginning of the 20th century. According to Rickert, Hegel designed the duality that he had discovered in the thinking as an antithesis, and, thus, the Other as the negation of the One. Rickert, on the other hand, argued for a priority of otherness over negation. He stressed that the negation as such does only destroy. It does not lead to anything positive at all. Therefore, it is not sufficient to deduct the Other from the One. It never owns such a magic power. Consequently, it is necessary to replace Hegel's antithesis by a heterothesis and assume that the thinking has at its disposal the One *and* the Other at one go. If this is the case, then, the designation of the Other within a contexture as well as the designation of the value of rejection can be explained through it.

So, it is the thinking subject who constructs alternative values out of a majority of given values and who names third values questioning these alternatives. Doing so, the thinking subject does not only generate a new space but rather opens a new position for his- or herself. What can all be imagined beyond the scope of the colonial/indigenous though, is, of course, up to the reader's fantasy and power of imagination.

NOTES

1. Hegel, G.W.F. *Wissenschaft der Logik*. (Faksimile nach der Erstausgabe von 1812). Göttingen: Vandenhoeck & Ruprecht, 1966. 78.
2. Hegel, G.W.F. *Wissenschaft der Logik II*. Frankfurt am Main, Suhrkamp 1983. 55.
3. Hegel, G.W.F. "Fragment zur Philosophie des Geistes." *Berliner Schriften 1818–1831*. Frankfurt am Main: Suhrkamp, 1980. 517–550. 531.
4. Bhabha, Homi K. *The Location of Culture*. London, New York: Routledge, 1994. 26.
5. Ibid. 25.
6. Ibid. 25.
7. Ibid. 28.
8. Ibid. 37.
9. Ibid. 258–259.
10. Günther, Gotthard. *Logik, Zeit, Emanation und Evolution*. Opladen: West-deutscher Verlag, 1967. 17.
11. Ibid. 68
12. Ibid. 85–86
13. Hegel quoted in Günther, Gotthard. "Das Problem einer Formalisierung der transzendental-dialektischen Logik: Unter besonderer Berücksichtigung der Logik Hegels." *Hegel-Studien*, suppl. 1 (1964): 65–123. 82.
14. Günther, Gotthard. "Das Janusgesicht der Dialektik." *Hegel-Jahrbuch* (1974): 89–117. 103.
15. Günther. *Logik, Zeit, Emanation und Evolution*. 86.
16. Günther. "Das Janusgesicht der Dialektik." 102.
17. Quine, Willard V.O. *Methods of Logic*. New York: Holt, Rinehart and Wilson, 1964.
18. Günther. "Das Janusgesicht der Dialektik." 102.
19. Günther. *Logik, Zeit, Emanation und Evolution*. 85.
20. Günther "Das Janusgesicht der Dialektik." 102–103.
21. Günther. *Logik, Zeit, Emanation und Evolution*. 86.
22. Günther, Gotthard. "Die Theorie der mehrwertigen Logik." *Beiträge zur Grundlegung einer operationsfähigen Dialektik*. Vol. 2. Hamburg: Meiner, 1979. 181–202.
23. Günther, Gotthard. "Life as Poly-Contexturality." *Beiträge zur Grundlegung einer operationsfähigen Dialektik*. Vol. 2. Hamburg: Meiner, 1979. 283–306.
24. Hegel. G.W.F. *Vorlesungen über die Philosophie der Geschichte*. Frankfurt am Main: Suhrkamp, 1985. 74.
25. Günther, Gotthard. "Die historische Kategorie des Neuen." *Beiträge zur Grundlegung einer operationsfähigen Dialektik*. Vol. 3. Hamburg: Meiner, 1980. 183–210. 190.
26. Bhabha. *The Location of Culture*. 25.
27. Ibid. 38.
28. Walcott, Derek. "The Schooner Flight." *Collected Poems 1948–1984*. New York: Noonday Press and Farrar, Straus & Giroux, 1986. 345.
29. Bhabha. *The Location of Culture*. 36.
30. Ibid. 145.
31. Park, Robert E. "Human Migration and the Marginal Man." *American Journal of Sociology* 33 (1928): 881–893.
32. Rickert, Heinrich. „Das Eine, die Einheit und die Eins: Bemerkungen zur Logik des Zahlbegriffs." *Logos* 2 (1911/12): 26–78; Rickert, Heinrich. *Das Eine, die Einheit und die Eins: Bemerkungen zur Logik des Zahlbegriffs*. Tübingen: J.C.B. Mohr 1924.

Part IV
Literizing the Third Space

7 Caliban's Voice
Writing in the Third Space

Bill Ashcroft

BEYOND CURSING

There is a moment in Shakespeare's final play *The Tempest* when we first encounter the monster Caliban. Caliban and Prospero have had a bitter exchange in which each call upon their respective powers to damn the other, when finally Caliban threatens to overwhelm Prospero by miscegenation— 'to people the isle with Calibans.' [Tmp I: ii 349][1] Although this is directed at Prospero, it is his daughter, Miranda, who replies:

> Abhorred slave,
> Which any print of goodness wilt not take,
> Being capable of all ill! I pitied thee,
> Took pains to make thee speak, taught thee each hour
> One thing or other: when thou didst not, savage,
> Know thine own meaning, but wouldst gabble like
> A thing most brutish, I endow'd thy purposes
> With words that made them known. But thy vile race,
> Though thou didst learn, had that in't which good natures
> Could not abide to be with; therefore wast thou
> Deservedly confin'd into this rock,
> Who hadst deserved more than a prison. [Tmp. I: ii 351–363].

Her speech defines the colonial relationship. Caliban is an 'abhorred slave', 'savage,' 'brutish,' 'vile.' Miranda's language has the power to construct Caliban, a power that reflects Prospero's very tangible control of his body, his actions, his destiny. The terms are those that produce a 'truth' about the colonial subject because that is the power of colonial discourse. Prospero and Miranda's treatment of Caliban stems from their belief that Caliban is no more than a barbarous brute who could not *know his own meaning* without their language. Their civilized and rational language entitles them to raise him to the level of competent slave. If he is recalcitrant he must be shown to be incapable of improvement: as Prospero says, he is 'A devil, a born devil, on whose nature/ Nurture can never stick' (Tmp. IV:

i 188–189).[2] The moral framework of the relationship is entirely determined by the dominant party. More specifically, the entire relationship is
constructed within the boundaries of colonial discourse: Caliban should
be grateful for having been taught the language because it has given him
meaning, it is capable of rendering him *human.*

Caliban's response to Miranda's diatribe is one of the most memorable
in literature and encapsulates the bitter reaction of many colonized peoples
to centuries of linguistic and political control:

> You taught me language; and my profit on't
> Is, I know how to curse. The red plague rid you
> For learning me your language [Tmp. I: ii 363–365].[3]

It is no wonder that Caliban rejects that language. It serves to confine him
in Prospero's power as surely as the magician's cloak. For the language is a
feature of Prospero's art itself. Caliban's response has been taken up time
and again as a rejection of the imperial tongue.

But in the physical and cultural space between Miranda and Caliban, a
space that seems to be unbridgeable, a space of time, geography and culture,
there is another space—a third space, what Homi K. Bhabha has called the
'Third Space of enunciation'.[4] For Bhabha cultural identity always emerges
in this contradictory and ambivalent space, a space that makes untenable
that purity and hierarchy of cultures so beloved by imperial discourse.
But this space is also a transcultural space, a 'contact zone,'[5] the excess of
fixed subjectivity—that space in which cultural identity develops. This is
pre-eminently the space of language—the space of postcolonial transformation. Shakespeare doesn't recognize this space. The concept of cultural
transformation beyond Prospero's art, particularly a *mutual* transformation, is inconceivable. After all, Prospero is a model for the playwright
himself, a creative authority at the height of his powers who looks back in
the play upon the capacity of creative art to change nature. The play, for
Shakespeare, was more likely an allegory of the power of art, the power of
civilized learning to improve on nature's mistakes. Caliban is not meant
to be the hero of the play for this is Shakespeare's swansong, a testament
to the virtues of order and good government and the ameliorating powers
of art.

Caliban will never step into this Third Space in *The Tempest*, for the
play provides him with no way in which he can make the language work
for him. He demonstrates that he is quite capable of answering back to
Prospero, he has the power of resistance—he cannily points out to Prospero
that he is the magician's *only* subject—and he has the power to reject the
way that language represents him. But his inability to appropriate the language of Prospero confines him as securely as does Prospero's art. It is this
acceptance of the link between Prospero's language and his art, and hence
the subtle acceptance of his domination, which traps Caliban.

But *The Tempest* is not a postcolonial play. It has become almost canonical to postcolonial theory because it accepts without question the tenets of imperial control that Prospero embodies. If Caliban is the model of the colonized subject, he is a model whose capacity for appropriating Prospero's language is yet to be realized.

Ironically, many postcolonial commentators have accepted Caliban's conclusion that the language is an inviolable agent of domination. George Lamming, who first broached the issue, believes that Prospero's language is always going to be a prison. Caliban 'can never be regarded as an heir of that language,' says Lamming, 'since his use of language is no more than his way of serving Prospero'.[6] This is an ironic contradiction. For Lamming to assert that Caliban will never be able to use Prospero's language for his own purposes is to deny Lamming's own achievement in writing widely read novels that have affected the way in which the Caribbean is viewed.

An alternative view was expressed by Janheinz Jahn, who suggests that 'if Caliban is no more than a part of nature, he will never be able to break out of the prison of Prospero's language'.[7] 'But suppose Caliban is also part of a culture, a different culture unfamiliar to Prospero?'[8] In that event Caliban's island is not simply nature but Caliban's culture. It is a very different culture from Prospero's but it can use Prospero's dominant arts for its own purposes:

> So he captures, in his own and Prospero's language, a culture Prospero did not create and cannot control, which he, Caliban, has recognized as his own. But in the process the language is transformed, acquiring different meanings which Prospero never expected. Caliban becomes a 'bilingual'. That language he shares with Prospero and the language he has minted from it are no longer identical. Caliban breaks out of the prison of Prospero's language.[9]

Jahn explicitly dates Caliban's appropriation of Prospero's culture, the 'successful revolt from the prison of Prospero's language' from the rise of the Negritudinist literary movement between 1934 and 1948.[10] According to Jahn, the escape was effected in three ways: in semantics, rhythm and subject matter. In particular, the use of French led writers such as Senghor, Damas and Césaire to construct a new literary culture, which reconfigured Africa as 'no longer exotic and "primitive" but as a specific culture'.[11] Caliban remained in Prospero's prison of language only as long as he could be deceived into believing it was a prison. The transformation of postcolonial literatures, which began in the Negritudinist movement, was one which saw that language was not the *repository* of culture but its *agent*.

This view of language is one that empowers Caliban to step into the space that separates him from Miranda, and in entering that space to take control of it *through the agency of her own language*. If Caliban is the model for the invaded and colonized subject, then he does, in those subjects, step into a third space that Shakespeare could not have conceived. In that space he appropriates Prospero's language and in that space both he and the colonizer are transformed.

LANGUAGE AND IDENTITY IN POSTCOLONIAL WRITING

This chapter will address two aspects of this question: the arguments over a colonized *language* which insist that Caliban can never move into that third space to use Prospero and Miranda's discourse of control; and the example of postcolonial *writing* which demonstrates that the transcultural space into which he moves is a powerful area of resistance through representation.

There are many forms of the argument against a colonial language, many ways of asserting that Caliban can do no more than curse, but one focused form of the argument is that between two Anglophone African novelists, the Kenyan Ngugi wa Thiongo and the Nigerian Chinua Achebe, who have engaged this issue longer, more often and more resonantly than other postcolonial writers. The debate between these two novelists represents a controversy that has raged for over fifty years: Do writers who continue to write in a colonial language remain colonized or can they appropriate the language as a tool for their own purposes? Does literature in a language such as English privilege Western cultural values, and with them the whole history of colonial oppression and control, or does such a literature use English as a tool to reveal the non-Western world and even record resistance to that colonial worldview? Does *any* communication in the dominant language imprison the subject in a dominant discourse?

Before we survey this debate it is useful to look at the language itself. The idea that a dominant language is a stable discourse that binds its speakers to an unchanging worldview overlooks something very crucial about the English language that Samuel Johnson recognized when he compiled his dictionary in 1755. In his preface to the dictionary Johnson reflects on the lexicographer's task, which is always to somehow 'fix' or stabilize the language. But he finds that any attempt 'to pursue perfection' in describing language is 'like the first inhabitants of Arcadia, to chase the sun, which, when they had reached the hill where he seemed to rest, was still at the same distance from them.'[12] At the very moment the English language was being institutionalized, its fluidity, its changeability and its exposure to 'alien' influence was confirmed. The lexicographer's view of the language has never been that of the imperialist, but it is the imperialist myth of language that many critics are misled into confronting.

We begin then with the startling claim that language *itself* occupies the Third Space of enunciation. This may appear both disruptive and extreme. So much cultural identity is invested in language that it appears imperative to most speakers that language be a stable discourse in which ontological certainty can be guaranteed. *My* language constitutes the avenue of my entry into an articulately experienced world. It is the language through which I came to have a family, a community, a society, a nation. For all intents and purposes, *my language is me.* Yet my language may be used by someone who is not me, my family or culture. How then does my language identify my difference?

The situation becomes extremely fraught when the language is a colonial one. Ngugi's position is stated early in his essay "Towards a National Culture" in which he expresses four general objections to the use of English.[13] (1) the colonial tongue becomes a province of the élite and thus the language itself reproduces colonial class distinctions; (2) language embodies the 'thought processes and values' of its culture; (3) learning a colonial tongue alienates a speaker from the 'values' of the local language and from the values of the masses (which to Ngugi are the same thing); (4) national language should not exist at the expense of regional languages which can enhance national unity 'in a socialist economic and political context.' To various degrees these objections apply today to the use of a global language.

Ngugi is right to suggest that colonialism has had a profound and often destructive effect on local cultures, disrupting social structures and initiating changes in cultural values. This is a process we see encapsulated in Miranda's speech to Caliban: 'Abhorred slave, / Which any print of goodness wilt not take.' But does Caliban remain a slave in the language because it was first used to enslave him? 'Those of us who have inherited the English language,' says Achebe,

> may not be in a position to appreciate the value of the inheritance. Or we may go on resenting it because it came as part of a package deal which included many other items of doubtful value and the positive atrocity of racial arrogance and prejudice which may yet set the world on fire. But let us not in rejecting the evil throw out the good with it.[14]

The position of most African writers is as pragmatic as Achebe's. The legacies of colonialism constantly need to be addressed, but, paradoxically, they may best be addressed by some of the tools taken from the colonizers.

I will address two major objections of the four Ngugi identifies, of which the most tenacious, most widely held and most erroneous is that: 'Language embodies the thought processes and values of a culture.' In *Decolonizing the Mind* Ngugi states that 'language, any language, has a dual character: it is both a means of communication and a carrier of culture.' Where English is concerned, 'it is widely used as a means of communication across many nationalities. But it is not the carrier of a culture and history of many of those nationalities.'[15] The key question here is 'how does a language "carry" a culture?' 'Is it impossible for a language to "carry" a culture different from the one in which it emerged?' Obviously what we mean by the term 'carry' will be critical in deciding this. Achebe believes that a language can 'carry' a different culture: 'I feel that the English language will be able to carry the weight of my African experience. But it will have to be a new English, still in full communion with its ancestral home but altered to suit new African surroundings.'[16] Clearly, what Ngugi and Achebe mean by the term 'carry' are quite different things, and this points out some of the difficulty of the debate, because many people believe that to 'carry' does not mean simply to 'bear', but to 'embody.' At the center of this conflict is the myth that a language embodies the essence of a culture. Hence, English, whether transported into a foreign language or settler culture, is profoundly inauthentic in its new place. If we were to regard an authentic language as one which somehow embodies cultural uniqueness in a way no other language could, then English would be linguistically inappropriate to the development of a non-British culture.

The idea that language embodies the essence of a culture and that essence cannot be conveyed in another language is possibly the most persistent myth about language and prevails in every postcolonial region. But let me look at one other besides Ngugi here: the Jamaican novelist and critic Jean D'Costa who has been very articulate about language issues. Her basic premise is that the polydialectical linguistic environment of the Caribbean evokes the essence of Caribbean culture: 'expression [. . .] forces the writer [. . .] to attain new levels of usage that evoke the essence of this unique world.'[17] '[W]hat can the writer do when faced with the need to express the multiple interrelated perceptions of a continuum culture?'[18]

At first glance, this notion of the essence of a culture seems relatively harmless. We all know what is meant by the term. But is essence simply a loosely used metaphor, or does it lie at the heart of a profoundly erroneous assumption about language and culture? Would this essence, for instance, exist in every manifestation of culture? Would it exist in every instance of polydialectical speech? How exactly does a specific language convey this essence? I will not dwell on this continuing argument except to say that in every case that we might detect a distinctive cultural feature, either of language, behavior or experience, it is not a sign of cultural essence but of cultural *difference*. Each sign obtains its identity only in its difference from other signs. On this distinction hinges a world of difference.

A culture is very much like a rope. Many strands overlap to form the rope, but no one strand runs through its center. We could observe a culture and say that it contained many distinctive features, but no single feature, no single 'strand' is present in every manifestation as essential to this culture distinct from all others.[19] Any one of these features may become a sign of the whole 'rope' and this is the way variants operate in cross-cultural literature, but no feature, or phenomenon or 'strand' can be said to be the essence of the culture. The signs obtain their value, they communicate the meaning of a culture by *difference*.

The question is: Is it impossible for signs of cultural difference to be communicated in a different language? If those signs communicate difference rather than essence, the answer must obviously be—no! In fact the very existence of a dynamic field of postcolonial literatures in English refutes this. The signs can accommodate various forms of difference. Language does not define a cultural boundary, but a region of intercommunication. The idea of an authentic relation between a language and a culture is a political concept, and as such, can be very useful, as Gayatri Spivak indicates in her use of the term 'strategic essentialism',[20] but it runs the risk of imprisoning writers into a belief in their inability to use the language authentically.

Achebe responds to the assertion that African writers will never reach their creative potential until they write in African languages, by reiterating the point that a writer's use of a language can be as culturally specific as he or she makes it. If we ask *Can an African ever learn English well enough to use it effectively in creative writing?* Achebe's answer is *yes*. But the secret such a writer has at his or her disposal is a healthy disregard for its traditions and rules. All writers have a creative sense of the possibilities of language, but the non-English speaking postcolonial writer has the added dimension of a different mother tongue, a different linguistic tradition from which to draw. If we ask, *Can he or she ever use it like a native speaker?* Achebe's answer is, 'I hope not'. His point is one which remains as true today as it was then. The appropriation of English by postcolonial writers is not only possible but extremely effective and enriches the language. 'The price a world language must be prepared to pay is submission to many different kinds of use.'[21]

Ngugi's purpose in *Decolonizing the Mind* is to draw attention to the political ramifications of using a colonial language. However there is a constant slippage between this political position, which confirms the ability of the individual speaker to make choices, and a position which sees the speaker as unable to avoid the view of the world the language seems to present. To assume that the colonial language inculcates the subject, incontrovertibly, into a way of seeing the world, is to accept, by implication, that the subject is either passive or helpless. This occurs when Ngugi claims of colonized African societies that 'it was language which held captive their cultures, their values and hence their minds'.[22] To assume that the speaker of a colonial language has a 'colonized mind' is to accept a theory of the subject as without agency, something that is refuted at every turn by postcolonial discourse.

Indisputably, language is grounded in a particular cultural reality. It provides the terms by which reality may be constituted, it provides the names by which the world may be known. Its system of values, representations and discriminations becomes the system upon which social, economic and political discourse is grounded. But whether these are incontestable acquisitions made by, or forced on, the colonial language learner, whether the language learner can make cultural distinctions between languages, is the real question at the heart of the considerable dispute over the efficacy of writing in English. To claim that language can hold the minds of the colonized captive, as Ngugi does when he exhorts the 'decolonization of the mind', is to deny the very capacity for resistance that his own writing invokes. Yet when we see the considerable cultural ethnography that a writer in English can produce we see that the novelist and poet can be used as ideal models for the engagement with a dominant discourse.

Indeed, cultural producers of all kinds have always recognized the utility of the tools at their disposal. Even where writers have used indigenous languages, the influence of English literary traditions is obvious. For instance, the emergence of novels and plays in languages like Wolof, Yoruba, Gikuyu in Africa, and Bengali, Kannada and Malayalam in India, has in each case required the invention of an audience, the creation of audiences of readers to consume literary works of a kind that had not previously existed in those languages. Ngugi is quite happy to 'utilize all the resources at our disposal—radio, television, film, schools, universities, youth movements, farmers' co-operatives' to create a different kind of society. But language is held to be different because it somehow mysteriously embodies the thought processes, values and cultural history of a culture.

In answer to Ngugi, Achebe makes the point that it is the way the language is *used* that counts.[23] He quotes a passage from his novel *Arrow of God* in which the Chief Priest tells one of his sons why it is necessary to send him to church:

> I want one of my sons to join these people and be my eyes there. If there is nothing in it you will come back. But if there is something there you will bring home my share. The world is like a Mask, dancing. If you want to see it well you do not stand in one place. My spirit tells me that those who do not befriend the white man today will be saying *had we known* tomorrow.

Now supposing I had put it another way, he says. Like this for instance:

> I am sending you as my representative among these people—just to be on the safe side in case the new religion develops. One has to move with the times or else one is left behind. I have a hunch that those who fail to come to terms with the white man may well regret their lack of foresight. The material is the same. But the form of one is *in character* and the other is not.

We might add that one is also more poetic. This is a convincing example of the fact that what we often take to be a *property* of language is in fact a *function of its use.* The Africanness of the first passage is a function of the way in which the English language is used. It is no more an embodiment of Africanness than the English language is an embodiment of Englishness.

What is at stake here is not whether the choice of language can revitalize some lost cultural essence or exorcise some colonial taint, but whether the use of English materially aids the process of decolonization. Does it substantially alter the audience addressed? Does it subvert the function of literature as a means of addressing only an élite controlled by its place in the social power structure? Does its use, therefore, challenge the institutional practices of the new ruling class in a genuinely subversive way? The answer to these questions will be very different in different societies, in Kenya as opposed to South Africa, in India or Singapore, and no one answer will serve for all. But it is clear that for writers such as Achebe the answer is yes.

Speaking of the changes in what it means to be an 'Indian' writer Salman Rushdie says:

> Many have referred to the argument about the appropriateness of this language to Indian themes. And I hope all of us share the view that we can't simply use the language in the way the British did; that it needs remaking for our own purposes. Those of us who do use English do so in spite of our ambiguity towards it, or perhaps because of that, perhaps because we can find in the linguistic struggle a reflection of other struggles taking place in the real world, struggles between the cultures within ourselves and the influences at work upon our societies. To conquer English may be to complete the process of making ourselves free.[24]

The corollary to the idea that language embodies the thought processes of a culture is that: 'Writing in a colonial language alienates a writer from his or her culture.' Achebe approaches this question with remarkable directness. 'Is it right that a man should abandon his mother tongue for someone else's?' he asks. 'It looks like a dreadful betrayal and produces a guilty feeling.' His answer has become famous in its simplicity: 'I have been given this language and I intend to use it.'[25] Although there will always be writers who write in their mother tongue, and it is good that they do so, Achebe sees great excitement in the possibilities for English use. His feeling about language, the sense that English was an alien language and reflected none of his experience leads him to quote James Baldwin who wrote in the *London Observer*:

> My quarrel with the English language has been that the language reflected none of my experience. But now I begin to see the matter another way [. . .]. Perhaps the language was not my own because I had never attempted to use it, had only learned to imitate it. If this were so,

then it might be made to bear the burden of my experience if I could find the stamina to challenge it, and me, to such a test.[26]

This is a very astute perception of the relationship of writers to language. The problem with many users of a colonial language is the problem of *imitation* which is very different from original *use*. This reiterates the point that language is a tool to be used and it is that use which can convey cultural specificity. Baldwin's statement has become one that Achebe repeats and remains true for all postcolonial writers; English can be 'made to bear the burden of my experience.' In some ways this sums up Achebe's view of his relationship to English, because it can be made to 'bear the weight of my African experience.' At base it is a refutation of the idea that culture is a property of language, a statement that language is a tool that can be used for many purposes. It is, significantly, the creative writer who can best show how the language can be used, how it can be made to bear the burden of a different cultural experience. This, indeed, is a primary value of postcolonial writing itself.

A crucial consideration in the link between language and culture is whether a culture can be pinned down to a particular set of beliefs, values and practices, as Ngugi asserts, or whether in fact cultures experience a perpetual process of internal change and transformation. Achebe identifies this changeability with the resonant phrase 'We lived at the crossroads of cultures.' These crossroads have a dangerous potency 'because a man might perish there wrestling with multiple-headed spirits, but also he might be lucky and return to his people with the boon of prophetic vision.'[27] The metaphor of the crossroads doesn't fully indicate the extent to which cultures may become changed by the intersection. Indeed no culture is static, but is a constant process of hybrid interaction and change. This is the Third Space of enunciation. It is the space of transculturation, a contact zone in which both cultures—colonizing and colonized—are changed. It is within this Third Space—the Third Space of language itself—that the transcultural work of postcolonial literatures is performed. This work occurs by means of the processes of appropriation and transformation that enable the Third Space to become a space of resistance as well as a space of sharing.

A superb example of the importance of language in colonial resistance is provided by Selwyn Cudjoe's analysis of the politics of language in the speeches of Trinidadian statesman and writer Eric Williams. Here is a classic example of the capacity of the colonized to acquire the cultural capital, and thus the power inherent in the dominant language, which can be 'recirculated' back against the dominant power. On the occasion of his ejection from the Caribbean Commission, Williams gave a speech in which 'he establishes his intellectual and moral superiority over his superiors and, in the process, describes how he rendered the former speechless; that is, for a moment, he had taken away his speech'.[28]

This is perhaps the pivotal act of empowerment through the acquisition of the dominant tongue. To render the colonizer silent is to reverse the power inherent in the possession of the dominant language, to use the 'master's tools' to obtain mastery over the master:

> In fact, Mr X, his superior, had not only become speechless, he was at a loss even to construct meaning [...]. Williams had literally beaten his superior (both figuratively and literally) at his own game and rendered him mute, one of the major weapons that the colonizer always held over the heads of his subjects.[29]

Williams's famous speech *Massa Day Done* owes its power, according to Cudjoe, to his perception that language should be regarded not in terms of meanings but rather in terms of a constant battle for power between speakers.[30] This characterizes very well his confrontation with the Caribbean Commission, but his range widened to take in the *Trinidad Guardian* and others 'who controlled the word and the way they represented the colonized people'.[31] The power of language to literally silence one's opponents is well known and widely used. That it should be employed against the colonizer in the colonizer's own language is a particularly resonant example of the transformative power of language appropriation. But the 'battle for power' is an extraordinarily ambivalent one because it occurs within a space of meeting, the Third Space of language, of enunciation, of cultural transformation.

The strategies by which a colonial language is transformed are extremely varied. Apart from direct glossing in the text, either by explanation or parenthetic insertions, such devices include syntactic fusion, in which the English prose is structured according to the syntactic principles of a first language; neologisms, new lexical forms in English which are informed by the semantic and morphological exigencies of a mother tongue; the direct inclusion of untranslated lexical items in the text, ethno-rhythmic prose which constructs an English discourse according to the rhythm and texture of a first language, and the transcription of dialect and language variants of many different kinds, whether they come from diglossic, polydialectical or monolingual speaking communities.[32]

If we look closely at these inter-cultural linguistic devices and the commentary which surrounds them, we can see that the role they propose for themselves is often that of power words, power syntax and power rhythms, which *reproduce* the culture by some process of metaphoric embodiment. Evidently many writers believe that by such means they are keeping faith with their own culture and *transporting* it into the new medium.[33] Thus the untranslated words, the sounds and textures of the language are vaguely held to have the power of the culture they signify by a process of ontological union. The historical privileging of metaphor in identity is manifested yet again by this propensity to see truth predicated on a process of cultural incorporation. Such uses of language are *metonymic*. They are *put for* a certain cultural experience which they cannot hope to reproduce but whose difference is at least validated in the new situation. To be precise the language bears a synecdochic relationship with the original culture, the part of the culture which stands for the whole.

PROSPERO'S BOOKS

When we talk about the use of language for empowerment, when we discuss the issue of language and authenticity, when we talk about the use of a dominant language in a global setting, we are talking mostly about writing. When Caliban is cast out from his home his revenge upon Prospero focuses on Prospero's books, which Caliban identifies as the source of his power, and which he seeks to destroy.

> Remember
> First to possess his books; for without them
> He's but a sot as I am, nor hath not
> One spirit to command. (Tmp. III: ii 88–90)[34]

Shakespeare uses the term 'books' here, as he has done in *Merry Wives of Windsor* (Wiv. IV: i 14)[35] to refer to not only Prospero's physical collection of books, but his book learning, his scholarship or study. Thus when he says: 'I'll to my book; / For yet, ere supper-time, must I perform / Much business appertaining' (Tmp. III: i 94–96).[36] He refers to his book learning and the magic arts that books confer. There is a subtle connection between the imperial language, which teaches Caliban 'how to name the bigger light and how the less,' Prospero's art, by which he keeps Caliban under control, and the books which Caliban 'recognizes' as the source of Prospero's power.

Prospero's books stand as a metaphor for power in the Third Space, but this power operates in precisely the same way as language. Power at its simplest means the capacity to change the behavior of another. Our usual assumption is that power works repressively, by the exertion of force by the strong over the weak. Thus, we assume, colonized subjects are, by definition, the weak. However, Foucault has demonstrated that power circulates:

> And not only do individuals circulate between its threads; they are always in the position of simultaneously undergoing and exercising power. They are not only its inert or consenting target; they are also always the elements of its articulation. In other words, individuals are the vehicles of power, not its points of application.[37]

Language therefore becomes the site of a dynamic power engagement. The transcultural space of language enables both powerful and powerless participants to act, to either perpetuate power or disrupt it, to entrench it or transform it. The operation of a colonial language works in precisely this way and it is postcolonial *writing* which demonstrates this most clearly. The colonized subjects who occupy the Third Space of enunciation operate in a constant state of potentiality, they may *use* the language, for whatever purpose they use it, they are 'exercising power,' as Foucault says. The language does not repress speaking subjects in and of itself. It provides the medium within which power circulates and that power can be usurped, appropriated and used as cultural capital. This is the Third Space in which Caliban may find his voice if he chooses. And if he finds his voice he may also find that the magic of Prospero's books is also his to use.

This perception of language as the scene of a power dialectic elaborates the very important link between language and writing in the colonial exchange. But it also raises to prominence the issue of the associated technologies of communication, particularly global electronic ones. Prosperos' books stand for much more than books today, just as they did in Shakespeare's time. But where they suggested scholarship, learning and erudition, today they suggest technology, the means of communication and information capital. Caliban's problem was not the language that represented him as a slave but the fact that he was allowed only an incomplete access to Prospero's discourse (he is never allowed to touch the 'books'). Caliban's partial literacy renders him incapable of engaging his master in a war of words—and thus he is forced to adopt physical violence as an alternative—an alternative that we soon realize is inadequate given Prospero's frequent demonstrations of magical power. The significance of this for the theme colonial resistance is poignant—particularly in the present world dominated by a hyperpower ever ready to invade weak nations in case they may be thinking about conflict. The option of violent political resistance to colonial control simply invites the exertion of even greater force. But the capture of the source of Prospero's power offers the true means of social and political transformation. In this one fact we discover the very center of the postcolonial method of transformative resistance.

The ideological assumption of the power of print is replicated in *The Tempest* in the power that accrues to Prospero from his books. The play imprisons Caliban in a colonizer's view of the colonial subject in two ways: first, it describes Caliban's unquestioned acceptance of the fact that Prospero's power, his superior technology, is located in a superior culture, which is embodied in the written word, in his books; and second, it denies Caliban any opportunity to appropriate Prospero's technology. He is constituted by the play as bestial, ugly, monstrous, lowly, little more than an object of the civilizing influence of Prospero's art. The play specifically denies him the opportunity to be nurtured by this art, because, as an unreconstructed natural man, a 'devil,' he is one 'on whose nature Nurture cannot stick.'

The actual function of these books is a source of extreme ambivalence in the colonial relationship. Ideologically, when Lord Macaulay in his infamous Minute to Parliament, says that English gives one access to a 'vast intellectual wealth,' he is merely intoning one of the cultural assumptions which interpellate colonial subjects the way Prospero's discourse interpellates Caliban.[38] But *strategically*, if Caliban were to acquire those books rather than burn them, would he not have access to an empowering counter-discourse? Because Caliban in the play is the unreceptive object of Prospero's civilizing ministrations rather than a subject capable of engaging colonial dominance, this opportunity is denied him. The underlying Eurocentrism of the play abandons Caliban to an unresolvable despair: all Prospero's and Miranda's language can teach him is how to curse. However, beyond the play, beyond the initial colonial encounter, a very different story unfolds. The example of postcolonial literatures reveals that however cursed may be the linguistic relationship of colonizer and colonized, the response available to Caliban is to take hold of the language and re-constitute it as a tool of empowerment. This is because it is not just language with which Caliban has to contend. Language is one key feature of a set of relations of power that constitute imperial discourse. Rejecting the language will not alter the fundamentally productive power of the discourse itself.

The continuing and heated debate in postcolonial studies over the use of the colonial language occurs because language is imputed to be the embodiment of culture identity *par excellence*. Yet what postcolonial writing demonstrates is that language itself is a zone of difference, struggle and transformation rather a zone of identity. Language, most notably in the transcultural performance of postcolonial writing, is a Third Space of enunciation between the poles of cultural identity, a space within which cultural identities themselves are transformed.

NOTES

1. Shakespeare, William. "The Tempest." *William Shakespeare: The Complete Works.* Ed. Peter Alexander. London, Glasgow: Collins, 1989 [1951]. 1–26, 6.
2. Ibid. 21.
3. Ibid. 6.
4. Bhabha, Homi K. *The Location of Culture.* London, New York: Routledge, 1994. 36–39.
5. Pratt, Mary Louise. *Imperial Eyes: Travel Writing and Transculturation.* London, New York: Routledge, 1990. 7. Pratt writes: 'contact zone' is an attempt to invoke the spatial and temporal copresence of subjects previously separated by geographic and historical disjunctures, and whose trajectories now intersect. By using the term 'contact,' I aim to foreground the interactive, improvisational dimensions of colonial encounters so easily ignored or suppressed by diffusionist accounts of conquest and domination. A 'contact' perspective emphasizes how subjects are constituted in and by their relations to each other. It treats the relations among colonizers and

colonized, or travelers and 'travelees,' not in terms of separateness or apartheid, but in terms of copresence, interaction, interlocking understandings and practices, often within radically asymmetrical relations of power.

6. Lamming, George. *The Pleasures of Exile*. Ann Arbor: Michigan UP, 1992 [1960]. 110.
7. Jahn, Janheinz. *A History of the Neo-African Literature: Writing in Two Continents*. London: Faber and Faber, 1968. 240.
8. Ibid. 240.
9. Ibid. 242.
10. Ibid. 242.
11. Ibid. 244.
12. Johnson, Samuel. "Observations on the Present State of Affairs, 1756." *Political Writings: The Yale Edition of the Works of Samuel Johnson*. Ed. Donald Greene. Vol. 10. New Haven: Yale UP, 1977. 180–196. 188, 186.
13. Ngugi wa Thiongo. "Towards a National Culture." *Writers in Politics: Essays*. London, Exeter, NH: Heineman Educational Books, 1981. 1–26.
14. Achebe, Chinua. *Morning Yet on Creation Day*. London: Heineman, 1975. 58.
15. Ngugi wa Thiongo. *Decolonizing the Mind: The Politics of Language in African Literature*. London: James Curry, 1981. 13.
16. Achebe. *Morning Yet on Creation Day*. 62.
17. D'Costa, Jean. "Expression and Communication: Literary Challengers to the Carribean Polydialectical Writers." *Journal of Commonwealth Literature* 19 (1984): 123–141. 123.
18. Ibid. 129.
19. Wittgenstein, Ludwig. *Preliminary Studies for the 'Philosophical investigations': Generally known as the Blue and Brown books*. Oxford: Blackwell, 1969, *The Blue Book* #19; *The Brown Book* #87; Wittgenstein, Ludwig. *Philosophical Investigations*. Trans. G. E. M. Anscombe. Oxford: Blackwell, 1974. #67, #116. (eg. 'What ties the ship to the wharf is the rope and the rope consists of fibres, but it does not get its strength from any fibre that runs through it from one end to the other, but from the fact that there is a vast number of fibres overlapping'. *Brown Book*, #87). # refers to numbered paragraphs in text.
20. Spivak, Gayatri, "Criticism, Feminism and the Institution: Interview with Elizabeth Gross." *Thesis Eleven* 10/11 (November/March) (1984–5): 175–187.
21. Achebe. *Morning Yet on Creation Day*. 61.
22. Ngugi. *Decolonizing the Mind*. 32.
23. Achebe. *Morning Yet on Creation Day*. 61–62.
24. Rushdie, Salman. *Imaginary Homelands*. London: Granta, 1991. 17.
25. Achebe. *Morning Yet on Creation Day*. 62.
26. cited in Achebe. *Morning Yet on Creation Day*. 62.
27. Achebe. *Morning Yet on Creation Day*. 67–68.
28. Cudjoe, Selwyn R. *Eric Williams Speaks: Essays on Colonialism and Independence*. Wellesley: Calaloux, 1993. 61.
29. Ibid. 61.
30. Ibid. 80.
31. Ibid. 80.
32. Ashcroft, Bill, Gareth Griffins, and Helen Tiffin. *The Empire Writes Back: Theory and Practice in Postcolonial Literatures*. London, New York: Routledge, 1989. 61–77.
33. Achebe. *Morning Yet on Creation Day*. 61–62.
34. Shakespeare. "The Tempest." 16.

35. Shakespeare, William. "The Merry Wives Of Windsor." *William Shakespeare: The Complete Works*. Ed. Peter Alexander. London, Glasgow: Collins, 1989 [1951]. 53–82. 73.
36. Shakespeare. "The Tempest." 15.
37. Foucault, Michel. *Power/Knowledge: Selected Interviews and other Writers 1972–1977*. New York: Pantheon, 1980. 98.
38. Macaulay, Thomas Babington. "Minute of the 2nd of February 1835." *Speeches by Lord Macaulay, with his Minute on Indian Education*. Ed. G. M. Young. London: Oxford UP, 1935. 349–350.

8 Crossing into a Mexifornian Third Space

Karin Ikas

INTRODUCTION

For good or ill, Mexifornia has become one of America's most popular buzzwords in this New Millennium. The term insightfully points at the substantial changes currently underway in the United States where U.S. Latinos/as in general and Mexican-Americans in particular are significantly on the rise.[1] Some of them are becoming steadily more integrated, others—mostly newly arrived legal and illegal immigrants from Mexico, Latin and South America who stay first and foremost in their *barrios*, so called Spanish-speaking Hispanic neighborhoods with its own identity as a semi-community—, are not. This rising tide of Hispanic residents does undeniably challenge established power structures in the United States and exposes available self-images as ideologies. An identity politics that means a break with sharp contrasts and allows for multiple subject positions to emerge is obviously needed here. With their idea of a Third Space respective Thirdspace, postcolonial scholar Homi K. Bhabha and spatial critic Edward W. Soja have given us a good tool at hand for such endeavors. By and large, they understand the Third Space respective Thirdspace as a metaphor for an alternative space that is emerging once people of different cultures try to negotiate and transgress the boundaries between Self and Other. The Third Space is neither physical nor entirely spiritual. Rather, it is something else that manifests itself as a plurality of realities that must be endured in a world increasingly marked by cultural multiplicity, hybridity, and cross-border traffic. All this is enacted in the Mexican-American Borderlands to which we will turn our attention in this study. On the whole we perceive this Southwestern part of the U.S.A. bordering Mexico as a classic example for a real and imagined space in-between. The majority of the protagonists who make up the Mexican-American Borderlands have more than one physical, ethnic and cultural background and thus face the challenge of how to communicate more successfully in a situation in which hybridity is indeed the order of the day. After a brief glimpse at the heated debate on Mexifornia as well as on the socio-cultural situation in the U.S.A. as such and the Mexican-American Borderlands in particular, we will turn our attention to the Third Space resp. Thirdspace debate originating from Bhabha and Soja. Last but not least, we examine how all this is enacted in Cherríe Moraga's dramatic piece about the Mexican-American Borderlands entitled *The Hungry Woman: The Mexican Medea.*

MEXIFORNIA

Latest figures and statistics show that we can certainly speak of a hispanization or latinization of the U.S.A. in the Third Millennium. According to the newest U.S. Census survey findings of the over 296.4 million people who resided in the U.S.A. as of July 1, 2005, more than 14.4 percent are Hispanics.[2] This makes people of Hispanic origin, also called U.S. Latinos/ as, the largest ethnic/race minority in the U.S.A. The revenue generated by the 1.6 million Hispanic-owned businesses rose by 19 percent to $222 billion in 2002 while the rate of growth of Hispanic-owned businesses inbetween 1997 and 2002 is 31 percent and hence triple the average rate.[3] More than 65 percent of the U.S. Latinos/as today are Mexican-Americans or Chicanos/as, the rest trace their origin to Central and South America (14 percent), Puerto Rico (12 percent) and Cuba (4 percent). With 31 million U.S. household residents who speak Spanish at home, Spanish speakers constitute a ratio of more than 1-in-10 U.S. household residents. Among all those who speak Spanish at home, more than one-half say they speak English very well. Code switching as well as language mixtures—such as Spanglish, Chicano English, and Chicano Spanish, are also very common among Mexican-Americans. Then there are dialects and street languages like Caló as well as a renewed interest in Pre-Columbian native languages such as the Aztec Nahuatl.[4] Last but not least, latest population estimates expect the projected Hispanic population of the United States as of July 1, 2050 to be about 102.6 million in other words, U.S. Latinos/as would constitute about 24 percent of the nation's total population on that date.[5]

Given all these striking numbers, it is not surprising to find that today, more than a decade after America had observed the 500th Anniversary of the encounter between the Old and the New Worlds, also known as the Discovery of America, its so-called dominating political, economic and intellectual élite has made a new discovery: The Coming of Mexifornia.[6] If Victor David Hanson is right, 'Mexifornia'—that is a state in the making which is 'not quite Mexico and not quite America either'[7]—is currently emerging within the geopolitical borders of the United States. Right now, Mexifornia is most likely equated with America's most populated state, California, where Hispanics make up more than one-third of the population today (approximatetly 12.4 million Hispanics). Yet, for Victor David Hanson and his cronies Samuel Huntington and Patrick J. Buchanan not only is California currently on the verge of transforming into a primarily Spanish-speaking Mexifornia but the United States as a whole is at risk.

They put forward that skyrocketing (il)legal Mexican and Latino immigration rates and an increasing failure of the dominant élite's intellectuals to integrate the subjugated groups of the U.S.-Latino and Hispanic people into mainstream America by instilling the traditional U.S.-American notion of national identity into them efficiently, has already produced a social and civic debacle in California that is about to swamp over the whole nation. In other words, Mexiamerica or Mexamerica as the U.S.A.'s new state of becoming is just around the corner because a long-time constrained minority people is not only gaining a numerical superiority but also the vigor and strength to formulate a Mexifornian counter-narrative of nation that casts a shadow over the traditional self-image of U.S. America. Whereas Samuel Huntington, author of the highly criticized and much debated (for its sensationalism and lack of substance) *Who Are We? America's Great Debate*[8] fears mainly for the future of Anglo-Saxon democracy in the United States whilst the Hispanic people venture out to emancipate themselves from historical objects of a traditional nationalist pedagogy to the modern subjects of the national signification process—to put it in Bhabha's terminology[9]—, Victor David Hanson worries especially about the rise of a primarily Spanish-language Mexifornia, which he feels would infect America with Latin America's dysfunctional social, political and cultural patterns. It seems that one rationale behind this black mood of despair is the anxiety of Anglo-America's neo-conservative élite to lose power and control. This comes along with an apparent fear of a world in which one might become a stranger to oneself after descending into what Bhabha has described as the alien territory in between the self and the other, a territory which would permit ambivalence as well as the exchange of cultural knowledge and the negotiation of difference in favor of an 'international culture.'[10] As Maria Antònia Oliver Rotger appropriately puts it:

> The immense attention given to Latinos/as in the cultural and commercial spheres of this country, as well as their increasing social and political pressure upon the government (with its concomitant backlashes on the part of neo-conservative political groups) have brought white, Anglo, protestant American identity to a crisis. [. . .] recent demographic figures about Latinos have originated a 'collective panic' about a possible 'Hispanic threat' to an old sense of 'Americanness'.[11]

In other words, as Bhabha aptly writes in *The Location of Culture*,

> the problem is not simply the 'selfhood' of the nation as opposed to the otherness of other nations. We are confronted with the nation split within itself, articulating the heterogeneity of its population. The barred Nation *It / Self*, alienated from its eternal self-generation, becomes a liminal signifying space that is *internally* marked by the discourses of

minorities, the heterogeneous histories of contending peoples, antagonistic authorities and tense locations of cultural difference.[12]

Before we go on, let's cast a quick glance at how the Hispanic/Mexican-American and the Anglo-American cultures differentiate from each other in a broad way. Vergilio Elizondo and John Haddox have illustrated this subject matter in detail, so we will just attend to some of the most striking differences here.[13] Generally speaking, Mexican-American culture is marked by a pride in the past whereas Anglos put emphasis on change. Although life is perceived as tragic, marked by hard choice and suffering, it is still enjoyable in the Mexican-American mindset and has to be accepted as it is, its hard blows included. Anglos do not face life with that kind of fatalism. Believing in having control over their destiny, they understand life as a success story; it is epic, with good struggling against evil. For Hispanic Americans, being comes before doing, relationships and people come before things, emotion appears to be stronger than pure logic, and the traditional practice of folk medicine and healing (*curanderismo*) is still quite important. Most work to live, and have extended families, which are the basis for society giving meaning to the life of the individual. For the majority of Anglos, on the other hand, things, careers, logic, efficiency, rugged independence, and personal convenience is very important. Most Anglos live to work, and nuclear families are quite common even though this might bring about loneliness and frustration to the individual in the end. Differences can also be found with regard to religious attitudes and denominations.[14] First of all, it has to be outlined that although about 63.7 percent of all U.S. Americans consider themselves 'Protestants', there is no one church or church group that speaks for all Protestants; rather, they are distributed among many different independent churches. That's why the Roman Catholic Church, with about 22.2 percent of all Americans as members, is by far the single largest denomination in the U.S.A. Whereas the number of Hispanics within Protestant ranks is only slightly rising, the majority of Hispanics are Roman Catholic. Currently about forty percent of all U.S. Catholics are Hispanic, and it is estimated that by 2010 half of all Roman Catholics in the U.S.A. will be Hispanic. Most Hispanics, though, do not simply adopt the rules and conventions of the institutional churches in the U.S.A., but they link Christianity in general and Roman Catholicism in particular with Mesoamerican religious beliefs and transform both traditions according to their needs. Apparently, this does not only bring about a greater mixture of European Catholic, Mexican Catholic and indigenous traditions within the Catholic Church in the U.S.A. and beyond, yet it has also repercussions on the religious landscape in the U.S.A. in general.[15] U.S. Hispanic theologian Virgilio Elizondo's thesis might thus hold true that even in the religious context *The Future is Mestizo*.

To sum it up, we can indeed assess that the transformations currently underway are manifold and substantial. Today, more than ever, the U.S.A.'s dominant definition of national identity is challenged internally by an emerging Hispanic minority that has already become a majority in many parts of the Southwest. Another important issue that comes into prominence here is that of segregation. More precisely, does this rapidly growing group of Hispanics or rather U.S. Latinos/as follow in the footsteps of their forefathers, the rather militant Chicano activists of the Chicano Civil Rights Movement of the 1960s and 1970s, and also call for a separate nation, the so-called nation of Aztlán, as Rodolfo 'Corky' Gonzales and others did at the *First National Chicano Liberation Youth Conference* in Denver in 1969 where *El Plan Espiritual de Aztlán* was passed[16]? Well, not really. This is because hardly any Mexican-American today truly believes in the realization of a manifesto that calls for expelling the Anglo-Americans and for forming Aztlán as a separate and autonomous though primarily patriarchal and heterosexual Chicano nation above the Rio Grande. Rather than being a battle cry to violence and segregation, Aztlán is nowadays generally understood as a spiritual vision of a desired new society of mixed-race people. Moreover, it is a symbol of cultural pride and an inspiration that keeps contemporary Chicanos/as going to gain justice and equality for their own people after their homeland had been seized by the U.S.A. in the mid 1850s.[17] In fact, many of the people of Mexican ancestry living in the U.S. Southwest today, did not actually migrate to the United States. From the time the Spaniards arrived in this land in the early 18th century, they mixed with the natives, and thus gave birth to the original mixed-race people in the Southwest, the so-called mestizo. So they were already living here when the first immigrants from the east eventually arrived. Only when the U.S. took this territory over from Mexico with the *Treaty of Guadalupe-Hidalgo* in 1848 and with subsequent contracts after Mexico's loss of the Mexican-American War (1846–1848), these people became foreigners on their own land, exiles who actually never left home. This also explains why they are often referred to as an adopted minority. Interestingly enough, however, even those people who have migrated from Mexico to the U.S. Southwest, or rather the U.S. Borderlands, in the subsequent years, feel that this area in the Mexican-American Borderlands is their homeland. In spite of everything then, the Mexican-American Borderlands will always belong to its native inhabitants and their mestizo descendants, that is the Hispanic people or *La Raza*, the so-called mestizo race; if only in a spiritual sense. In view of all this, it is quite understandable that U.S. Hispanics, although most do not call for segregation, nonetheless refuse to succumb any longer to a national pedagogy[18], which only aims at keeping them in a colonized minority position. That's why its intellectuals have begun their dissemination of the national narration in the sense of what Bill Ashcroft, Gareth Griffiths and Helen Tiffin once identified as *The Empire Writes Back* strategy.[19] Doing so, they drive a wedge between demands of the pedagogical part that all members of the nation adopt the dominant national consciousness that had been constructed, and they urge U.S. America into distancing itself from its very own positions.

Thus, via traditional media and communication channels, face-to-face panel discussion as well as cyberspace,[20] scholars, politicians and common people from all walks of life and ethnic backgrounds have launched a debate on how to cope with these changes while trying to avoid the traps of populism and segregationist talks.[21] All in all, there is an increasing awareness that neither any claim to a hierarchical purity of cultures nor any exoticism of cultural diversity does take us very far in the global era where communication between members of different cultures has become a most important affair.[22] Scholars and writers have repeatedly demonstrated that this also means that beyond fixed cultural—that is ethnic, gender, and class-related—identities so called hybrid identities are created by asymmetrical translations and negotiations. And indeed, for most people residing in the U.S. states along the Mexican-American border—e.g. Texas, California, New Mexico, and Nevada—identity has never been something permanent, simple and obvious. They aren't able to categorize themselves into one or two pigeonholes of the identity politics because continuous (im)migration and emancipation movements as well as patterns of dislocation, miscenegation and transculturation impede upon their attempts to locate and negotiate a self between social and cultural entities and even nations to this very day. This is particularly true for Mexican-Americans, the largest group residing here. Their experience is shaped by three borderline aspects: a history of native origin in the Southwestern territory right before it was annexed by the United States after the Mexican-American War (1846–1848); a(n) (im)migrant experience; and a present post-modern Chicano/a experience. In contemporary discourse, arts and literature, this is usually depicted in two ways. Firstly, the space adjoining the U.S.-Mexico border is perceived as a danger zone and this affects both dominant ethnic groups residing here: (il)legal Mexican-American (im)migrants for whom the dialectics of difference[23] does not give rise to assimilation, synthesis and resolution but to conflicts; and Anglo-Americans who feel increasingly threatened by their increasing sway of power coupled with the never-ending influx of Spanish speaking Latinos immigrants and the subsequent transformation of the U.S.-Mexico border region into what they suspiciously call Mexifornia. Secondly, and most interestingly though, the border is increasingly perceived as a hybrid site of cross-fertilization where a complex process of inter- and transcultural relations comes to pass.[24] Borrowing Mary Louise Pratt's notion of the 'contact zone,'[25] José David Saldívar, for example, perceives the two-thousand-mile-long border between the United States and Mexico as a paradigm for a '*Transfrontera* contact zone.'[26] For him this means a 'social space of subaltern encounters, the Janus-faced border line in which peoples geopolitically forced to separate themselves now negotiate with one another and manufacture new relations, hybrid cultures, and multiple-voiced aesthetics.'[27]

Even more pointedly than José David Saldívar, Bhabha acknowledges the Mexican-American Borderlands as a case in point for an alternative space where communication between cultures and negotiation of identities assumes new dimensions. Actually, in the context of Bhabha's critique the space of the borderlands is defined as a third sphere of action and representation, which opens up when the U.S.-American society and the Chicana/o nationalists expose their self-definition on the post-colonial field of tension in the borderlands. Bhabha demonstrates this already in the opening section of his study *The Location of Culture* where he points at the significance of the Mexican-American Borderlands culture for a critical assessment of the Third Space. The Mexico/U.S. border, Bhabha argues, is the prolific site for a 'borderline work of culture' where 'art does not merely recall the past as a social cause or aesthetic precedent; it renews the past, refiguring it as a contingent "in-between" space, that innovates and interrupts the performance of the present. The "past-present" becomes part of the necessity, not the nostalgia, of living.'[28] Glimpses at particular productions of Mexican-American performance artist Guillermo Gómez-Peña as well as at certain literary works by Chicano author Tomas Ybarra-Frausto, among others, are used by Bhabha to substantiate his view that the signs used for what Eric Hobsbawn and Terence Ranger called the invention of tradition[29] are variant and subject to changing times, in particular once they are performed or rather reiterated and deferred by emergent minorities. By contesting the meaning of both, their own traditions and the dominant national narration, the speakers of minorities, in this case the Mexican-American people, get the process of a deferring and scattering of meaning, the so-called dissemination, going until everything moves into one another and a Third Space of enunciation emerges. For Bhabha, the driving force behind this transformation process is the eventual ability of minority speakers to detach themselves not only from the dominant national narration but also from their very own position through performative utterance. This is what makes them agents of a new hybrid national narration.

A somehow similar tactic is applied by American scholar Soja, who is another key player in this currently *en vogue* interdisciplinary debate on space, the spatiality of human life and the concept of Thirdspace as an alternative mode of thinking. In his study *Thirdspace: Journeys into Real and Imagined Places*, Soja appears to be inspired by 'the border work being done'[30] by U.S. Latino critics and writers, namely Guillermo Gómez-Peña as well as Gloria Anzaldúa and María Lugones. Moreover, stressing the significance of the latter, namely the postcolonial feminists Anzaldúa and Lugones, he takes a particular stand for the postmodern spatial feminist critique in his transdisciplinary exploration of the real and imagined worlds of Thirdspace: 'Here, in the overlapping borderlands of feminist and postcolonial cultural criticism is a particularly fertile meeting ground for initiating new pathways for exploring Thirdspace and also for the later journeys to a real-and-imagined Los Angeles.'[31] Besides some references to Edward Said and bell hooks, Soja grounds his description of a 'trialectics' of spatiality that threads through all subsequent real and imagined journeys undertaken at the turn of the century mostly in Henri Lefebvre's conceptualization of the social space as conceived, perceived, and lived. By and large, we can assess that for Soja social spatiality functions as form, configured materially as things in space, and also mentally, as thoughts about space; furthermore, it is a process, a dynamic force that is actively being produced and reproduced all the time, and as such inseparable from society.[32]

So far so good. Although Soja and Bhabha have different foci here—the former approaches the Thirdspace via physical space searching for something that is neither entirely physical nor entirely spiritual; the latter approaches the thematic through literature and language viewing it mainly as a question of how we translate and negotiate cultural multiplicity so that hybrid identities emerge in the Third Space of enunciation—each of them understands the Thirdspace respective Third Space as an opportunity, as a process that opens up and broadens horizons for translating and communicating the multiple elements and experiences of the self and the other that are simultaneously present and thought to interact in a contact zone. This, of course, implies a break with clear-cut contrasts, e.g. contrasts between such opposing couples as man-woman, reason-emotion, subject-object and those especially associated with the colonial and postcolonial space, namely 'nature-culture, chaos-civility,'[33] margin-center and so on. Even though difference as such is not denied in the Third Space critique's point-of-view, the focus is on the reciprocity of any pair of such definitions. In other words, it is all a question of how each of the pair influences the other in a both-and instead of an either-or relationship. This is closely related to Arjun Appadurai's position, namely that 'culture does imply difference, but the differences now are no longer, if you wish, taxonomical; they are interactive and refractive.'[34] In his studies on the mutuality and interdependence of cultures in the colonial and postcolonial process Bhabha's thesis is that 'cultural difference is not the acquisition or accumulation of additional cultural knowledge; it is the momentous, if momentary, extinction of the recognizable object of culture in the disturbed artifice of its signification, at the edge of experience.'[35] The idea of hybridity as 'camouflage, as a contesting, antagonistic agency functioning in the time-lag of sign/symbol, which is a space in-between the rules of engagement'[36] occupies a central place here. In Bhabha's view, hybridity is important because it opens up a third dimension or a third sphere for the production of meaning that goes beyond fixed cultural identities in the relation and negotiation of two systems in an ever changing network of cultures and traditions.[37] To speak with him: 'For me the importance of hybridity is not to be able to trace two original moments from which the third emerges, rather hybridity to me is the "Third Space", which enables other positions to emerge.'[38] And in "The Commitment to Theory" he adds:

it is that Third Space, though unrepresentable in itself, which constitutes the discursive conditions of enunciation that ensure that the
meaning and symbols of culture have no primordial unity or fixity;
that even the same signs can be appropriated, translated, rehistoricized
and read anew.[39]

Although I am aware of the problematic history of the term hybridity[40]
as well as of the criticism Bhabha has received for not sufficiently conceptualizing the material and historical conditions that would appear within
a colonial discourse analysis framework,[41] his insight as to the role of a
hybrid identity and the Third Space are useful because they enable us to
see recurrent misunderstandings occurring in interactions across languages
and cultures as opportunities to create something new out of a plurality
of realities that must be endured. Papastergiadis sums it up well when he
describes the role of the hybrid identity as 'a lubricant' in the conjunction of cultures.[42] This is also our point of departure for the final part of
this paper. We will call on Bhabha's aforementioned notions of 'hybridity'
and 'Third Space' to find out what these concepts mean for a particular
dramatic piece on the Mexican-American Borderlands that does not just
point its fingers at Anglo America's dominating élite but also at Chicano
nationalists for formulating Aztlán as a counter-narrative of the nation that
brings out similarly questionable ethnic, gender and sexual discrimination
and evokes reactionary politics.

For our endeavor we have chosen *The Hungry Woman: A Mexican
Medea* (2000), one of the first insightful dramatic pieces published in the
Third Millennium by well-known controversial Chicana lesbian author
and critic Cherríe Moraga. In our analysis we argue that Moraga uses
hybridization, which emerges in various forms throughout the play, as
a strategic device to open up an imagined space and signify a reading of
identities that defies any imposition of fixed, unitary identifications. This
is compatible with Bhabha's idea that the production of meaning in the
relations of two systems requires a Third Space, which is in fact the space
of hybridity itself.

CHERRÍE MORAGA'S HUNGRY WOMAN AND THE
NEW AZTLAN AS A MEXIFORNIAN THIRD SPACE

At first glance, Moraga's *The Hungry Woman: A Mexican Medea* seems
a little out of touch. The small volume—with its violet-green and rather
whimsically macabre cover—depicts a light-bearing uncanny one-eyed
witchlike figure with apparel reminiscent of Latin America's patron saint
La Virgin de Guadalupe. Hence, on the surface the jacket seems to give
more notice of a blood-thirsty crime thriller produced by a horror-struck
author with iconoclastic endeavors than of a work that has something to

contribute to the Third Space debate. But, as is often the case with horror, you can't help but wonder what is going on inside. And indeed, on closer inspection and with an eye on the mythological roots of Mexican-American culture and power structures, we learn that the image on the cover is, in fact, Chicana artist Celia Herrera-Rodriguez' extravagant version of Omecihuatl, the Aztec creator-goddess and source of all life. Grounded in Mesoamerican mythology and also shaped by non-indigenous folklore and traditions, Herrera-Rodriguez has interpreted Omecihuatl as a crossroad character at the edges of experience: she is a hybrid, grief-stricken and battle-hardened symbol for all those exiles and women today, who, as Irma Mayorga aptly put it in her critical essay "Homecoming" (2001), 'suffer the legacy of their antepasados in the injustices of patriarchy and hunger for empowerment' in a society continuously favoring binary structures to hybrid forms of existence.[43]

Moraga herself has experienced the Mexican-American Borderlands hitherto as a neo-colonialist space where dominant concepts of nation, culture, and even religious affiliations—although they are increasingly put to the test these days—prevail. This is because they are not only upheld by a dominant Anglo-American élite but also by a radical and revolutionary Chicano élite invoking nativist concepts in their endeavor to make a reality of Aztlán, the mythic patriarchal Chicano nationalist homeland dreamt of since the 1960s. For Moraga, the latter goes hand in hand with a reactionary sexual and gender politics that continues to push especially mixed-race queer citizens to the margins, making life very difficult for lesbian and multiethnic migrant citizens and writers such as Moraga herself. Like the hungry mythic women 'La Llorona, Coyolxauhqui, Coalticue' whom she worships and relates to in her foreword as 'the mutilated women of our indigenous american history of story'[44], she had endured various forms of discrimination throughout the first three decades of her life when she was too white to be accepted by her Mexican mother's ethnic group, too brown to fully belong to her Anglo father's ethnic community, too unwomanly as a lesbian and—after becoming a queer mother of a heterosexual son—too much mother and hence too un-homosexually woman to be a real lesbian.[45] And in this struggle for meaning—which is marked by a continuous longing for rootedness in an uprooted world or rather a place called home, as well as the desire to transgress or even blur the boundaries between the self and the others at last—, playwriting has become Moraga's most significant ally. In an interview she describes her mission as a playwright as follows:

> for me writing theatre is somehow a bit like writing a novel. The characters are talking to you, and you have to listen to them. If you try to superimpose your ideology of that time, the work gets very flat. So I never am concerned about how the audience is going to respond. I never censor anything based on who the audience is. I write for my

ideal audience that is probably made up of people who are not homophobic, not racist, people who are open-minded. So if you assume your audience is open-minded, and you write well and with enough depth, then whoever is in the audience—white person, person of color, whatever—will be able to see the other-maybe for the first time in their life-just as humans.[46]

To achieve this effect and at the same time remind the spectator in the audience that the play *The Hungry Woman: A Mexican Medea* is just a representation of reality and not reality itself, Moraga employs techniques from the epic theatre outlined by Bertolt Brecht in his *Little Organum for the Theater* [original German title: *Kleines Organon für das Theater*, 1948].[47] The techniques adopted by Moraga from the epic theatre to 'force[d] the spectators to look at the play's situations from an angle that they necessarily became subject to his criticism'[48] consist of unnatural stage lighting, exaggerated costumes and masks, songs, a chorus—here CIHUATATEO: EL CORO that performs in the traditional style of Aztec danzantes—, fictional representations and tellings of semi-historical as well as mythical archetypes and events from the Mesoamerican and Mexican-American as well as the Western tradition. From the former these include the Mesoamerican goddess Coatlicue, the Cihuatateos, who are female incarnations of the divine spirit thought to transport the soul of women lost in childbirth to the sun; pseudo-historical female action and revenge heroes like *the Hungry Woman* or the Weeping Woman La Llorona, and last but not least the legendary story of the pseudo-historical place Aztlán[49]; from the latter these comprise in particular the Christian messiah concept, and the pieta motif. Implementing her idea of myth as '[. . .] an opening into the past, told in character and image, that can provide a kind of road map to our future'[50], Moraga recovers these myths, presents them, however, not in pure but rather hybrid forms in a transcultural—and transnational—milieu. The somehow bizarre cover image with the multi-leveled mythic crossover character Omecihuatl already points to Moraga's strategic *mythopoeia* as a conscious creation of transcultural myths that emerge from, yet also go beyond mere, hybridizations. This is even more apparent in the play's complex title *The Hungry Woman: A Mexican Medea,* which implies a metaphorical reference to elements of pre-Columbian, Mexican and European mythology. Moraga blurs and reworks this Western and non-Western mythical material to make her *Hungry Woman: A Mexican Medea* heroine a crosscut of the pre-Columbian moon deity Coyolxauhqui, the Mexicano/a weeping woman La Llorona and the Greek Medea. In that sense she signifies that what had seemed to belong to the ageless tradition of a particular culture and made up its collective consciousness, is subject to change and transculturation in the contemporary age where 'world culture does not present itself as uniform but can be rather described as "organized diversity", that is, a web of various local cultures which are not necessarily anchored to a geographical territory', as Sabrina Brancato rightly puts it.[51]

Nonetheless, the stage directions for the opening scene make perfectly clear that so far the borderlands—which are introduced here as a 'muy Blade Runner-esque' metaphysical border zone between Gringolandia (U.S.A.) and Aztlán (Mechicano country) where decay, pollution, and chaos prevails—is anything else but such an organized diversity for negotiating transcultural identities and communicating in-between cultures and ethnicities.[52]

Right from the beginning the protagonist's displaced and victimized status is attributed to asymmetrical power relations and numerous forms of betrayals. The later have occurred while the transformation of the Mexican-American Borderlands into a rather disparate postmodern ensemble of four imagined and real spaces, namely Aztlán, Gringolandia, Phoenix also known as Tamoanchán, and a mythical realm inhabited by a spirit chorus of Aztec warrior women, took place. Although most people 'look lousy in' this increasingly disparate, crazy and ominous world, Medea's position is particularly problematic: as an indígena mexicana Medea she would have had 'the blood quantum' required for citizenship in Aztlán[53] and as a wife of a highly-respected Chicano leader also the family status requirements to be a proper woman in this Mechicano country. Nonetheless, her eventual outing as a brown activist lesbian lover and mother—whereby she conducts a serious breach of the prescribed etiquette—puts her into exile. Her exile is a lunatic asylum in an in-between country also known as '"Tamoanchán," which means "we seek our home".' It is a 'gypsy ghetto' like place where 'the seeking itself became home' [after] 'los homos became peregrinos [. . .] como nomads, just like our Aztec ancestors a thousand years ago' (cf. conversation between Savannah, one of Medea's warden nurses who also performs as the Aztec mythic character Mama Sal, and Medea's son Chac-Mool[54]). For Moraga the link between mythical transformation, liberation and identity formation is indeed a seminal one. It's the trigger to finally open an alternative space that goes beyond the numerous confinements that mark the borderlands spaces in the here and now. We can see this in scene eight when Luna, Medea's lesbian lover, explicitly refers to the Hungry Woman creation myth as follows:

Creation Myth. In the place where the spirits live, there was once a woman who cried constantly for food. She had mouths everywhere. [. . .] And every mouth was hungry y bien gritona. To comfort la pobre, the spirits flew down and began to make grass and flowers from the dirt-brown of her skin. From her greñas, they made forests. From those ojos negros, pools and springs. And from the slopes of her shoulders and seños, they made mountains y valles. At last she will be satisfied, they thought. Pero, just like before, her mouths were everywhere [. . .] They would never be filled. Sometimes por la noche, when the wind blows, you can hear her crying for food.[55]

This passage, for which Moraga draws on John Bierhorst's critical account of *The Hungry Woman: Myths and Legends of the Aztecs*[56], clearly shows that spatiality cannot be considered apart from memory, desire, and enunciation. Throughout the play, desire shapes the process of remembering whereas memory lies rooted in bodies and spaces, and all this has to be unearthed through enunciation. The following scene serves as an excellent example:

MEDEA:	[. . .]. I do miss my Luna.
NURSE:	Why don't you tell her that when you see her? You never talk to her.
MEDEA:	No. I only want to be an Indian, a Woman, an Animal in the Divine Ecosystem. The jaguar, the bear, the eagle.
[. . .]	
MEDEA:	During the day when Jasón was at work. [. . .] I could hear Chac-Mool outside talking to the stonemason. It was paradise.
NURSE:	The stonemason?
MEDEA:	Yes. The woman, the migrant worker my husband Jasón hired to put in the garden patio. [. . .].

[LUNA and CHAC-MOOL appear in MEDEA's memory]

LUNA:	You should plant corn.
CHAC-MOOL:	My mom didn't say nothing about no corn.
LUNA:	What's a garden without corn?
CHAC-MOOL:	She's gonna plant medicine.
LUNA:	Your mom makes medicine?
CHAC-MOOL:	Yeah, she learned from my Bisabuela.
LUNA:	Plant corn. A single corn plant can produce enough grain to feed a person for a day.
MEDEA:	And the stonemason's voice entered me like medicine. Medicine for my brokenness.[57]

Here the ancient knowledge of the Bisabuela—Medea's Spanish named grandmother—and the stonemason—the migrant laborer in the borderlands, is deployed to cultivate—in a metaphorical sense—the garden at the edges of contact and do the borderland work of culture. To pull out the weeds of neo-colonial power relations, assimilative technologies, and notorious claims to authenticity is once again the most tedious and difficult part of the job as Jasón's behavior illustrates. Earlier in the play we learned that his problems of life at the borders emerge from the fact that he lacks 'the blood quantum'[58] requested for citizenship in the new Chicano country of Aztlán after the latter had been reestablished along the lines of a presumed indigenous authenticity. And, what is even more, Jasón also lacks the insights and sensibility to utilize his resources and cross into an alternative space attuned to hybridity 'from which something begins it presencing'[59] instead. Without the ability to recognize the potential of his and other people's hybrid existence, he is practically living life like a blind man who careens towards an existence where his only possibility to satisfy his recurrent need for power is to participate in what has always occurred in hierarchically structured societies all along: to kick at those perceived as weaker and more disadvantaged members of society in order to seize a share of power. This is beautifully evoked in the scene just quoted when Jasón pushes the colored female stonemason back into her postcolonial status *quo ante* by recognizing her first and foremost as a subjugated brown migrant woman laborer employed to do the dirty manual work.

The themes of postcoloniality, acculturation, hybridity, and mythical transformation are climaxed and underscored in the final scenes of the play where the stories of Medea, the Hungry Woman, and the Cihuatateo intersect with the Mesoamerican rite of making sacrifices and the Christian devotional theme of 'Our Lady of Sorrow', also known as the pieta motif. The latter found its most famous artistic expression in Michelangelo's marble Pietà sculpture (1499) in the St. Peter's Basilica in Rome. The critical stage is reached here when Medea—who remains very much caught up in the web of intra-cultural oppressions based on gender and sexuality in the final analysis—kills her son Chac-Mool right before his time of puberty begins. With this infanticide she literally goes beyond good and evil in her endeavor to save the people in the Mexican-American Borderlands from what she pictures as the dawning continuation of a primarily unilateral, patriarchal and homophobic era. Interestingly enough, however, this does not give rise to an instant of triumph over the presumed effacement of an antagonistic system. Rather, it brings about a moment of extraordinary devotion and lamentation for which Moraga employs the pieta motif in the following way:

> He [=CHAC-MOOL] passes out. It is a pieta image, MEDEA holding him limp within her arms. [. . .]. The CIHUATATEO enter, dressed in the traditional Aztec. They lift CHAC-MOOL and take him into the center of the field. [. . .]. She becomes frenzied, a frightening image, her white nightgown flowing in the sudden wind. The pile of blue corn stalks have formed a kind of altar. The CIHUATATEO heave CHAC-MOOL's body on top of it.[60]

Apparently, this is very much designed along the lines of the ancient Aztecs' belief that welfare and survival of humankind depends first of all on the offering of blood to the divine deity. Nonetheless, with the explicit reference to the pieta and the iconoclastic transformation of the latter to a rather profane lesbian and brown-colored mother and defeated warrior gestalt that supports the body of the indigenous-named messiah-son Chac-Mool just shortly before the divine and noble Cihuatateo take over, the scene quickly turns from the original act as well as emotion of great love and loss together with a revering fear of a divine act of control into a transcultural field of redemption and transgression. In the play's final tableau this line of thought is fully developed when Moraga has the Christian concept of the messiah step in so that a resurrected Chac-Mool can return to the scene and act in the following way:

MEDEA: [. . .] Why have you come here?
CHAC-MOOL: To take you away.
MEDEA: Away . . . where?
CHAC-MOOL: Home.
MEDEA: Home.
[. . .]
[He leads her by the hand back to the bed. He holds a handful of powdered herbs and puts them into a small paper cup of water. [. . .]. CHAC-MOOL holds MEDEA's head while she drinks. She is instantly drowsy. CHAC-MOOL gathers her into his arms as she falls into a deep sleep. It is a piety image. The lights gradually fade. Only the shimmering moon remains, and the figure of the four CIHUATATEO dancing silently in its light.] [61]

According to Christian beliefs many of the messianic prophecies of the Old Testament were fulfilled in the mission, death and resurrection of God's son Jesus, the one and only savior, who repeatedly referred to himself in the New Testament as 'Son of Man'[62] and will therefore return to make the rest of the Messianic prophecy come true on doomsday. In the above-quoted epilogue this role of the messiah is, as expected, also taken over by the son, namely Chac-Mool. More surprising in this context, though, is the son's Pre-Columbian name Chac-Mool as it refers to a Mesoamerican religious character that is more used to offering human sacrifices to the gods than being sacrificed himself. Yet, a closer look at this prehistoric Chac-Mool reveals that he was not only involved in the Mesoamerican religious practices of human sacrifices but also perceived as an intermediary between human beings and the Gods of rain, water and fertility in a more general sense.[63] And this surely is the connecting line to Jesus, the Christian God's son who—as Son of Man—is a mediator between the divine and the earthly as well. So, Moraga's Chac-Mool incarnate holds especially two offices in these final scenes: he is an avenging angel and a savior. After his miraculous resurrection, he murders his own mother Medea in the same manner that he had been murdered by her before: death by poisoning. Through this matricide the former infanticide is avenged. Moreover, through her physical death Medea is redeemed from any form of eternal sin that she and others have inscribed on her body during her voyage through the dystopic borderlands. The apparent replacement of the Christian notion of redemptive sacrifice, which centers upon the belief that Jesus died an innocent death to redeem mankind from all sins, with the Mesoamerican concept of human expiatory sacrifice, hints at the implications for affirming the indigenous and migratory people's presence in the contemporary Mexican-American Borderlands: so, the core of the debate here is that non-Western religious concepts, myths, and cultural traditions infiltrate the Western ones and transform the dominant system from within through dissemination. This then maneuvers towards transculturality and a disseminated, more worldly notion of salvation. And all of this is couched in the final tableau's iconoclastic depiction of a reversed and multiply twisted pieta motif. Moraga's second pieta composition consists of the messiah-like messenger-son and matricide Chac-Mool mourning over his dead lesbian mother and infanticide Medea, whose spirit is already on the move to an interstitial space. On this journey to a home beyond the confinements of the real world, her spirit is accompanied by four Cihuatateos dancing silently in the moonlight. With this adumbration of a space floating in-between this world and the other where hybrid people living between culturally and ethnically defined dualisms can betake themselves to at last, Moraga's play comes to a close. Once again, Moraga sticks to exaggeration and continues her strange combination of the play's gests' in the mode of Brecht's epic theatre theory to ensure that the spectator in the audience does not emotionally identify with the action before him or her but rather feels alienated from it and treats it critically (= A-effect). It may be concluded then that Moraga uses the Alienation-effect in two ways: firstly, to allow the spectators in the audience of whatever ethnic group and religious affiliation to dissociate themselves from their very own positions; secondly, to motivate them to similarly detach themselves from the play's suggested deconstruction of binary oppositions and the subsequent dissemination of meaning from elements of the colonial and the colonized, the Christian and the Mesoamerican, the non-indigenous and the indigenous traditions that make up the two conflicting narrations of nationhood in the Mexican-American Borderlands. The thus double-detached spectator is requested to use his or her critical perspective to identify social ills at work in the world and go forth from the theatre and effect change. In other words, the A-effect is meant to provoke a rational self-reflection and critical view of the actions on the stage among the spectator in the audience. At best, the latter is then motivated to take the story's structures apart trying to find out how the processes in question might affect his or her own life, role, status and behavior while he or she goes forth from the theatre and gets down to formulate an alternative narrative that gives more credit to the state of affairs in the Mexican-American Borderlands of today.

CLOSING AND OUTLOOK

All in all we can assess that for Moraga crossing into a Mexifornian Third Space implies a transcultural knitting of a complex weave of mythical and religious interactions. That way, she unsettles the dominant Anglo-American national discourse as well as the reactionary nativist Chicano pathos of a New Aztlán that appears to be nothing else but the old wine of an asymmetrically structured patriarchal system in the new bottle of a pseudo-authentic and blood-rooted Chicano nation. While the lack of tolerance for sexual diversity and the myopic vision of many fundamentalist groups on either side—the Euro-American and the Mexican-American one—is largely held responsible for the chaos and troubled life in an imagined dystopic future of the Mexican-American Borderlands where the colored, the homosexual, and the female migrant others are pushed to the margins, it is exactly the exiled position from which a development towards a third emerges. In exile, Moraga's hybrid Chicana heroine gets down to construct an alternative and rather mythopoetic narrative of the Mexican-American Borderlands 'that is new, neither the one nor the other but something else besides, which contests the terms and territories of both.'[64] Hybridity is acknowledged as the most viable subject postion from which to negotiate and represent a condition of transcultural or rather transmythical mobility here, of people on the move who, as Bhabha aptly notes, 'will not be contained within the Heim of the national culture and its unisont discourse, but are themselves the marks of a shifting boundary that alienates the frontiers of the modern nation.'[65] In times like these, when the post-9/11 United States is not only at war in Iraq and conducts a military campaign against worldwide terrorism but also debates a continued fortification of its 2,000-mile border with Mexico while already erecting hundreds of more miles of walls there, this is a rather daring, though very significant, undertaking. As the discussion above has illustrated, neither a fortification of borders nor a global crusade against terror can't take people's attention away from the fact that the truly significant challenges U.S.-America faces in the Third Millennium are internal. Political conscious intellectuals of the U.S.A.'s largest growing ethnic minority group, a so-called evolving U.S. Latino/a élite, have an important contribution to make here. They are a driving force in the emerging construction of a new narration of nation that gives more credit to an internally more and more transformed U.S. America. Distancing themselves from the dominant and their very own positions, intellectuals such as Moraga—who also put the spectator in the audience in a double-detached position in the epic theatre-style designed socio-critical plays—can launch a process of negotiations whereby to reformulate the identities of the minority and majority actors involved in the process, so that something new that is neither the one nor the other but a third eventually comes into pass. While her hybrid and multiply twisted pietas surely won't knock the Statue of Liberty off her pedestal as a national symbol for U.S.-America in the coming years, they nonetheless give credit to the fact that the pieta motif has gained enormous significance as a symbol for the often pitiful and salvation-awaiting state of individuals struggling with the multiple challenges in the global village of today. Numerous artists, writers, movie directors, educators, journalists and even natural scientists all have utilized the pieta motif in the United States in recent years.[66] Two of the most interesting iconoclastic pieta interpretations surely are the monumental Southwest Pieta (1983), a fibreglass-sculpture by renowned Latino artist Luis Jiménez, and the American Pietà, a name given to a famous 9/11 Reuters photograph. The Southwest Pieta, which is located in

Albuquerque, New Mexico, and was declared a national treasure by President Bill Clinton in 1999, shows a mourning male brown Aztec warrior holding his dead female lover. While the pair as such represents a particular Mexican-American and Mesoamerican legend, namely the tragic Romeo-and-Juliet-like love story of the Aztec warrior Popocatepetl and the Atzec emperor's daughter Ixtaccihuatl, whom the gods had turned into volcanoes to be united for eternity, the eagle in the background, which is a significant national symbol for Mexico and Anglo-America alike, brings in a transcultural moment that might allow both sides to relate to the image and get something out of it for negotiations across boundaries.[67] The latter, the American pieta of 2001, depicts a policemen and four firefighters carrying the body of fire department chaplain Mychal F. Judge—one of America's new male heroes who was later exposed as a homosexual—out of the debris of the World Trade Center. With this tying in of a Mesoamericanized Catholic pieta (The Southwest Pieta) with a secularized male White Anglo Saxon Protestant fireworkmen Pieta, numerous borders are criss-crossed in religious, social, political and cultural contexts. Studying further how this popular iconography eventually intersects with discourses of sexuality, postcoloniality, national and religious ideology might help us to gain more insights into the multiple layers of the representation and negotiation of identities and the discursive implications of communicating the self and the other while moving towards a third in an internally multiply challenged post 9/11-American culture.

NOTES

1. In this study I use the terms 'Mexican-American' and 'Chicano/a' interchangeably to refer to a person of Mexican ancestry living in the United States, whether he or she refers to herself as Mexican, Mexican-American, Latino/a, Hispanic, Hispano/a or whatever. The term 'U.S. Latino/a' is used here to denote a person of Latin American ancestry. It acts as the umbrella term for all the subgroups that form the U.S. Latino/a population in the U.S.A. today, e.g. Mexican-Americans, Cuban Americans, descendents from El Salvador, Guatemala, Honduras, Puerto Rico, etc. For an overview of the forming of all these terms and possible ways to distinguish them further, consult Meier, Matt S., and Feliciano Rivera. *Dictionary of Mexican-American History*. Westport: Greenwood Press, 1981; and also chapter 1.2. in Ikas, Karin. *Die zeitgenössische Chicana-Literatur: Eine interkulturelle Untersuchung*. Heidelberg: Winter, 2000. 2–6.
2. This estimate doesn't include the 3.9 million residents of the dominion of Puerto Rico. For detailed info cf. U.S. Census Bureau. http://www.census.gov/Press-Release/www/releases/. Online releases.
3. Cf. http://www.census.gov/csd/sbo/.
4. Anzaldúa sums up the most frequent codes and language varieties used by Mexican-Americans in the Borderlands as follows: '1. Standard English, 2. Working class and slang English, 3. Standard Spanish, 4. Standard Mexican Spanish, 5. North Mexican Spanish dialect, 6. Chicano Spanish (Texas, New Mexico, Arizona and California have regional variations), 7. Tex-Mex, 8. *Pachuco* (called *caló*).' Anzaldúa, Gloria. *Borderlands/La Frontera*. San

Francisco: Aunt Lute Press, 1999. 77. See also, e.g. Peñalosa, Fernando. *Chicano Sociolinguistics*. Rowley: Newbury House Publishers, 1980.

5. See U.S. Census Data. Online accessible: http://www.census.gov/Press-Release/www/releases/archives/population/001720.html.

6. Cf. Ewing, Walter A. "Mexifornia. A State of Confusion." Online Publications of the American Immigration Law Foundation. http://www.ailf.org/ipc/Mexifornia.asp. No page numbers; Fonte, John. "Victor Davis Hanson's Second Thoughts on Immigration." Hudson Center for American Common Culture. Online. http://www.hudson.org/index.cfm?fuseaction=publication_details&id=2983. No page numbers.

7. Victor Davis Hanson, "Mexifornia: Five Years Later." *City Journal* (winter 2007). Cf. Online issue: http://www.city-journal.org/html/17_1_mexifornia.html. No page numbers.

8. Huntington, Samuel. *Who We Are? America's Great Debate*. New York: Free Press, 2005.

9. See Homi K. Bhabha. *The Location of Culture*. London, New York: Routledge, 1994. Also, Wagner, Gerhard. "Nation, DissemiNation und Dritter Raum: Homi K. Bhabhas Beitrag zu einer Theorie kollektiver Identität." *Dialektik* 1 (2006): 181–193.

10. Bhabha. *The Location of Culture*. 38.

11. Oliver-Rotger, Maria Antònia. *Battlegrounds and Crossroads: Social and Imaginary Space in Writings by Chicanas*. Amsterdam, New York: Rodopi, 2003. 105.

12. Bhabha. *The Location of Culture*. 148.

13. Compare Elizondo, Vergilio. *The Future is Mestizo*. Bloomington: Meyer-Stone Books, 2000; Haddox, John. *Los Chicanos: An Awakening People*. Southwestern Studies, Monograph 28. El Paso: Texas Western Press, 1970.

14. Despite the fact that the words 'In God We Trust' mark the U.S. currency and the U.S. Pledge of Allegiance states that the U.S. is 'one nation under God', from its very beginnings as a nation, Americans have been careful to separate state and church, government and religion. The First Amendment of the Constitution forbids the government to give special favors to any religion or to hinder the free practice of any religion. Consequently, there is no state-supported religion nor any official state church, no legal or official religious holidays nor any church taxes. Some nationally representative studies on religion and faith in recent years have revealed, however, that the U.S.A. is less secular that had been suspected and is in fact one of the most religious nations in the so-called developed world today. Some figures: just one in ten Americans (10.8 percent) is not affiliated with a congregation, denomination, or other religious group; and even 63 percent of the members of the non-affiliated group still believe in God or some higher figure. Roughly a third of Americans are rather conservative-oriented Evangelical Protestants by affiliation (33.6 percent) and fewer than 5 percent of the U.S. population claim a faith outside of the Judeo-Christian mainstream. Nearly half of all Americans (47.2 percent) identify themselves as Bible—believing, yet only a fifth believes that God favours the U.S.A. in worldly affairs (18.6 percent), while 12.8 percent are undecided and the rest disagrees. These figures are taken from the Baylor University's study on religion in the U.S.A. conducted in 2005. Compare here also footnote 15.

15. See, e.g., Catholic Glenmary Research Center, *The Religious Congregations and Membership in the United States, 2000*. Nashville: Catholic Glenmary Research Center Publications, 2000; Boorstein, Michelle. "Americans May Be More Religious Than They Realize." *The Washington Post*, 12 September 2006. A12.

16. Cf. McWilliams, Carey, and Matt S. Meier. *North of Mexico: The Spanish-Speaking People of the United States*. Westport: Praeger Publishers, 1990; and Alford, Harold J. *The Proud Peoples: The Heritage and Culture of Spanish-Speaking Peoples in the United States*. New York: David McKay Co., 1973.

17. De Leon, Arnoldo, and Griswold Del Castillo. *North to Aztlán: A History of Mexican-Americans in the United States*. Wheeling: Harlan Davidson, 2006.

18. As Gerhard Wagner has illustrated in full detail in his contribution to this anthology, the differentiation between 'the pedagogical' and 'the performative' is of great significance in the Third Space debate originating from Bhabha. Generally speaking, the 'pedagogical' signifies the disciplining of a subjugated people by the dominating people. The latter's intellectuals turn the people under restraint into an object of their education. The pivot of this education is to instill the dominating system's traditional discourse of the Western nation on the disciplined people. The 'performative', on the other hand, which goes back to Jacques Derrida's critique of John L. Austin's Speech Act Theory and designates the dissemination of the meaning of a meaningful sentence uttered whereby at last the meaning of the majority's tradition that lays beneath the dominant national identity, is disseminated, works for Bhabha to rehabilitate the subjugated people as the true national subject that constructs its own identity. It's due to this 'performative' and 'enunciatory present' (Bhabha. *The Location of Culture*. 178) that the narrative construction of the nation has been democratized in recent years.

19. Compare Ashcroft, Bill, Gareth Griffiths, and Helen Tiffin. *The Empire Writes Back: Theory and Practice in Post-colonial Literatures*. London, New York: Routledge, 1989.

20. Countless weblogs, internet forums, newswires, and websites provide ample proof of this. For a substantial and continuously updated overview of U.S. Latino related internet forums and weblogs cf. Juan Guillermo Tornoe. "Hispanic Trending". Online. http://juantornoe.blogs.com/hispanictrending/2004/09/spain_is_once_a.html.

21. For a brief overview of the current debate on the border cf. for example Singh, Amritjit, and Peter Schmidt "On the Borders Between U.S. Studies and Postcolonial Theory." *Postcolonial Theory and the United States*. Ed. Amritjit Singh and Peter Schmidt. Jackson: UP of Mississippi, 2000. 3–68.

22. See, e.g. *Chicana Literary and Artistic Expressions: Culture and Society in Dialogue*. Ed. Herrera-Sóbek, Maria. Santa Barbara: Center for Chicano Studies Publication Series, 2000; Gutiérrez, David G. "Migration, Emergent Ethnicity, and the 'Third Space': The Shifting Politics of Nationalism in Greater Mexico." *The Journal of American History* 86.2 (1999). Online: http://www.indiana.edu/~jah/mexico/dgutierrez.html. No page numbers. Also Saldívar, José David. *Border Matters: Remapping American Cultural Studies*. Berkeley: U California P, 1997.

23. Compare Saldívar, Ramón. *Chicano Narrative: The Dialectics of Difference*, Madison: U Wisconsin P, 1990.

24. See Oliver-Rotger. *Battlegrounds and Crossroads*. Also, Kaup, Monika. *Rewriting North American Borders in Chicano and Chicana Narrative*. New York, Frankfurt am Main: Peter Lang, 2001; and *U.S. Latino Literatures and Cultures: Transnational Perspectives*. Ed. Karin Ikas and Francisco A. Lomelí. Heidelberg: Winter, 2000.

25. Pratt, Mary Louise. *Imperial Eyes: Travel Writing and Transculturation*. London: Routledge, 1992. 4.

26. Saldívar, José David. *Border Matters: Remapping American Cultural Studies.* Berkeley: U California P, 1997. 13.
27. Ibid. 13–14.
28. Bhabha. *The Location of Culture.* 7.
29. See *The Invention of Tradition.* Ed. Eric J. Hobsbawn and Terence Ranger. Cambridge: Cambridge UP, 1984
30. Soja, Edward W. *Thirdspace: Journeys to Los Angeles and other Real-and-Imagined Places.* Oxford, Cambridge, MA: Blackwell, 1996. 14.
31. Ibid. 14.
32. For further insights consult Edward Soja's entry entitled "Thirdspace: Towards a New Consciousness of Space and Spatiality" in this volume (see 49–61).
33. Bhabha. *The Location of Culture.* 124
34. Appadurai, Arjun. "Global Ethnoscapes: Notes and Queries for a Transnational Anthropology." *Recapturing Anthropology: Working in the Present.* Ed. Richard G. Fox. Santa Fe: School of American Research Press, 1991. 191–210. 205.
35. Bhabha. *The Location of Culture.* 126.
36. Ibid. 193.
37. Ibid. 36.
38. Compare Rutherford, Jonathan. "The Third Space: Interview with Homi Bhabha." *Identity, Community, Culture, Difference.* Ed. Rutherford. London: Lawrence and Wishart, 1990. 207–221. 211.
39. Bhabha. *The Location of Culture.* 37.
40. For a brief though fruitful overview of the various interpretations, characteristics and applications of the term hybridity in the post-colonial context cf. chapter 27 "Hybridity" in *The Post-colonial Studies Reader.* Ed. Bill Ashcroft, Gareth Griffiths, and Helen Tiffin. London, New York: Routledge, 2006. 137–162. Also, Smith, Andrew. "Migrancy, Hybridity, and Postcolonial Literary Studies." *The Cambridge Companion to Postcolonial Literary Studies.* Ed. Neil Lazarus. Cambridge: Cambridge UP, 2004. 241–261; and Ha, Kien Nghi. "Die schöne neue Welt der Hybridität: Epistemologischer Wertewandel und kulturindustrielle Vermischungslogik im Spätkapitalismus." *Kultur in Zeiten der Globalisierung: Neue Aspekte einer soziologischen Kategorie.* Ed. Peter-Ulrich Merz-Benz and Gerhard Wagner. Frankfurt am Main: Humanities Online, 2005. 93–161.
41. Compare, e.g. Parry, Benita. "Problems in Current Theories of Colonial Discourse." *The Post-colonial Studies Reader.* Ed. Bill Ashcroft, Gareth Griffiths, and Helen Tiffin. London, New York: Routledge, 2006. 44–50; Wagner. "Nation, DissemiNation und Dritter Raum; and Mitchell, Katharyne. "Different Diasporas and the Hype of Hybridity." *Environment and Planning D: Society and Space 1997* 15 (1997): 533–553.
42. Papastergiadis, Nikos. "Tracing Hybridity in Theory." *Debating Cultural Hybridity: Multi-Cultural Identities and the Politics of Anti-Racism.* Ed. Pnina Werbner and Tariq Modood. London: Zed Books, 1997. 257–281.
43. Mayorga, Irma. "Homecoming: The Politics of Myth and Location in Cherríe L. Moraga's *The Hungry Woman: A Mexican Medea* and *Heart of the Earth: A Popul Vuh Story.*" Afterward to Cherríe L. Moraga. *The Hungry Woman.* Albuquerque, NM: West End Press, 2001. 155–165. 156.
44. Moraga. *The Hungry Woman.* VII–X.
45. Cf. Cherríe Moraga in an interview with Karin Ikas. Published in Karin Rosa Ikas. *Chicana Ways: Conversations with Ten Chicana Writers.* Reno, NV: U Nevada P, 2002. 153–172.
46. Ibid. 162–163.

47. Cf. also Brecht, Bertolt. „Die Strassenszene: Grundmodell einer Szene des epischen Theaters" (1938). Translated and published as "The Street Scene: A Basic Model for an Epic Theatre." *Brecht on Theatre: The Development of an Aesthetic.* Ed. John Willett. New York: Hill and Wang, 1964. 121–129.

48. Cf. Brecht. *Bertolt Brecht on Theatre.* 121.

49. The term Atzlán originates from the Nahua tribe in Mexico and designates a sense of mythic place and territory. In Chicano/a literature, art and folklore, Aztlán is often appropriated as the name for that portion of Mexico that was taken over by the United States in 1848 after the Mexican-American War (1846–1848), on the belief that this greater area represents the point of parting of the Aztec migrations. In the era of the Chicano Civil Rights Movement (1960s–1970s), this concept of Aztlán as an indigenous homeland inside the U.S.A. that had been taken over by the U.S.A. by war of conquest and is today California, Arizona, Nevada, New Mexico, Colorado, and Texas, was significant to strengthen a Chicano ethnic consciousness (cf. Cooper-Alarcón, Daniel. "Towards a New Understanding of Aztlán and Chicano Cultural Identity." *The Aztec Palimpsest: Mexico in the Modern Imagination.* Ed. Daniel Cooper-Alarcón. Tucson: U Arizona P, 1997. 3–35; also *Aztlán: Essays on the Chicano Homeland.* Ed. Rudolfo Anaya and Francisco A. Lomelí. Albuquerque: U New Mexico P, 1991). Like the Nahuas before them, today's Chicanos/as view this territory not only as their spatial home but more importantly also as the spiritual homeland of their ancestors. Moreover, as Mary Pat Brady notes: 'By renominating the Southwest as Aztlán, Chicanos/as not only denaturalized the U.S.-Mexico border, which had been naturalized through continually vibrant ideology of Manifest Destiny, but also signalled an ongoing relay between subjectivity and place' (see *Extinct Lands, Temporal Geographies: Chicana Literature and the Urgency of Space.* Durham, London: Duke UP, 2002. 146). The challenge Aztlán posed to America's Manifest Destiny during the Civil Rights Movement is obvious, and here lies a root for the worries of some of today's neo-conservative Anglo-Americans politicians and critics, namely the fear of a secession of the increasingly hispanicized Southwest to form a separate state. Together with fellow lesbian Chicana critics and writers such as Gloria Anzaldúa and Emma Pérez, Moraga reveals, however, that Aztlán as it has been envisioned by traditional heterosexual males is no paradise at all as long as the concept does not give credit to the need of homosexuals, Women of Color and all other people who, like herself, feel outsiders of the traditional patriarchal Mexican, Chicano and Anglo-European influenced borderland world.

50. Compare Cherríe Moraga. "Hungry for God." *The Hungry Woman.* IX–X.

51. Brancato, Sabrina. "'Glocality' and Cultural Identity." *This Century's Review* (04.2006). Online publication: Cf. http://www.thiscenturysreview .com/gloacality.html. No page numbers.

52. Moraga. *The Hungry Woman.* 6.

53. Ibid. 72.

54. Ibid. 24.

55. Ibid. 44–45.

56. See *The Hungry Woman: Myths and Legends of the Aztecs.* Ed. John Bierhorst. New York: Quill and William Morrow, 1993.

57. Moraga. *The Hungry Woman.* 12–13.

58. Ibid. 72.

59. Bhabha, Homi K. "Life at the Border: Hybrid Identities of the Present." *New Perspectives Quarterly* 14 (Winter 1997): 30–31. 30.

60. Moraga. *The Hungry Woman.* 91.

61. Ibid. 98–99.

62. See Mark 14:61b–62; Luke 22:66–70.

63. See Lawrence, G. Desmond. "Chacmool." *Oxford Encyclopedia of Meso-american Cultures.* Vol 1. Ed. David Carrasco. New York: Oxford UP, 2001. 168–169; Miller, Mary Ellen. "A Re-examination of the Mesoamerican Chacmool." *The Art Bulletin* 67.1 (1985): 7–17; Graulich, Michael. "Quelques observations sur les sculptures Mesoamericaines dites 'Chac Mool.'" *Annales Jaarboek* (1984): 51–72.
64. Bhabha, *The Location of Culture.* 28.
65. Ibid. 164.
66. Kozlovic, Anton Karl. "Christian Communication in the Popular Cinema." *Nebula* 4.1 (March 2007): 143–165; Schippert, Claudia. "Sporting Heroic Bodies in a Christian Nation-at-War." *Journal of Religious and Popular Culture* 5 (Fall 2003). Online web-based journal. Cf. http://www.usask.ca/relst/jrpc/art4-heroicbodies-print.html. No page numbers. Ford, Michael. *Father Mychal Judge: An Authentic American Hero.* Mahwah, NJ: Paulist Press, 2002. Flores-Turney, Camille. *Howl: The Artwork of Luis Jiménez.* Santa Fe: New Mexico Press, 1997; Klein, George. *Pietà: Mitleid, Compassion, Agape, Caritas.* Cambridge, MA: MIT Press, 1992.
67. Cf. Jiménez, Luis. *Man on Fire: Luis Jimenez/El Hombre en llamas.* Albuquerque: The Albuquerque Museum, 1994.

Part V
Locations and Negotiations

9 Transcultural Negotiations
Third Spaces in Modern Times

Frank Schulze-Engler

In the wake of Homi K. Bhabha's *The Location of Culture*, the figure of third space has become one of the main pillars of contemporary postcolonial theory: it has been taken up in a vast array of scholarship in literary and cultural studies as well as in the social sciences, but it has also become the focus point of heated debates on the alleged privileging of the migrant condition in Bhabha's work or on the displacement of other forms of critical theory (such as Marxism) in his writings.[1]

This chapter is neither concerned with a detailed exegesis of Bhabha's notions of third space nor with an elaborate account of the manifold theoretical responses they have given rise to. Instead, it seeks to highlight a peculiar presupposition that underlies both Bhabha's own account of third space and much of the postcolonial critical debate that has lionized or vilified his ideas: the suggestion that the concept of the third space is most productive in the context of the Western nation state and that its most important function is to disrupt the cultural and political homogeneity on which both the Western nation and the prevalent understanding of modernity are based. This limited rather than liminal view of nation, culture and modernity has severely restricted the uses to which the idea of third space can be put in literary studies, and the burden of this chapter thus lies on exploring new, transcultural dimensions of third space beyond the discursive perimeters of postcolonial theory that can help us to come to terms with the forms and functions of literature in a globalized world.

LIMITED SPACE: POSTCOLONIALISM, MODERNITY AND THE WESTERN NATION STATE

How, then, is third space constructed in Bhabha's *The Location of Culture*, and why does his exploration of this space inevitably land itself in the solitary confinement of the Western nation state? This question is best addressed by a brief reconstruction of the argument put forward in "The Commitment to Theory," where the most extensive discussion of third space in *The Location of Culture* is to be found. In this essay, third space is introduced via the problem of enunciation, which is set out in classical post-structuralist terms as a general problem of the ambivalence of language:

> The reason a cultural text or system cannot be sufficient unto itself is that the act of cultural enunciation—the *place of utterance*—is crossed by the *différance* of writing. [. . .] It is this difference in the process of language that is crucial to the production of meaning and ensures, at the same time, that meaning is never simply mimetic and transparent.[2]

From this general poststructuralist account of the inherent instability of meaning in language, the argument then moves on to a more specific consideration of the role of enunciation in the context of cultural performance. It is in this context that the third space enters the argument as a necessary requirement for the production of meaning, a requirement that at the same time ensures that meaning is always ambivalent:

> The linguistic difference that informs any cultural performance is dramatized in the common semiotic account of the disjuncture between the subject of a proposition (*énoncé*) and the subject of enunciation, which is not represented in the statement but which is the acknowledgment of its discursive embeddedness and address, its cultural positionality, its reference to a present time and a specific space. [. . .] The production of meaning requires that these two places be mobilized in the passage through a Third Space, which represents both the general conditions of language and the specific implication of the utterance in a performative and institutional strategy of which it cannot 'in itself' be conscious. What this unconscious relation introduces is an ambivalence in the act of interpretation.[3]

Third space is thus introduced in terms of a peculiar relationship between 'the general conditions of language' and 'the specific implication of the utterance in a performative and institutional strategy of which it cannot "in itself" be conscious.' While this definition clearly signals towards a universal theory of 'cultural performance,' the argument subsequently takes an astonishing turn by endowing the general idea of third space with the specific telos of the disruption of the Western nation:

> The intervention of the Third Space of enunciation, which makes the structure of meaning and reference an ambivalent process, destroys this mirror of representation in which cultural knowledge is customarily revealed as an integrated, open, expanding code. Such an intervention quite properly challenges our sense of the historical identity of culture as a homogenizing, unifying force, authenticated by the originary Past, kept alive in the national tradition of the People. In other words,

the disruptive temporality of enunciation displaces the narrative of the Western nation which Benedict Anderson so perceptively describes as being written in homogeneous, serial time.[4]

How do we account for this sudden narrowing of focus in Bhabha's account of third space and what are its consequences for theorizing the postcolonial? Since the text itself simply enunciates this contraction without providing further arguments, possible answers have to be sought in their own 'discursive embeddedness and address,' their own 'cultural positionality.' An obvious major determinant of this positionality is the postmodern critique of Western modernity on which Bhabha rests his own case for the postcolonial disruption of that modernity. In his essay on "The Postcolonial and the Postmodern" Bhabha situates his own usage of post-structuralist theory in the context of a 'postcolonial prerogative' based on experiences of a 'postcolonial contramodernity':

[M]y use of poststructuralist theory emerges from this postcolonial contramodernity. I attempt to represent a certain defeat, or even an impossibility, of the 'West' in its authorization of the 'idea' of colonization. Driven by the subaltern history of the margins of modernity—rather than by the failures of logocentrism—I have tried, in some small measure, to revise the known, to rename the postmodern from the position of the postcolonial[5].

While one trajectory of this postcolonial critique of Western modernity has led Bhabha towards the history of colonialism and an analysis of the 'ambivalence of colonial discourse',[6] of the 'sly civility'[7] of the colonized and of the subversive features of colonial 'mimicry' as 'an immanent threat to both "normalized" knowledges and disciplinary powers',[8] another important facet of this critique has focused on the contemporary world and the unsettling presence of the postcolonial within the West. In his introduction to *The Location of Culture*, Bhabha notes the potential Eurocentricity of the postmodern critique of Western modernity, which could turn postmodernism into 'a profoundly parochial exercise' if it remained 'limited to a celebration of the fragmentation of the "grand narratives" of postenlightenment rationalism',[9] and sets out his perspective on the relationship between the postmodern and the postcolonial in the following terms:

The wider significance of the postmodern condition lies in the awareness that the epistemological 'limits' of those ethnocentric ideas are also the enunciative boundaries of a range of other dissonant, even dissident histories and voices—women, the colonized, minority groups, the bearers of policed sexualities. For the demography of the new internationalism is the history of postcolonial migration, the narratives of cultural and political diaspora, the major social displacements of peasant and aboriginal communities, the poetics of exile, the grim prose of political and economic refugees.[10]

This identification of the contemporary postcolonial with migration, exile and diaspora sets up a peculiar relationship between the postcolonial and the Western nation state: what seems most significant about marginal people is indeed their capacity to unsettle the unisonance of the Western nation state. In "DissemiNation," Bhabha highlights

> a relatively unspoken tradition of the people of the pagus—colonials, postcolonials, migrants, minorities—wandering peoples who will not be contained within the *Heim* of the national culture and its unisonant discourse, but are themselves the marks of a shifting boundary that alienates the frontiers of the modern nation.[11]

It is this interest in the capacity of 'the people of the pagus' to challenge Western modernity by subverting the cultural homogeneity of the Western nation—an interest autobiographically fuelled by having experienced life 'in the nations of others'[12]—that lies at the heart of Bhabha's identification of third space with an interstitial challenge to the cultural fixity of the Western nation state:

> It is significant that the productive capacities of this Third Space have a colonial or postcolonial provenance. [. . .] the theoretical recognition of the split-space of enunciation may open the way to conceptualizing an *inter*national culture, based not on the exoticism of multicultural-ism, or the *diversity* of cultures, but on the inscription and articulation of culture's *hybridity*. To that end we should remember that it is the 'inter'—the cutting edge of translation and negotiation, the *in-between* space—that carries the burden of the meaning of culture. It makes it possible to begin envisaging national, anti-nationalist histories of the 'people'. And by exploring this Third Space, we may elude the politics of polarity and emerge as the others of our selves.[13]

What, then, are the consequences of this confinement of a universal-istically conceived category in the interstices of the Western nation state for postcolonial theory? First and foremost, it firmly welds the postcolo-nial to a postmodern/poststructuralist critique of Western modernity; sec-ondly it suggests that the most important dimensions of the contemporary postcolonial are to be found in the exilic/diasporic/migrant dynamics that have brought the postcolonial physically and conceptually into the heart of the West; and thirdly it intimates that the subversion of the unisonance of Western modernity and its primary habitat, the Western nation state, is the primary purpose of postcolonial culture and literature. All three assump-tions have had a major influence on the development of postcolonial theory;

in the field of postcolonial literary studies, they have inspired an extensive interest in the counter-discursive functions of postcolonial literature, which the authors of *The Empire Writes Back* have classically defined as 'the project of post-colonial writing to interrogate European discourse and discursive strategies from its position within and between two worlds':

> Thus the rereading and rewriting of the European historical and fictional record is a vital and inescapable task at the heart of the post-colonial enterprise. These subversive manouevres, rather than the construction of essentially national or regional alternatives, are the characteristic features of the post-colonial text. Post-colonial literatures/cultures are constituted in counter-discursive rather than homologous practices.[14]

From the point of view of a transcultural comparative study of the new literatures in English (from which this chapter takes its cue), all three assumptions are highly problematic, however.

First and foremost, the notion that the postcolonial (not as a set of theories, but as a set of countries, societies, cultures, literatures or people) should primarily be defined by its proximity to a poststructuralist critique of Western modernity has little inherent plausibility: the idea that centuries of colonial oppression and anticolonial resistance as well as many decades of post-independence history in some two thirds of the world derive their ultimate meaning from the fact that they allegedly were poststructuralist *avant la lettre* may seem probable enough in postcolonial literary studies, but is unlikely to raise much enthusiasm elsewhere.[15]

Secondly, the transnational and transcultural dimensions of the new literatures in English are evidently of vital importance. These dimensions are not necessarily tied to experiences of migration, exile or diaspora, however, but are frequently related to cultural and social change on the ground; as Ulf Hannerz has suggested, 'meanings find ways of travelling even when people stay put'.[16] The suggestion that the literature with the highest productive capacities is a postcolonial literature exploring third spaces within the context of Western nation states is an unnecessarily restrictive one.

Thirdly, the idea that postcolonial literatures are primarily dedicated to the subversion of the unisonance of Western modernity is hard to reconcile with the realities of literary history. What is arguably at issue in contemporary writing in English from non-Western locations is not a sustained counter-discursive strategy of dismantling the hegemonic reach of Western master discourses, but an exploration of internal and external conflicts, risks and chances in complex societies and cultures that form part of a globalized world of modernity. Instead of pressing these literatures into a preordained counter-discursive function, it thus seems more productive to explore the relationship of these literatures to a network of transnationally and transculturally linked modernities.

How, then, can the concept of third space be explored in the context of the new literatures in English—beyond the poststructuralist confinement into which it has been placed by Bhabha and much of postcolonial theory? A major contribution for extending its usability would seem to consist in edging the concept away from poststructuralist grand narrations of Western modernity. In recent decades, a wide variety of new theories have contributed to a reconceptualization of modernity in the context of a global risk society or transnational connections;[17] Eurocentric perspectives on modernity have been supplanted by models of a decentered and globalized modernity;[18] and the idea of a singular modernity has been challenged by a spate of theories of multiple or alternative modernities.[19]

> One of the most important implications of the term 'multiple modernities' is that modernity and Westernization are not identical; Western patterns of modernity are not the only 'authentic' modernities, though they enjoy historical precedence and continue to be a basic reference point for others.[20]

> The undeniable trend at the end of the 20th century is the growing diversification of the understanding of modernity, of the basic cultural agendas of different modern societies—far beyond the homogenic and hegemonic visions of modernity prevalent in the 1950s. [. . .] All these developments do indeed attest to the continual development of multiple modernities, or of multiple interpretations of modernity—and, above all, to attempts at 'de-Westernization', depriving the West of its monopoly on modernity.[21]

In a similar vein, Peter Taylor has postulated that the era of conceiving of modernity in terms of a 'Whig-diffusionism' that sees modernity as an inherently European phenomenon that has beneficially spread over the rest of the globe has come to an end:

> The alternative to a Whig-diffusionist story-and-map, whether of the virtuous modern morality or deterministic modern technology variety, is to emphasize discontinuities in *both* time and space. Modernity does not just appear as a result of any 'natural' evolution; there are many discontinuities, with both the rise and the development of the modern world creating quite different forms of what it is to be modern. Similarly, the modern does not simply exist as a continuous geographical gradient from high to low; there are discontinuities between core and periphery zones of the system creating quite different forms of what it is to be modern. In short there are different modern times and different modern spaces in a world of multiple modernities.[22]

There are thus numerous theoretical resources that open up new directions in exploring the relationship between contemporary literatures and globalized modernity beyond an exclusive focus on the unsettling of a unitary Western modernity embodied in the Western nation state. The wider picture includes a broad variety of internal conflicts and negotiations taking place within the context of multiple modernities as well as an equally broad variety of transnational connections that link modern lifeworlds across cultures. In this context, the notion of third space needs to be pluralized and expanded to cover the manifold transcultural negotiations contemporary literatures are engaged in.

THIRD SPACES IN MODERN TIMES

In the main part of this chapter, I would now like to take a closer look at four sociopolitical arenas located beyond the normative framework of the Western nation state, and at literary texts engaging in an exploration of third spaces related to these arenas. These arenas are the transnational collective memory of modern slavery and its legacy in Europe, Africa and the New World; the civil war in Sri Lanka; indigenous Maori culture in Aotearoa/New Zealand; and colonial modernity in Africa. In all of these arenas, it is not the normative framework of the modern Western nation state that is centrally at issue (although modern nation states are undeniably part of the picture), and consequently the third spaces explored in the literary texts are not structurally ones that subvert homogenous notions of the nation, but spaces enabling new, critical perceptions amidst long-standing interactions and conflicts that often seem to freeze social reality into a static pattern of binary oppositions. In these contexts, the literary texts themselves performatively constitute third spaces: rather than simply reflecting practices already to be found in the social world, they become testing grounds of the social imagination and fictional locations where new perceptions can be negotiated.

TOWARDS A TRANSATLANTIC COLLECTIVE MEMORY: CARYL PHILLIPS'S *CAMBRIDGE* AND *CROSSING THE RIVER*

The novels and essayistic writings of the British-Caribbean writer Caryl Phillips can be read as a protracted intervention intended to nurture transnational collective memory and to counter transnational historical amnesia. At the same time, they are engaged in coming to terms with the genesis of modern world society and with the social, political and cultural legacies of one of the first examples of a truly globalized system of production: modern transatlantic slavery. In exploring the manifold links that bind the history of modernity and the history of transatlantic slavery together, Phillips eschews a rhetoric of blame aimed at evoking Western liberal guilt; instead he seeks to stimulate insights into the legacy of a common history shared by Africa, Europe and the New World alike, and to overcome an historical amnesia with regard to this legacy that blocks insights not only into the making of the Black Diaspora in the New World, but also into central aspects of African, European, and American/Caribbean history. The basic structure of many of Phillips's novels is thus not predicated on a 'dominant' 'Western' history that has to be confronted with its slave 'other', but on a sustained negotiation of the meaning of history in a transnational context.

In Phillips's novel *Cambridge* (1991),[23] this negotiation is effected by contrasting three historicized narratives (the travel journal of Emily Cartwright modeled on 19th century women travelogues, the life story of Olumide/David Henderson/Cambridge modeled on slave narratives such as Olaudah Equiano's *Interesting Narrative*, and a report in the manner of a 19th century colonial journal) that are framed by a prologue and epilogue. As many commentators have noted, the multiple narration is the central message of the novel;[24] the three narratives are placed side by side, with no metanarration to reconcile them or to impose diegetic order. The third space of transnational historical memory in Phillips's novel is thus a literary one that ultimately has to be (re)constructed by the reader.

While at first sight, the two major texts, Emily's Journal and Cambridge's life story written shortly before his death, may seem like a classical example of colonial discourse on the one hand that is dismantled by the testimony of one of the oppressed on the other, both texts are, in fact, much more complex. Emily, who has come to the Caribbean to visit her father's plantation, represents the white ruling class in the colonial system, but as a woman in colonial society is also regarded as inferior to men; Cambridge, who already was a free man, but was criminally reenslaved and brought to the Caribbean, naturally has the contemporary readers' sympathies on his side even when he finally kills the white overseer who tormented him for so long, but also manages to alienate these sympathies by his intransigent Christianity that results in his over-assimilation while in England and leads him to regard the behavior of his wife on the Caribbean plantation as 'paganism'.[25] The historical verities of colonial discourse are obviously undermined in the text (for example in the travesty of truth presented in the journal article that reduces Cambridge's story to the tale of a treacherous slave whose 'soul was dark within'[26]), but at the same time the question of historical truth is raised; the third space explored in this novel is thus intimately related both to overcoming historical amnesia with regard to the legacies of transatlantic slavery and to sensitizing the reader to the fact that historical truth can only be reconstructed in a polyphonic manner.

Polyphonic narration is also the hallmark of *Crossing the River* (1993).[27] The novel begins and ends with the reflections of a transhistorical African father figure who sold his own children into slavery; the main part metaphorically follows the journey of the three children and consists of the story of Nash Williams, a freed American slave who is sent to Sierra Leone by his philanthropic master to spread Christianity and eventually disappears; that of Martha Randolph, another former slave who goes west as a Black pioneer and dies in a small midwestern town on her way to California; the journal of James Hamilton, a cruel slave trader and tender husband who bought the three children from their African father; and Joyce, a young English woman who falls in love with Travis, a black American GI, during World War II. The third space in this novel (which once again is fabricated by the reader who has to assemble the different parts of the text into a coherent whole) is the space of a yet to be written transnational world history that would encompass the perspective of Africans who sold others into slavery, the crimes of the slave traders and the Middle Passage, the struggle for survival of the African slaves in the new world, and the transatlantic struggle to come to terms with post-slavery modernity. The ultimate aim of such a history would not only be to deflate Western master discourses, but also to explore the contribution of modern slavery to the emergence of a globalized world. In the final reflections of the African father who reaches across diasporic centuries to embrace Joyce as his daughter, a glimpse of such a transnational world history becomes visible:

> I hear a drum beating on the far side of the river. [...] I wait. And then listen as the many-tongued chorus of the common memory begins again to swell, and insist that I acknowledge greetings from those who lever pints of ale in the pubs of London. Receive salutations from those who submit to (what the French call) neurotic inter-racial urges in the boule-vards of Paris. [...] For two hundred and fifty years I have listened. To the haunting voices. Singing: Mercy, Mercy, Me. (The Ecology.) Insisting: Man, I ain't got no quarrel with them Vietcong. Declaring: Brothers and Friends. I am Toussaint L'Ouverture, my name is perhaps known to you. [...] I have listened to the sounds of an African carnival in Trinidad. In Rio. In New Orleans. On the far bank of the river, a drum continues to be beaten. A many-tongued chorus continues to swell. And I hope that amongst these survivors' voices I might occasionally hear those of my own children. My Nash. My Martha. My Travis. My daughter. Joyce. All. Hurt but determined. [...] There are no paths in water. No sign-posts. There is no return. A desperate foolishness. The crops failed. I sold my beloved children. *Bought 2 strong man-boys, and a proud girl.* But they arrived on the far bank of the river, loved.[28]

BEYOND LONG-DISTANCE NATIONALISM: CHANNA WICKREMESEKERA'S *DISTANT WARRIORS*

If Phillips's version of third space is intimately tied to a textual perfor-mance of transnational cultural memory, the third space explored in Channa Wickremesekera's novel *Distant Warriors* (2005) opens up amidst an overabundance of historical memory, albeit of an extremely restricted and obsessive kind.[29] Set among the Sinhalese and Tamil communities in present-day Melbourne, *Distant Warriors* recounts a particularly corrosive form of long-distance nationalism that relocates the internecine strife of the Sri Lankan civil war in the Sri Lankan diaspora in Australia.[30] While the novel focuses on ethnic suprematism and hatred among the Sinhalese and Tamil communities, it also registers the interactions of both communities with Australian society at large; what emerges is a complex picture of a contested transculturality that only comes into its own in the impossible subjectivity staged in the text, but that nevertheless embodies a social imagination that could potentially become a valuable resource in an eventual reconciliation process.

According to Benedict Anderson, long-distance nationalism constitutes a form of 'nationalism that no longer depends as it once did on territorial location in a home country';[31] in a globalized world characterized by mass travel and ubiquitous media networks, nation states have to reckon with the transnational

> political participation of often unrealistic co-nationals living outside their political borders; this participation can reach toxic levels or assume corrosive forms in the modalities of money for certain political figures, nationalist propaganda, and weapons, although it can be restricted to the more benign activities of lobbying and fund-raising for humanitarian undertakings.[32]

Wickremesekera's novel chronicles a spiral of first semantic and then physical violence that ultimately reaches a toxic level when Sinhalese nationalists invade a Tamil fundraising event in a Melbourne suburb. Both sides draw on long-standing ethnic hatred fuelled by events in their 'home country' across the Pacific; the Sinhalese feel provoked by the terrorism of the Tamil Tigers, while the Tamils deplore the violence unleashed in Tamil areas by the Sri Lankan army. The discourse of ethnic strife leaves no room for more nuanced views: while the self-righteous Sinhalese lawyer Seneviratne absolutely refuses to acknowledge that the Tamil population in Sri Lanka may have reasons for their political protest, dismisses all Tamils as criminal terrorists and sees the Tamil Tigers in Sri Lanka and the Melbourne Tamil diaspora as one 'despicable enemy', the Tamil doctor Bhanu Nagalingam regards all Sinhalese as 'thugs' and accuses his son Rajan of being 'a lover of the Sinhalese' when the latter dares to mention the fact that the Tamil Tigers also committed atrocities in the Sri Lankan civil war.[33] While not all Sri Lankan characters share in this vilification of the ethnic Other, there hardly seems room for them to speak, and thus it is only outsiders (such as the Russian girlfriend of one of the protagonists) that probe into the solid collective identity built on ethnic homogenization.

Distant Warriors employs three major strategies to open up a third space that undermines the self-righteousness of both camps and allows a different perspective to emerge. The first one consists in an ironic portrayal of a cultural memory that obsessively returns to centuries of history reinvented in ever more trivial invocations of past grandeur. Pinpointing one of the key facilitators of long-distance nationalism, electronic communication, the novel derides Seneviratne's frustrated search for an email address that would adequately express his Sinhalese patriotism:

> Seneviratne was well aware that Australia in general and Melbourne in particular, were full of Sri Lankans with such e-mail addresses, proclaiming their Sri Lankan-ness. Many had e-mail addresses with the names of ancient kings and heroes, so much so that Seneviratne himself had been hard-pressed to find a suitable name for his own e-mail address. He had picked Perakhumba, the name of an ancient Sinhala king, but Hotmail said that the name was already taken (. . .). All the heroes and kings were taken. Even Kandula, the war-elephant, was claimed. Finally, Seneviratne had to settle for the relatively lightweight and somewhat awkward Lion-king, a direct translation of Rajasinha.[34]

While the 'cultural memory' evoked in cyberspace where 'too many people [were] masquerading as dead kings and heroes'[35] thus becomes closely associated with a grim disneyfication of history, the novel uses a second strategy of querying long-distance nationalism by highlighting the refusal of both Sinhalese and Tamils to come to terms with the new realities of their transnational existence. Both cling to the idea of patriotism and a national homeland (although in the Tamil case this is no longer Sri Lanka but Tamil Eelam, the independent country they hope to establish in the Tamil areas) and resolutely refuse to acknowledge the fact that after several decades their lifeworld in Australia has become more than just a form of temporary exile. Thus the Nagalingam family assiduously nurtures the idea of a return to Tamil Eelam, which ironically enough is constantly evoked by the younger son Naveen who was born in Australia, and it is only the elder son Rajan who realizes that this myth of homecoming preempts an acknowledgement of the new realities created by the parents' successful professional careers in Melbourne and the children's socialization into Australian society. In a conversation with Father Anton, a Tamil priest and activist whose visit to Melbourne as guest-of-honor at a Tamil fundraising event sparks off the plot that culminates in a deadly confrontation between the two groups of distant warriors, Rajan recognizes the desire of the Tamil population in Sri Lanka for self-determination and peace, but at the same time insists on the reality of his own existence:

> It's a good thing to want to be free. To be able to do what you want without anybody telling you what to do or think. To have self-determination.

[. . .] But is self-determination only for your people in Sri Lanka? Do I
have no freedom to choose my destiny? Even when I could do so, by living
here, in Melbourne![36]

The third strategy of deflating the obsessive binary conflict in the novel
hinges on the narration that juxtaposes the intransigent warriors' perspectives and thus relativizes them, and on the plot that emphasizes the
conscious staging of long-distant nationalism in Australia. Both the Tamil
fund-raising and the Sinhalese assault on it have decidedly theatrical qualities, but the slightly farcical scenario turns into a fatal grotesque when a
young man in the Sinhalese raiding party draws a gun (that tellingly turns
out to have been a toy gun later on) and is killed by the police. In a scene
verging on a mise en abyme, Rajan—who witnessed both the raid and the
young man's death—reflects on the theatrical qualities of the events in *Distant Warriors* in the following manner:

> How bizarre it all was. The passionate speeches, the Sinhalese assault,
> the resulting pandemonium and now, this tragic ending. Throughout the
> event, he had felt like an alien, witnessing customs and rites that were
> strange, yet fascinating. Then the boy's antics on the stage added a dan-
> gerous and insane twist to the whole plot. Strangely, the arrival of the
> police seemed like an infusion of reality, a comforting sense of order to
> chaos. The gun-shot put a terrible end to the agony and the farce.[37]

This histrionic undercurrent in the plot of the novel is directly related
to the inability or refusal of most participants to come to terms with their
transnational lifeworld on the one hand and the realities of Australian society on the other, which in turn reinforces stereotypes of violent and out-
landish strangers among the majority population:

> As they approached the gate, Rajan saw the Australians on the street
> staring at them. There was no sympathy or recognition in their faces
> but only cold disdain. 'Why don't you go back to wherever you came
> from and kill each other?' a female voice asked, the hostility and con-
> tempt cutting through the air like a thick, heavy blade. He turned in
> the direction of the voice but saw only a group of blank faces, white in
> the dark summer night.[38]

The complicated relationship to the Australian host society that emerges
in the final passages of the novel serves as a reminder that Tamil-Sinhalese
relations in Melbourne are part of a larger, more complex picture in which
the roles assigned to Asians in Australian society also influence the course
of events. Yet the third space explored in Wickremesekera's novel cannot be
reduced to a postcolonial challenge that Tamils and Sinhalese pose to the
putative unisonance of the Australian nation state; instead, it is clearly related

to the necessity to overcome the ethnic binarism that underlies the workings of long-distance nationalism. Since the text does not present characters to the reader that could serve as carriers of a vision of reconciliation, the third space cleared in the novel remains a strictly literary one, but undoubtedly the social imagination at work in the novel provides a new mode of perceiving not only the lifeworlds of expatriate Sinhalese and Tamils, but also the central conflict in Sri Lanka itself: a move beyond an ossified cultural memory and towards a possible process of negotiated reconciliation.

TRANSNATIONAL GAY INDIGENALITY: WITI IHIMAERA'S *THE UNCLE'S STORY*

Yet another form of third space comes into sight in a recent novel by one of the best-known Maori authors from Aotearoa/New Zealand. In Witi Ihimaera's *The Uncle's Story* (2000) this third space is not designed to overcome a corrosive form of cultural memory that keeps two ethnocultural groups apart, but to enable a subject position to emerge that so far has been kept silent in the self-assertion of Maori culture.[39]

This self-assertion has often been closely tied to a reaffirmation of the warrior ideal that characterized traditional Maori society. When Arapeta, the patriarchal head of the Mahana family and former World War II veteran, sends his son Sam to fight in the Vietnam war, he expects him to assert Maori honor (*mana*) on the South East Asian battlefield, just as he himself had done as an officer in the Maori Battalion on the battlefields of Europe. The front-lines appear clear-cut: on one side an indigenous population that has been oppressed and marginalized during the colonization of New Zealand and is now reviving its culture and reasserting its traditions and rights, on the other a majority society that once thrived on this oppression and marginalization and now has to learn to come to terms with this new Maori self-confidence. Right at the centerer of this sociocultural reassertion, Ihimaera opens up a new conflict line, however: the struggle for recognition of gay and lesbian Maoris.

While fighting in Vietnam, Sam discovers his own homosexuality and falls in love with the American helicopter pilot Cliff Harper. When Cliff visits Sam in New Zealand after the war, their relationship is discovered and Sam is cruelly punished by his autocratic father who believes that Maori culture and homosexuality are mutually exclusive:

'In traditional times, son, people like you never existed,' Arapeta said. 'They would have taken you outside, gutted you and left your head on a post for the birds to eat. Men like you abuse the sperm which is given to man for only one purpose. The very sperm that died inside my mates when they were killed on the battlefield. The sperm that is for the procreation of children. Don't you know that the sperm is sacred?'[40]

After Arapeta has asserted his patriarchal view of normative Maori heterosexuality by vindictively humiliating his son, there is literally no space left for Sam in Maori society; he decides to leave New Zealand altogether, but is killed in an accident on the way to the airport where Cliff is waiting for him. When Sam's body is brought home, his father buries him in an unmarked spot in the wilderness and thus banishes him into the total oblivion of *te kore*, the absolute void beyond the cycle of generations which Sam dreaded being thrown into once he had been expelled from the spiritual community of the Maori: 'He had disconnected him from the umbilical cord of whakapapa, and sent him falling head over heels like a spaceman trailing his severed lifeline through a dark and hostile universe to oblivion'.[41]

Things change a generation later, however, when Michael Mahana, Sam's gay nephew, has his coming out in his parents' home; Aunt Patty, Sam's sister, hands over Sam's diary (which she secretly kept for decades) to Michael, who begins to reconstruct his uncle's story that has so long been expunged from family history. Michael decides that he will not let himself be pushed out of Maori society into the void and embarks on a self-confident passage towards a Maori modernity that can encompass both being Maori and being gay: he openly challenges the cultural tradition that sees Maoriness and homosexuality as mutually exclusive, fights for his right to openly live as a gay Maori, and makes a political commitment 'to change the Maori world'.[42] Interestingly enough, the third space the novel delves into also has a transnational dimension:[43] as a political activist, Michael increasingly becomes aware of the common predicaments of indigenous peoples in various parts of the world, and the decisive turning point in his life occurs when he publicly demands recognition for deviant indigenous sexualities at a conference on the cultural and social survival of indigenous peoples held in Canada:

> I am a gay man. Of all the children of the gods, my kind–gay, lesbian, transvestite and transsexual–inhabited the lowest and darkest cracks between the Primal Parents. We, now, also wish to walk upright upon this bright strand.
>
> To do this, we must make a stand. For those of us who are First Peoples, this is not something to be done lightly nor without knowledge of risk. In my country, my own Maori people are among the most homophobic in the world. They are a strong, wonderful people but their codes are so patriarchal as to disallow any inclusion of gay Maori men and women within the tribe. As long as we do not speak of our sin openly, we are accepted. But if we speak of it, if we stand up for it, we are cast out. My own uncle was cast out. I have been cast out. Many of us, in all our cultures, have been cast out. [. . .] But there is another way. Only you, however, can sanction it. This is why I am standing today.[44]

In the final passages of the novel, the opening up of a third space for indigenous homosexuality is staged in a central location of Maori tradition, when Waka, a young gay Maori activistist who died of AIDS, is brought back to his home town in order to have his death acknowledged in the communal meeting place (*marae*) and to have him buried according to traditional Maori protocol. Once more, there seems no space for this traveler between the worlds (the name Waka alludes to the great canoes in which the Maori journeyed across the Pacific to Aotearoa/New Zealand) when part of the Maori community refuses to let the funeral procession enter the *marae*, but this time round Michael and the others are determined to have their gay indigeneity acknowledged:

> 'We'll wait all day and all night if we have to,' I said. 'It is Waka's right to be buried in the place where he was born. He is Maori as well as gay. We're here to make sure his right is honored.' [. . .] 'We are a people. We are a tribe. We bring our dead. If tradition has to be broken, then I will break it. Nobody will stop us from burying our own among the people where they belong. The time for hiding ourselves and our dead is past. The time for burying them in some anonymous cemetery is over.'[45]

The fact that the combative mourners prevail and that the plot of *The Uncle's Story* thus ultimately endorses the vision of a 'gay tribe' formulated by Michael and his co-campaigners highlights the activist, even interventionist quality of Ihimaera's novel. An important aspect of this activism is undoubtedly an assertion of indigenous priorities and rights, a desire to move beyond 'the borderlands of White society' and a life lived 'only by the White man's leave within White structures that are White driven and White kept'.[46] The tribulations of Sam and Michael staged in the text, however, do not derive their ultimate significance from serving as a postmodernist challenge to Western post-settler culture: what makes them *unheimlich* is not their fleeting presence in the Western nation state, and the void they struggle against is not the poststructuralist gap between the opacity of language and the world created by discourse. Once more, the significance of the third space constituted in the text far exceeds the problematic of an interstitial dismantling of the New Zealand nation state, and can more productively be read in terms of the arduous task of redefining indigenous modes of modernity that continue to braid what Ihimaera has referred to as 'the Rope of Man' by adding distinctly new fibers to the common thread.[47]

COLONIAL MODERNITIES IN A GLOBALIZED WORLD: WOLE SOYINKA'S *ÌSARÀ: A VOYAGE AROUND 'ESSAY'*

Despite its postmodernist vocabulary, much of contemporary postcolonial theory has been characterized by a reductive focus on colonialism and on the conflict between colonizers and colonized; the most popular modes of projecting this focus onto the cultures and literatures of the postcolonial world have been the explicit or tacit adoption of the vocabulary of anticolonial resistance on the one hand and the postmodernist deconstruction of colonial discourse on the other. What has often been overlooked in this postmodern binary are the specific forms of modernity created by colonizers and colonized alike: by the machinations of colonial administrations and education systems as well as by various modes of social agency that not only formed tributaries to the mainstream of anticolonialism, but also branched out into the transformation of non-Western societies, economies and knowledge systems. In this context, third space can be perceived as a move beyond the binary oppositions of colonialism and anticolonialism, towards an understanding of the concrete predicaments and interventions of those who began to shape modernity under conditions of European colonialism.

Wole Soyinka's *Ìsarà: A Voyage Around 'Essay'* (1990), the second work in a series of autobiographical writings begun with *Aké: The Years of Childhood* (1981) and since continued with *Ibadan: The Penkelemes Years* (1994) and *You Must Set Forth at Dawn: A Memoir* (2006), focusses on Soyinka's father and a circle of school-friends of his generation.[48] Set in the Nigerian 1940s in the eponymous small town of Ìsarà, Soyinka's voyage is anything but an exercise in sentimental nostalgia: far from simply being part of an embarrassing prehistory redeemed only once anticolonialism had successfully overthrown colonialism, the activities of the generation of Soyinka's father are presented as contributions to a vibrant process of sociocultural transformation.[49] This transformation necessarily entails confrontations with the colonial system, but its significance reaches beyond the agenda of political anticolonialism. As Soyinka points out in his "Author's Note," both the intellectual agenda and the incisive involvement of the characters he portrays are not just of historical interest, but can serve as an *aide-memoire* for a disconcerted Nigerian present:

> Life, it would appear, was lived robustly, but was marked also by an intense quest for a place in the new order, and one of a far more soul-searching dimension than the generation they spawned would later undertake. Their options were excruciatingly limited. A comparison between this aspect of their time and their offsprings,' when coupled with the inversely proportionate weight of extended family demands and expectations, assumes quite a heroic dimension.[50]

Ìsarà thus brings to life the determination of the intellectuals of his father's generation to modernize their society, to set up an independent African business life and to defend their achievements both against colonial authoritarianism and a stifling traditionalism incapable of solving the pressing problems of the day. The protagonists of the story, who were educated in a seminary at Ilesa and whom Soyinka in punning diction refers to as

Ex-Ilés, are certainly no perfect heroes, but their social idealism and professional dedication stand in stark contrast to the corruption and unproductive greed that has characterized so much of recent Nigerian history.

In one of the most fascinating developments in the novel, Soyinka's father, the village teacher variously called 'Tisa', 'Soditan' or 'Essay' learns to see his social, economic and political environment as a dynamic modernity in its own right. Initially the wide world out there conjured up in the letters of his traveling pen-friend Wade Cudeback from Ashtabula, U.S.A., seems somehow more real or significant to him than his own Nigerian surroundings, but in the course of the novel he begins to grasp the interconnectednesss of his own concerns and aspirations with the wider world. 'Ashtabula' thus becomes Africanized, while his own struggle for a civil modernity in Nigeria achieves a transnational dimension. This chiastic development reaches its apex when Wade Cudeback arrives on a surprise visit to Ìsarà and 'Essay' is faced with the challenge of devising an adequate greeting. When his planned ironic reenactment of the colonial courtesy once performed by Stanley and Livingstone is preempted by his visitor, 'Essay' settles for an astonishing gesture acknowledging both the transnational space generated by the year-long exchange of letters between the two teachers and the transnational third space of his modern Nigerian lifeworld that finally has acquired a significance of its own and can no longer be contained in the colonial site allotted to it by the segmentary logic of Empire:

> As he set eyes on the visitor, Soditan was mildly disconcerted to find that the white teacher in no way resembled his handwriting, neither did he emit the slightest aura which evoked the places and adventures he so richly conveyed in his letters. Saaki gave Wade Cudeback a massive wink as Soditan stepped forward to shake hands with him. The Ìsarà teacher had decided on the form of the greeting he would use for this encounter. It would certainly raise a laughter of approbation from the Ex-Ilés and his guest, break the ice and set everyone at ease. But Wade Cudeback beat him to the salute: 'Teacher Soditan, I presume?'
>
> In the few seconds of grace provided by the knowledgeable laughter, Soditan thought rapidly. His response, he would later acknowledge, emerged in spite of himself. Astonished, he heard himself say, and with a feeling of inner composure:
> 'Welcome to Ashtabula.'[51]

CONCLUSION

As this chapter hopes to have shown, the multitude of third spaces to be encountered in the New Literatures in English can no longer be contained in the poststructuralist framework in which they have habitually been perceived by postcolonial theory. One of the reasons why academic commentators have begun to address the question of an impending 'end of postcolonial theory'[52] and have registered 'a sense of exhaustion in postcolonial studies'[53] may well lie in the fact that key concepts of postcolonial theory (such as third space) today often seem to obstruct rather than to encourage encounters with cultural and literary realities in a world of globalized modernity. In his contribution to the debate referred to above, Simon Gikandi has suggested that postcolonial studies has 'bifurcated' into 'the task of reading texts that emerge in the crisis of postimperial Europe and the task of accounting for the narratives of decolonization in the nation-states that emerged after decolonization'.[54] This conceptual bifurcation may significantly have contributed to the exhaustion of postcolonial studies by channeling interest into a bipolar system that promotes endless rehearsals of Western self-criticism on the one hand and is structurally incapable of perceiving anything but 'decolonizing narratives' in 'nation states that emerged after decolonization' on the other. Focussing attention on the variety of third spaces created in the context of globally interlinked multiple modernities and transnational connections can arguably contribute towards overcoming this impasse and opening up literary studies to an interdisciplinary dialogue where seminal questions about the contours and trajectories of these modernities can be raised. Ironically enough, it is today the third space beyond the poststructuralist grand narrations of postcolonial theory and the bifurcated verities of conventional postcolonialist practice where some of the answers may be found.

NOTES

1. For an example of the former critique, see Schmidt-Haberkamp, Barbara. "The Appropriation of the Third Space: Considerations upon the Mediating Function of Migrant Writers." *Anglistentag 1999 Mainz: Proceedings*. Ed. Bernhard Reitz and Sigrid Rieuwerts. Trier: WVT, 1999. 301–311; for examples of the latter, see Parry, Benita. "Signs of the Times." *Postcolonial Studies: A Materialist Critique*. Abingdon: Routledge, 2004. 55–74; and Phillips, Lawrence. "Lost in Space: Siting/citing the in-between of Homi Bhabha's *The Location of Culture*." *Scrutiny 2: Issues in English Studies in Southern Africa* 3 (1998): 16–25.
2. Bhabha, Homi K. *The Location of Culture*. London: Routledge, 1994. 36.
3. Ibid. 36.
4. Ibid. 37.
5. Ibid. 175.
6. Ibid. 85–92. 102–122.
7. Ibid. 93–101.
8. Ibid. 86.
9. Ibid. 4.
10. Ibid. 4–5.
11. Ibid. 164.
12. Ibid. 139.
13. Ibid. 38–39.
14. Ashcroft, Bill, Gareth Griffiths, and Helen Tiffin. *The Empire Writes Back: Theory and Practice in Post-Colonial Literatures*. London: Routledge, 1989. 196.

15. See ibid. 12: "The impetus towards decentering and pluralism has always been present in the history of European thought and has reached its latest development in post-structuralism. But the situation of marginalized societies and cultures enabled them to come to this position much earlier and more directly".

16. Hannerz, Ulf. *Transnational Connections: Culture, People, Places*. London: Routledge, 1998. 8.

17. Beck, Ulrich. *World Risk Society*. Cambridge: Polity, 1999; Hannerz. *Transnational Connections*.

18. Giddens, Anthony. *The Consequences of Modernity*. Oxford: Polity, 1990; Giddens, Anthony. *Runaway World: How Globalization is Reshaping Our Lives*. London: Profile, 1999.

19. Eisenstadt, Shmuel N. "Multiple Modernities". *Daedalus* 129 (2000): 1–29; Gaonkar, Dilip Paramshwar, ed. *Alternative Modernities*. Durham, London: Duke UP, 2001; Probst, Peter, Jan-Georg Deutsch, and Heike Schmidt, ed. *African Modernities: Entangled Meanings in Current Debate*. Oxford: James Currey, 2002.

20. Eisenstadt. "Multiple Modernities". 2–3.

21. Ibid. 24.

22. Taylor, Peter J. *Modernities: A Geohistorical Interpretation*. Minneapolis: Minnesota UP, 1999. 12.

23. Phillips, Caryl. *Cambridge*. London: Picador, 1992.

24. See, for example, Eckstein, Lars. "Dialogism in Caryl Phillips's *Cambridge*, or the Democratisation of Cultural Memory." *World Literature Written in English* 39 (2001): 54–74; Eckstein, Lars. *Re-Membering the Black Atlantic: On the Poetics and Politics of Literary Memory*. Amsterdam, Kenilworth: Rodopi, 2006; Ledent, Bénédicte. "The 'Aesthetics of Personalism' in Caryl Phillips's Writing: Complexity as a New Brand of Humanism." *World Literature Written in English*, 39 (2001): 75–85; Sharrad, Paul. "Speaking the Unspeakable: London, Cambridge and the Caribbean." *De-Scribing Empire: Post-Colonialism and Textuality*. Ed. Chris Tiffin and Alan Lawson. London: Routledge, 1994. 201–17.

25. Phillips. *Cambridge*. 163.

26. Ibid. 173.

27. Phillips, Caryl. *Crossing the River*. London: Faber and Faber, 2000. For a detailed analysis of polyphonic narration in this novel, see Ledent, Bénédicte. "'Overlapping Territories, Intertwined Histories': Cross-Culturality in Caryl Phillips's *Crossing the River*." *Journal of Commonwealth Literature* 30 (1995): 55–62; Lenz, Günter H. "Middle Passages: Histories, Re-Memories, and Black Diasporas in Novels by Toni Morrison, Charles Johnson, and Caryl Phillips." *Crabtracks: Progress and Process in Teaching the New Literatures in English*. Ed. Gordon Collier and Frank Schulze-Engler. Amsterdam, Atlanta: Rodopi, 2002. 235–52.

28. Phillips. *Crossing the River*. 235–237.

29. Wickremesekera, Channa. *Distant Warriors*. Colombo: Perera Hussein, 2005.

30. For a general discussion of long-distance nationalism see Anderson, Benedict. *The Spectre of Comparisons: Nationalism, Southeast Asia and the World*. London: Verso, 1998. 58–76; for an analysis of Tamil long-distance nationalism see Fuglerud, Oivind. *Life on the Outside: Tamil Diaspora and Long Distance Nationalism*. London: Pluto, 1999.

31. Anderson, Benedict. "Western Nationalism and Eastern Nationalism: Is There a Difference That Matters?" *New Left Review* 9 (2001): 31–42. 42.

32. Kox, John K. "Zlatko Skrbis, Long-distance Nationalism: Diasporas, Homelands and Identities" [Review]. *Slovene Studies* 22 (2003): 188–191. 189.

33. Wickremesekera. *Distant Warriors.* 61. 109. 107.
34. Ibid. 8–9.
35. Ibid. 9.
36. Ibid. 91.
37. Ibid. 215.
38. Ibid. 217.
39. Ihimaera, Witi. *The Uncle's Story.* Honolulu: Hawai'i UP, 2000.
40. Ibid. 257.
41. Ibid. 322.
42. Ibid. 358.
43. For a discussion of the local and the global in contemporary Maori literature see Moura-Kocoglu, Michaela. "Manifestation of Self and/or Tribal Identity? Māori Writing in the Global Maelstrom." *Transcultural English Studies: Theories, Realities, Fictions.* Asnel Papers 12. Ed. Frank Schulze-Engler and Sissy Helff. Amsterdam, Kenilworth: Rodopi, in print [2008]; Riemenschneider, Dieter. "Contemporary Maori Cultural Practice: From Biculturalism towards a Glocal Culture." *Journal of New Zealand Literature* 18–19 (2000–2001): 139–160. Frank Schulze-Engler, "Witi Ihimaera, *The Uncle's Story*: Indigenous Literatures in a Globalized World." *A History of Postcolonial Literature in 12 ½ Books.* Ed. Tobias Döring. Trier: WVT, 2007. 51–69.
44. Ihimaera. *The Uncle's Story.* 343–344.
45. Ibid. 364–365.
46. Ibid. 326.
47. In a recent novel, Ihimaera has described 'the Rope of Man' in the following terms: "Some Maori believe that with the coming of the Pakeha [the white New Zealanders] it became frayed and almost snapped during the New Zealand Wars. [. . .] It renewed itself, thickened, matted with strong twisting fibres and was as strong as it had been originally. But it was a *different* rope"; see Ihimaera, Witi. *The Rope of Man.* Auckland: Reed, 2005. 191.
48. Soyinka, Wole. *Aké: The Years of Childhood.* London: Rex Collings, 1981; Soyinka, Wole. *Ìsarà: A Voyage Around "Essay".* London: Minerva, 1991; Soyinka, Wole. *Ibadan: The Penkelemes Years—A Memoir, 1946–1965.* Ibadan: Spectrum, 1994; Soyinka, Wole. *You Must Set Forth at Dawn: A Memoir.* New York: Random House, 2006.
49. For discussions of the implied relationship between colonial history and contemporary realities in Soyinja's text see Bodunde, Charles. "Beyond Biography. Characters and Journeys in Soyinka's *Isara*." *Commonwealth Essays and Studies* 23 (2001): 39–46; Cribb, Tim. 2003. "African Autobiography and the Idea of the Nation." *Resistance and Reconciliation: Writing in the Commonwealth.* Ed. Bruce Bennett, Susan Cowan, Jacqueline Lo, Satendra Nandan, and Jennifer Webb. Canberra: Association for Commonwealth Literature and Language Studies, 2003. 63–73.
50. Soyinka. *Ìsarà.* vi.
51. Ibid. 262.
52. Yaeger, Patricia. "Editor's Column: The End of Postcolonial Theory? A Roundtable with Sunil Agnani, Fernando Coronil, Gaurav Desai, Mamadou Diouf, Simon Gikandi, Susie Tharu, and Jennifer Wenzel." *PMLA* 122 (2007): 633–651.
53. Jennifer Wenzel in Yaeger. "Editor's Column: The End of Postcolonial Theory?" 634.
54. Yaeger. "Editor's Column: The End of Postcolonial Theory?" 635.

10 Two Nations in the Third Space
Postcolonial Theory and the Polish Revolution

Gerhard Wagner *

INTRODUCTION

Postcolonial and postmodern literary scholar Homi K. Bhabha has drafted a theory of nation which, he claims, goes beyond the theoretical concept of nation formulated in the social sciences.[1] Bhabha criticizes the social sciences for providing an inadequate description of nation building: in his view, they are all too fixated on the perspective of the dominating élite, which seeks to indoctrinate the people with its own idea of national identity. He contends that such an approach cannot even adequately address the situation of the 19th century, let alone that of a contemporary world in which globalization poses a permanent challenge to existing power structures, and millions of migrants unmask existing national self-images as mere ideology. For Bhabha every nation is subject to dissemination; national identity can only be thought of as the result of a negotiation that emerges in a third space between dominant élites, who speak for the majority of the people, and newly arrived minorities.

Bhabha's theory is quite significant for the social sciences.[2] His idea of negotiation need not be restricted to relations between majorities and minorities nor to those between residents and migrants. In principle, it can be applied to all those cases in which a dominant definition of national identity is challenged by an alternative that cannot be simply ignored. Unfortunately, Bhabha's writing is both full of unexamined presuppositions and is not sufficiently complex, and this creates significant problems for the reception of his theory. Social scientists in search of inspiration from his writings put them aside with a shrug of their shoulders after wading through pages of exegesis of postcolonial literature. Students of culture versed in postcolonial discourse, on the other hand, have to take great pains to figure out precisely what a nation is supposed to be. All this puts a heavy strain on Bhabha's concept of the third space, which ultimately degenerates into an umbrella term for everything possible. Understanding the potential of Bhabha's theory will clearly require a fair amount of explanatory work.

In the following we will thus start by reconstructing the philosophical and sociological foundations of Bhabha's theory. Next, we will determine the general conditions of possibility that have to be satisfied to allow negotiation to take place at all. Finally, we will give a concrete example of such a negotiation. For reasons of theoretical and political relevance, however, our example will not be taken from the Anglophone world that so typifies postcolonial discourse. Instead, the Polish nation has been chosen as example, a nation that managed to free itself from Soviet 'colonization' in the course of the 1980s and was apparently genuinely able to redefine itself in the course of a process of negotiation.

THE NATION'S TWO PEOPLES

Bhabha claims that *'there is no given community or body of the people.'*[3] For him the people that constitute a nation 'are not simply historical events or parts of a patriotic body. They are also a complex rhetorical strategy of social reference.'[4] In making this claim, he follows the constructivist approach that has won acceptance in the social sciences since the 1980s. This approach no longer views the nation as an entity or essence (*Wesenheit*) whose integration comes about naturally, as it were, from pregiven cultural, ethnic and social factors. Instead, the nation is seen to be a construct.[5] Accordingly, it is usually intellectuals who identify special characteristic features that are thought to be shared by a given people (to be understood in the mere sense of a population). In this process, they establish the notion of national identity (which may as easily include cultural, ethnic, or social factors as political ones) by inventing a tradition. This tradition harks back to an origin that either grants meaning to the present, such as it is, or confronts the present with an alternative that has yet to be re-attained (a Golden Age). Intellectuals present the people with a narrative based on this invented tradition as a source of identification. If the people accept this offer a sense of community (an 'us') emerges that integrates the nation and motivates collective action. Bhabha himself has edited a reader to clarify the connections between nation and narration.[6]

On the other hand, however, Bhabha also critically sets himself apart from this social-scientific mainstream. According to Bhabha the mainstream fails to view the construct in terms of the relation of power (the structure of domination) manifest in it. For him, the rhetorical strategy of social reference is so complex as to support two opposing significations:

> the people are the historical 'objects' of a nationalist pedagogy, giving the discourse an authority that is based on the pre-given or constituted historical origin *in the past*; the people are also the 'subjects' of a process of signification that must erase any prior or originary presence of the nation-people to demonstrate the prodigious, living principles of the

people as contemporaneity: as that sign of the *present* through which national life is redeemed and iterated as a reproductive process.[7]

The first signification is that of a ruling élite on whose behalf intellectuals create a tradition-based notion of national identity in order to instill it in a disempowered people, a people stripped of their independent capacities: 'The pedagogical founds its narrative authority in a tradition of the people [. . .] that represents an eternity produced by self-generation.'[8] The social sciences focus on this kind of signification. The second signification relates to that of a subjected people, who, in an open discourse, formulate a 'counter-narrative of the nation.'[9] Making use of the terminology of John L. Austin's speech act theory (a theory that has also been used by other critical discourse theories and that initiated a paradigm change in the cultural and social sciences),[10] Bhabha terms this second signification performative: 'The performative intervenes in the sovereignty of the nation's *self-generation* by casting a shadow *between* the people as "image" and its signification as a differentiating sign of Self.'[11] This is the signification that Bhabha aims to rehabilitate with his theory.

To do so he uses the term 'liminality' in order to emphasize the transitional character of the oppositional relationship between the two significations.[12] He seems to be projecting Jacques Lacan's distinction between *moi* and *je* onto the nation. This is supported not only by his designation of the people as the 'national subject,' but also by his pointing out that the pedagogical side creates an 'image' of this subject and by doing so indulges in 'narcissistic neuroses.'[13] According to Lacan the *moi*—the reflexive form of I—is the primary, but as such deficient subject, because it is an imaginary and speculative subject.[14] It is imaginative because it obtains its identity from an image (*imago*), and it is speculative because it involves a mirror image (*speculum*). Like Narcissus, who looks into the water and falls in love with his own image, the child who looks into a mirror gains an integrated experience of itself, insofar as it is able to piece together its fragmented bodily experiences. Nothing more, however, is possible. The *moi*, which due to its reflexive structure is its own object,[15] remains an imaginary narcissistic subject that reproduces its own image. In order to become the *je*, which is, as Lacan claims, the true subject, the image has to yield to language and the reflexive circle has to be broken by the incorporating of others.

In Lacan's scheme of the imaginary, Bhabha finds the principle on which all definitions of national identity are based and which the social sciences have undoubtedly correctly described by pointing out that intellectuals 'imagine' a 'self-image' of their nation.[16] Even if this has to be taken metaphorically, since this imagination is narrative in character, occurring as it does in the medium of language, this self-image is also a mirror image insofar as intellectuals refer to those self-images that have been imagined by their forefathers. And though the tradition on which they found their self-image is an invention, this invention of tradition is itself part of a tradition of invention.[17] In this way, every invented tradition is actually a reflexive representation of a self-generated eternity: 'The object and characteristic of "traditions," including invented ones, is invariance.'[18] Bhabha contrasts the pedagogical side of the national subject (which is limited to the *moi*) with its performative side. The latter is supposed to advance the construction of the national subject qua *je* in that it—as the other—breaks the self-reflexive circle:

> The problem is not simply the 'selfhood' of the nation as opposed to the otherness of other nations. We are confronted with the nation split within itself, articulating the heterogeneity of its population. The barred Nation It / Self, alienated from its eternal self-generation, becomes a liminal signifying space that is *internally* marked by the discourses of minorities, the heterogeneous histories of contending peoples, antagonistic authorities and tense locations of cultural difference.[19]

THE THIRD SPACE OF ENUNCIATION

While the adjective 'pedagogical' denotes the disempowerment of the people into an object of education, the forcing of the people to accommodate themselves to a notion of national identity dished out to them by intellectuals in the name of the ruling élite, the adjective 'performative' rehabilitates this very people as the true national subject that constructs its own identity. This democratizes the construct. Nonetheless, this is not to say that intellectuals are no longer important here. In fact, Bhabha uses the examples of the Algerians who resisted French colonial policy, and the women of British miners who fought against the neoliberal policies of Maggie Thatcher, to show that in principal each and every person is capable of a 'theoretical commitment,' and that this can also be the basis for the construction of a national identity.[20] For Bhabha minorities are especially important here. They are supposed to get the construction of the national *je* going by criticizing the dominant national narrative and confronting it with their own notions and ideas:

> The language of critique is effective not because it keeps forever separate the terms of the master and the slave [. . .] but to the extent to which it overcomes the given grounds of opposition and opens up a space of translation: a place of hybridity, figuratively speaking, where the construction of a political object that is new, *neither the one nor the other*, properly alienates our political expectations, and changes, as it must, the very forms of our recognition of the moment of politics.[21]

Bhabha terms the opening of this place of hybridity through the language of criticism as the 'intervention of the Third Space of enunciation.'[22] Utterances made by minority speakers who criticize the dominant national narrative, step in-between the pedagogical and the performative. Since criticism, however, is only possible from the standpoint of one's own position, this inevitably also means that voice is given to one's own notions, up to and including one's own traditions. For Bhabha this 'articulation of the antagonistic or contradictory' in the narratives of the confronting two sides is necessary: 'The production of meaning requires that these two places be mobilized in the passage through a third space.'[23] Bhabha speaks metaphorically with Frantz Fanon's words in deeming this a 'zone of occult instability' where the people in a 'fluctuating movement' get in touch with both poles to articulate them.[24] Here he is not thinking of an overcoming or sublation of this antagonistic relationship. He replaces the 'thirdness in the structure of dialectical thought' (which he knows that the Marxist critic Frederic Jameson conceived of as 'the third space') with a very specific concept of '*negotiation*': 'By negotiation I attempt to draw attention to the structure of *iteration* which informs political movements that attempt to articulate antagonistic and oppositional elements without the redemptive rationality of sublation or transcendence.'[25]

Quite obviously, Bhabha refers to Jacques Derrida's concept of *différance* here. He has to, for otherwise this articulation would only be possible in a pedagogical sense, and not in the performative sense he has in mind. This is also supported by the fact that Bhabha views the concept of the performative, which comes from speech act theory, exclusively in Derrida's terms. In his critique of speech act theory Derrida places particular emphasis on the insight he has gained from his critique of Ferdinand de Saussure's philosophy of language, namely, that the iteration of a sign in no way guarantees that the sign maintains its meaning. Clearly, there has to be 'a minimal remainder' (*restance*); otherwise a sign cannot be repeated at all. It is wrong, however, to assume that a sign possesses a permanence that is unaffected by change over time.[26] Iteration always leads to a temporal differentiation of the sign from itself—a *différance*—resulting in a shift of meaning: 'the time and place of the other time already at work, altering from the start the start itself, the first time, the at once.'[27] This is true for all signs, including those used for the inventions of tradition. These signs are anything but invariant. That they are repeatedly used within the course of traditions of invention merely means that they endure over time, not that they remain identical to themselves outside of time. The *différance* that makes itself felt in the mere articulation of signs ensures 'that the meaning and symbols of culture have no primordial unity or fixity; that even the same signs can be appropriated, translated, rehistoricized and read anew.'[28]

For Derrida the concept of *différance* is followed by that of *dissémination* to describe a process of distribution or dispersal where the meaning of its starting point is already shifted into other channels.[29] For Bhabha it is thus logical to entitle the speech in which he puts forth the idea that minorities, as agents of the new, should criticize the ruling notion of national identity 'DissemiNation.'[30] As previously mentioned, since this criticism can only come from one's own position, it always results in its dispersal. Those elements that are antagonistic or contradictory to the signs of the dominant narrative are those signs that constitute the narratives of the minorities and that also undergo a change in meaning due to the articulation that the confrontation compels. This articulation is *necessary* because the narratives of the minorities are the Other that break the self-reflexive circle of the national *moi* and at the same time enable the production of that new narrative which brings about the new national identity qua *je*. The minorities articulate the dominant national narrative as well as their own traditions—which can certainly be quite national—until their meanings, which become ever more dispersed, become interwoven with one another and a new hybrid national narrative emerges.

A NATIONAL CONTRACT

In fact, what we are dealing with here is a Third Space of *enunciation*. The spokespersons of the minorities themselves remain on the outside. Their criticism is first made *possible* simply because their intention does not require them to dissociate themselves from their own positions—which de facto they nevertheless already do just by making their utterances. As Derrida has demonstrated, there is always a difference between intention and utterance because it is a condition of the possibility of communication that the speaker *qua speaker* dissociates him- or herself from his or her utterances. To utter something means in fact to place it outside of oneself. Words can turn into repeatable signs and thus language into a social fact only in their 'absence' from the speaker's individual intention and the speaker's position, a position that may be more or less politically, culturally, ethnically and/or socially formed. Just as a sign is never completely identical with itself, the subject making an utterance is never totally identical with the subject of that utterance. For Bhabha, Derrida's reference to the 'disjuncture between the subject of a proposition *(énoncé)* and the subject of the enunciation' is very significant here: it enables the spokespersons of minorities to express their criticism and then later, if appropriate, to distance themselves from their position.[31]

For Bhabha in any case the formulation of a new national narrative involves a two-fold process of detachment. This is also illustrated by his examples of the Algerians and the miners' women. The Algerians fought against colonialism, but proved unable to elude the influence of the French. They thus gave up their own traditions, the very traditions that provided them with support during colonial times. The miners' women protested against Thatcherism, but were attracted by the opportunities it offered women. They thus also discarded their class-specific notions of family:

> Here the transformational value of change lies in the rearticulation, or translation, of elements that are *neither the One* (unitary working class) *nor the Other* (the politics of gender) *but something else besides*, which contests the terms and territories of both. There is a negotiation between gender and class, where each formation encounters the displaced, differentiated boundaries of its group representation and enunciative sites[32].

It is thus also plausible to assume that those spokespersons of minorities who criticize the dominant national narrative distance themselves from their own positions. At the very latest this would be the case once the people agree to the new national narrative which the minorities qua spokespersons present to them as a source of identification.

It is telling that Bhabha takes his definition of the term 'nation' from Ernest Renan's influential theory (1882). According to Renan, a nation is a 'large-scale solidarity.' Its existence is based upon the will of the people who identify themselves with it: 'A nation's existence is, if you will pardon the metaphor, a daily plebiscite.'[33] Bhabha puts it as follows: 'The national subject is produced in that place where the daily plebiscite—the unitary number—circulates in the grand narrative of the will.'[34] That sounds rather cryptic, but in fact means that the individual members of a people agree to belong to a nation by identifying with their very own—and in that sense 'grand'—narrative. This also makes clear why Bhabha designates the aspect of criticism as performative. It will be recalled that this term originates from speech act theory. In contrast to constative utterances, which are used to claim that something is true or false, performative utterances are used to carry out (perform) actions, which can either succeed or fail.[35] The standard example here is that of marriage. The person who says: 'I do!' at the registry office establishes a marriage by uttering a promise. To perform a deed is to implement it, to enact it. Analogously, Bhabha pictures the members of a people establishing a nation through performative utterances. Even for Renan, the 'clearly expressed desire to continue a common life'—which can be expressed as follows: 'Yes, I do belong to the nation!'—was constitutive for the nation.[36] For Bhabha it is likewise 'the daily pleciscite which represents the performative discourse of the people.'[37]

This agreement calls to mind that other agreement with which people make a contract with one another. In fact, shortly after the publication of Austin's *How to Do Things with Words*, political philosophers began to interpret the classical works of contract theorists like Thomas Hobbes in accordance with speech act theory and to understand the concluding of a contract as an obligation in the sense of a performative utterance.[38] The reference to contract theory is truly instructive here because it enables us to understand this process of disassociating (or distancing oneself) from one's own position which is made possible by the disjunction between the subject of an utterance and the subject of the enunciation. Contract theory is based upon the notion of isolated individuals, a notion that can be traced back to Plato and his reflections on the creation of a state following a great flood.[39] During the times of the religious and civil wars following the Reformation, this idea of a fresh start became the basis for modern contract theories, with Hobbes' *Leviathan* surely the most prominent example.[40] Hobbes tries to solve the problem of how the state of war can be brought to an end by interpreting peaceful co-existence within a state as an expression of interests. Once you can count on interests, you need not assume any other bonds prior to the concluding of the contract, because a contract is a purely voluntary unifying act and constitutes the state as a formal realm of political decision making. Conversely, however, this also means that all existing bonds have to be neutralized, which is why Hobbes pushes them into the realm of conscience. In this way (wo)man is divided into a public and a private part. In the one, he or she is a citizen; in the other, a Catholic or Protestant, or bound together in some other way or manner—be it by language, ethnicity, standing, or corporation. Yet, with regard to his or her status as a citizen, these bonds are null and void.

Ever since then, contract theorists have stuck to that neutralization of the cultural, ethnic, and social statuses of individuals, which they cloak beneath a veil of unknowing.[41] Contract theory has no use for individuals as they exist in all of their diversity prior to and outside of the contract. They are betting that people have an interest to define themselves anew, outside of their statuses. And Renan is betting the same thing. He defines the concept of nation without reference to any cultural, ethnic, or social commonalities as a large-scale (community of) solidarity based on the will. Here he had in mind the French nation, which came into being in 1789 as a 'nation of citizens' on the basis of 'equality of civil rights and the procedure of democratic legitimation of rule by the citizens.'[42] Even though he noted that a nation is not a 'community of interest' in the sense of a 'tariff union,' requiring instead affective ties,[43] Renan counted on man's interest in a nation, which excludes 'the original or natural relations of human beings to each other.'[44] This holds for those citizens who belong to the *bourgeoisie*, since the economy works best once economic actors represent nothing more than 'a multitude of mere persons who are capable of delivering something and consequently of promising something.'[45] The same also holds for the great majority of remaining citizens, since the relationship to cultural and ethnic minorities can in principle be regulated in such a nation without any associational prohibitions or any measures of forced assimilation, and political and legal procedures can be institutionalized for resolving social conflicts.[46] Renan's theory also allowed him to intercede in the disputes between France and Germany over Alsace-Lorraine. Viewing the dispute from a cultural, ethnic, or social point of view provided no basis for choosing one side over the other. Nonetheless, by referring to the will, Renan was able to justify considering the inhabitants of this hybrid region, who had lived under German occupation ever since the war of 1870/71, as members of the *grande nation*. Bhabha finds himself in a similar situation. For him too, it is the minorities who cannot be integrated by reference to cultural, ethnic, and social commonalities; rather, this can only be accomplished in terms of their own volition, their will. It is thus plausible to assume that Bhabha adopts Renan's theory of nation, and that he follows Derrida in insisting upon the disjunction between the subject of a proposition and the subject of enunciation, which allows the members of minorities to dissociate themselves from their own positions.

THE POSTCOLONIAL BIAS

It would be unacceptable for Bhabha if only the members of minorities and of those people for whom minorities speak were to drop their veils. He must also require a similar striptease from the representatives of the pedagogical side. Only this allows the nation to be established qua *je*. Viewed from the perspective of the philosophy of language, the educators are also in the position to do this. By at least responding to the minorities' criticisms, they can contribute to the Third Space of Enunciation. In this way, Bhabha's concept of negotiation would no longer need to be taken in a purely metaphorical sense. In principal, educators can get involved here in a constructive way, in order to ultimately distance themselves from the ruling position. From a sociological point of view, of course, their theoretical commitment is hardly to be taken for granted. Conditions are best in those nations of citizens in which the integration of minorities is possible with relatively few problems, since they possess institutionalized procedures for conflict resolution (it is no accident that contract theory enjoys great popularity in these nations). Spokespersons for minorities are not only able to express their criticism freely, but they usually receive a response from the pedagogical side.[47] Although it has undergone a structural transformation, the public sphere in these nations is still intact.[48] As his association of the term 'nation' with the adjective 'Western' reveals, Bhabha does indeed have the citizen nations in Western Europe and North America in mind. That he nonetheless describes their ruling structures as repressive has to do with the sensibility of certain minorities. As we all know, Western nations have been instrumental in colonizing the globe. Now the Empire strikes back as masses of migrants set off to settle in these very nations. The intellectuals among them are not willing to succumb to the national pedagogy because it reminds them of their disempowered colonial status. Accordingly, they start their dissemiNation of national narratives—what Bill Ashcroft, Gareth Griffith, and Helen Tiffin have termed 'The Empire Writes Back'[49]—in order to move Europeans and North Americans into distancing themselves from their own positions in the sense of a national *je*.

This postcolonial perspective also explains Bhabha's rhetorical claim that the pedagogical side demands from the members of a nation that they homogenize: 'The boundary that marks the nation's selfhood interrupts the self-generating time of national production and disrupts the significa-tion of the people as homogeneous.'[50] By doing so, he foists Herder's old theory onto the citizen nations. This theory was used in the 19th century to lay the basis for the 'folk nations' (*Volksnationen*) in Central Eastern Europe, nations whose structures were in fact more suitable for repressive measures.[51] The fact that citizen nations could emerge in Western Europe and North America whereas folk nations established themselves in Central Eastern Europe has to do with the different basic political constellations of the 19th century. In the West there were states where nations could consti-tute themselves on the basis of the equality of civil rights and the procedures of democratic legitimation of rule that bourgeois revolutions had success-fully brought about. Members of these nations were those people who—in Renan's sense—wanted to be citizens of the ruling folk. The narratives told within the scope of the invention of tradition were foundational. They accorded the present meaning, as seen in the light of the past. By contrast, in the East there were either no states at all, or, if they existed, they stood under foreign rule. Nations here could only be established on the basis of other commonalities their members shared. This is the way in which the 'folk nations' emerged. They constituted themselves via the belief in a com-mon 'ancestry' or descent:

> The folk is conceived as a prepolitical essence; the individual is sub-sumed under this collectivity on the basis of the identity ascribed to his properties. The nation does not develop as a politically constituted solidarity association of citizens. On the contrary, it appears as prepo-litical essence that has a higher status than the individual.[52]

Members of these nations were those people who shared the belief in this common ancestry and who were willing to get involved on behalf of the desired state. The narratives told within the framework of this invention of tradition were 'counterpresent': they pointed out the deficiencies of the present in the light of the past and aimed to transcend them. The higher sta-tus accorded the folk could function not only to stimulate the individual's willingness to make sacrifices 'in the name of the realization of the folk's interests that were legitimated by means of a philosophy of history and interpreted by the dominating élites'; rather, it also served to 'justify the limitation of individual rights to freedom and democratic procedure', as soon as the folk had (re-)gained the desired state.[53]

The same holds for the 'class nations' which constituted themselves by means of the 'equality of class position' of their members and were able in the 20th century, due to this structural affinity, to replace a fair number of folk nations:

> As in the case of the folk nation, the idea of the class nation shifts the determination of the characteristics of the nation to a collectivity. 'Folk' and 'class' are categories that have similar functions: they make possible the ascription of individuals to collective beings whose superiority, grounded in a philosophy of history, legitimizes a reduction of individual civil rights.[54]

In folk nations and class nations the collective entity (be it the folk or the class), however, is not only ranked higher than the individual, it is also to be ranked higher than other peoples, something which results in wars and the discrimination of minorities. Folk nations and class nations that were able to unify as a state are therefore not the preferred destinations of migrants. In such nations the voice of criticism can be silenced even before it has had a chance to create a Third Space of enunciation. In view of these conditions, Bhabha's association of citizen nations with the demand for homogeneity appears to be nothing more than a morally opportunistic rhetorical effect, an effect that is apparently meant to increase the political significance of his postcolonial theory.

Although Bhabha rightfully criticizes the social sciences for insufficiently discussing the problem of power in the construction of national identity, he himself fails to take up concrete relations of power, something that other postcolonial theoreticians have already criticized him for.[55] Instead of getting caught up in trite discussions in university English departments in the West,[56] it would have been more logical and more productive for Bhabha to deal with those nations in which the performative is not so self-evident. In such nations, there are many more preconditions for negotiations in which each formation is supposed to encounter the displaced, differentiated boundaries of its group representation and enunciative sites. Indeed, Bhabha's theory is no help here. His reference to the 'displaced' is reminiscent of Gilles Deleuze's theory of deterritorialization and reterritorialization, but it is too abstract for our purposes.[57] Michel Callon's 'sociology of translation' works much better here. Callon is a proponent of the Actor Network Theory. The latter first gained popularity in the sociology of science, but it can be used whenever problems need to be analyzed that can only be solved if heterogeneous actors with quite different interests can be successfully incorporated into a network of cooperative relationships. Callon calls this incorporation a 'translation' and it involves a process of displacement, 'during which the identity of actors, the possibility of interaction and the margins of manoeuvre are negotiated.'[58] Thus, Callon's concept of translation is more than just the transfer of signs from one language into another. Rather, Callon presents a sociological specification of the dissociation from one's own position that arises in the course of negotiation and results in the assumption of a representative function:

> To translate is to displace [. . .]. But to translate is also to express in one's own language what others say and want, why they act in the way they do and how they associate with each other: it is to establish oneself as a spokesman. [. . .] At the beginning the [actors] were separate and had no means of communication with one another. At the end a discourse of certainty has unified them, or rather, has brought them into a relationship with one another in an intelligible manner. But this would not have been possible without the different sorts of displacements and transformation [. . .] the negotiations, and the adjustments that accompanied them.[59]

In the following we will use the example of the Polish nation to illustrate this process of translation.

POLAND'S FIRST AND SECOND REPUBLIC

It is truly surprising that the literary scholar Homi K. Bhabha does not make reference to Benjamin Disraeli's 1844 novel *Coningsby* to illustrate his idea of a nation divided. In this novel, Disraeli anticipates Karl Marx's fundamental idea, whereby society is split into two hostile camps. Disraeli called this phenomenon 'the two nations.'[60] Norman Davies used this expression to come to terms with the Polish situation in the 1980s, which apparently really was characterized by an opposition between the pedagogical and the performative:

> For thirty-six years, Polish politics had taken little account of the people in whose name the Party reigned. Thirty-six million people were the passive object of politics. In 1980, they rose up determined to become one of its active subjects. The *Solidarity* Movement was the incarnation of that determination. The ruling Party suffered a stroke from which it was unlikely to recover.[61]

The People's Republic of Poland—where the events took place—was constructed as a class nation in 1944. It replaced the folk nation which had emerged in the 19th century from the remnants of the failed First Republic. The supporters of *Solidarity* used this tradition as the basis for their protests. By the time they came to power in the 1990s their critique of the class nation had also caused an erosion in support for their folk nation. Consequently, they constituted themselves in the Third Republic as a national *je*, which was in fact neither the one nor the other but a third thing in opposition to both, namely, the first Polish citizen nation. To understand this process, a brief glimpse at Polish history seems in order.[62]

The First Republic consisted of the United Kingdom of Poland-Lithuania. Called the *Rzeczpospolita*, it existed between 1569 and 1791 as an aristocracy. Ten percent of the population, roughly equivalent to one million people, formed the nobility, the *Szlachta*. It elected kings who were less constitutional monarchs and more general managers. They formed the Polish nation as a nation of nobles, which did not include the entire population, but only that part enjoying political representation. While it claimed for itself the values of freedom and equality, the *Szlachta* suppressed the Polish *bourgeoisie* and kept the majority of the population, craftsmen and farmers, in serfdom. This as well as its numerical size was rather characteristic for Central Eastern Europe, where the notion that farmers possess human dignity, which had prevailed in the Western European feudal system, was not recognized. This sense of superiority was particularly strong in Poland because the *Szlachta* established itself not only as a feudal estate but also as an ethnic group, claiming descent from the Sarmatians, an Indo-Iranian nomadic people from the Black Sea. The identification of a feudal estate with an ethnic group proved an easy fit: 'The conviction of the excellence of one's own customs and the inferiority of alien ones, a conviction which sustains the sense of ethnic honor, is actually quite analogous to the sense of honor of distinctive status groups.'[63] In both cases the characteristics one believes to hold in common with others are only community-forming if other collectives are nearby from whom one can distinguish oneself , and despise:

> behind all ethnic diversities there is somehow naturally the notion of the 'chosen people,' which is merely a counterpart of status differentiation translated into the plane of horizontal co-existence. The idea of a chosen people derives its popularity from the fact that it can be claimed to an equal degree by any and every member of the mutually despising groups.[64]

The sense of ethnic honor is an honor of the masses, for it is accessible to anybody who believes in their common ancestry. This enabled the members of the *Szlachta*, a rather heterogeneous social group, to consider themselves as 'a race apart from mankind': 'Nowhere in Europe was the mystique of "blue blood" more cherished than in Poland, and later commentators have talked of "Noble Racism."'[65]

By the end of the 18th century, the *Szlachta* had become completely immobilized due to the power of veto with which each individual member of the Polish parliament, the *Sejm*, was able to block legislation. In 1791, this led to a democratization, yet not to a loss of power of the nobility. Admittedly, the partitioning powers—Russia, Prussia, and the Habsburg monarchy—abolished the legal status of the *Szlachta* in 1795. Nonetheless, in the face of foreign rule, their descendants were able to appoint themselves champions of the cause of the Polish people and thus determine the

identity of a nation now encompassing the entire population. In contrast
to Western European nations, which enjoyed the advantage of being able
to constitute themselves as citizen nations within existing states, the lack
of a state forced Polish intellectuals to come up with other features held in
common and to compensate for their disadvantage with the help of a specific philosophy of history. In this way the Polish nation turned into a folk
nation, based upon the belief in a common ancestry and oriented towards
a better future:

> The sense of dignity of the negatively privileged strata naturally refers
> to a future lying beyond the present, whether it is of this life or of an-
> other. In other words, it must be nurtured by the belief in a providen-
> tial mission and by a belief in a specific honor before God. The chosen
> people's dignity is nurtured by a belief either that in the beyond 'the
> last will be the first,' or that in this life a Messiah will appear to bring
> forth into the light of the world which has cast them out the hidden
> honor of the pariah people.[66]

In so doing, the intellectual descendants of the *Szlachta* defined the Polish nation with reference to the common ancestry of its members, now
traced back not so much to the Sarmatians as to the baptism of Prince
Mieszko I, the leader of the Piastes, in 965. Clearly, Catholicism was a
constant factor in the history of Poland. After the conquest of Constan-
tinople by the Turks in 1453, Poland was not only ready to be the bulwark of Christian Europe (*antemurale Europae christianiae*), it actually
fulfilled this task in front of the gates of Vienna in 1683. When roughly
100 years later Polish intellectuals lost their state, they were forced to set
their hearts on a future beyond their present miseries. In 1832, the Polish-
Lithuanian poet Adam Mickiewicz in his *Books of the Polish People and
the Polish Pilgrimage* revisited the old idea of Poland as the bulwark of
Christian Europe. He granted this topos, arising from Poland's location on
the periphery of Europe, a significance in terms of a philosophy of history,
by glorifying the partitioning of Poland as a sociohistorical reflection and
fulfillment of the history of Christ. Like Christ, the Polish nation had been
killed, and like Christ, it will arise again, in order to free all the peoples of
Europe from oppression:

> And the Polish people was tortured to death and buried in its grave,
> and the kings called out: we have killed freedom and buried it. But
> their cry was dumb . [. . .] For the Polish people has not died; its body
> lies in the grave, and its soul moved out of the earth, i.e., out of the
> public life of the peoples, into hell, i.e., into the everyday lives of the
> peoples who suffer slavery in their own land . [. . .] But on the third
> day the soul returns to its body, and the people will rise and free all the
> peoples of Europe from slavery.[67]

It was to take almost 150 years until that third day dawned. The Polish nation played its part in this, insofar as it was a folk nation. The emphasis on the collectivity of the people at the expense of the individual was stimulating for the almost proverbial willingness of Poles to sacrifice their lives for the sake of one's country and its mission. On the one hand, it made a culture of resistance possible and this enabled the Poles to survive the long period of partition. On the other hand, however, it also abetted relations of totalitarian rule, which followed the brief experiment with independence in the 1920s. The Polish nation as a folk nation exhibited a structural affinity to the totalitarian regimes under which Poland suffered in the 20th century. The *Third Reich*, which one fought against, was a state-unified folk nation. The People's Republic of Poland, self-constituted in 1944, was a class nation, and it constituted itself on the basis of its members' equality of class position. Yet it could only be established and survive for several decades because it displayed the same ruling structure with which the Poles were all too familiar. Like the folk nation, the class nation transfers the defining characteristics of the nation to a collective that is held to be of higher value than any given individual, legitimizing the curtailment of individual civil rights. Moreover, it is the same 19th century philosophy of history-based reasoning, itself a secularized form of salvational history, that served as a basis for Mikiewicz's messianism and Marx's communism. Both cases involve Gnostic mass movements.[68] While messianism formed the basis for the Polish folk nation, which had itself been oppressed, but remained true to its mission to free all the peoples of Europe, communism formed the basis for the Polish class nation, which participated, under the aegis of the Soviets, in the proletarian world revolution for which sacrifices had to be made as well.

As in any class nation, in Poland, too, class interest was disconnected from the particular interests of individuals. Its interpretation was appropriated by a political élite, which used it to legitimate the absolute rule of the Party. By claiming that the working class, the Party of the working class, and the rule of the Party of the working class were all one and the same, and by restricting the formation of political associations to class interest, this élite prevented the democratic participation of the members of the class nation, who were, by definition, all workers. Paradoxically it was precisely free unions that could not be permitted, since that would have been the same as admitting the existence of internal class conflict, and this would have been incompatible with the legitimating construct of rule. In this sense the *Nomenklatura* ruled in a pedagogical sense very reminiscent of the *Szlachta*: 'The Party bosses treated the state as their private property, in the manner of medieval barons; and they treated the common citizens as the chattels of their fief. The gulf between the ruling élite and the masses was wide. The existence of the "two nations" was a reality.'[69] While the élite represented the class nation, the masses began to call to mind their suppressed existence as a folk nation, which possessed a culture of resistance and had a mission to fulfill.

TOWARD A CITIZEN NATION

The general conditions that led to revolution in the early 1980s have already been described and analyzed adequately elsewhere; the same holds true for the course of the revolution and its consequences.[70] Here we are only interested in finding out whether the interaction between the élite and the masses can be reconstructed as a translation in Callon's sense, which, as outlined above, is employed as a sociological specification of Bhabha's concept of negotiation. And that appears to be the case. There are four moments in the process of translation that can be analytically distinguished, even if they overlap in reality: (1) the 'problematization' elevates a circumstance into a problem in a way that allows other actors to be able to define this problem in the same way; (2) the 'interessement' defines and stabilizes the identity of the actors in the sense of this problematization; (3) the 'enrolment' associates the actors into cooperating nodes of a network; and (4) the 'mobilization' results in the taking on of representative roles.[71]

The starting scenario is the rapidly deteriorating economic situation at the end of the 1970s to which the Party could not respond adequately. Yet another dramatic increase in food prices led to a wave of protest in July 1980, which quickly spread throughout the country. Just as quickly, though, it became clear that the situation would not escalate into violence. Right from the beginning, the protesters, who primarily vented their dissatisfaction by means of strikes, made every endeavor to keep their actions within certain limits, in order not to provoke a violent response on the part of the regime or even a possible invasion of the troops of the Warsaw Pact. It was by this means that they first became acceptable at all as negotiating partners. In their capacity as *primum movens*, their spokesmen (who were far from being intellectuals themselves, though they did receive the support of intellectuals) were then able to voice criticism. By pursuing a 'problematization', they opened a Third Space of Enunciation. With the political crisis so evident, it did not prove difficult for them to define the problematic situation in a way that allowed other actors to relate. Their actual achievement was to define the identity of these other actors in such a way that they themselves were the central node in an emerging network of relationships: 'They determined a set of actors and defined their identities in such a way as to establish themselves as an obligatory passage point in the network of relationships they were building.'[72]

Which actors were involved? On the one side, the pedagogical side, we had the Party and the Kremlin, and on the other, the performative side, we had the Church and the protest movement, which called itself *Solidarity* and directed the action. With regard to the Party the strikes of *Solidarity* put it under such massive pressure that the Party's first secretary Edward Gierek had no choice but to approve the Gdansk Agreement of August 30, 1980. Even though he had the leading role of the Party certified in writing in this agreement, in return he had to yield on another point, assenting to the demand for independent and self-governed unions. With this displacement he *de facto* deprived the Party of its basic legitimation. The class nation began to dissolve. The agreement was rightfully regarded as the basis for a new 'social contract.'[73] With regard to the Kremlin, *Solidarity* acknowledged Poland's loyalty to the Warsaw Pact in the Gdansk Agreement and avoided any disruption of Soviet interests, ensuring, for example, that the lines of communication to East Germany were never cut off. This may have contributed to Moscow moving from its course, by not moving at all. It departed from ('displaced') its own tradition of marching into its satellite states in times of political crisis. With regard to the Church, however, it was only necessary to show one's solidarity. Ever since the election of the Archbishop of Krakow, Karol Wojtyla, as Pope John Paul II in 1978 and his triumphal visit to Poland the following year, the moral authority of the Polish Church had grown so enormously that the Church was able to liberate ('displace') itself from its oppressed position within the state and openly support the cause of *Solidarity*. The Pope's visit was also significant in a further important way:

> It provided the people of the country with the opportunity to openly profess their beliefs without being controlled and choreographed by the regime. With one stroke contact was created between individuals: everyone could see with his own eyes to what extent his feelings were shared by others. At the same time this also laid the foundation for the strikes in Gdansk the following year.[74]

Finally with regard to *Solidarity* itself, it was forced to distance itself ('displace' itself) from the aspired role of union in order to become the political advocate for an oppressed Polish folk nation awakened from its long sleep by the big bell of St. Peter's, as Juliusz Słowacki, another national poet of the 19th century, had prophesized in his poem "The Slavic Pope." With its growing membership rolls, which ultimately exceeded 10 million, *Solidarity* 'represented almost every single family in the land, and thereby expressed the will of the overwhelming majority of the Polish nation.'[75]

According to Callon the next moment of translation is the 'interessement':

> Interessement is the group of actions by which an entity attempts to impose and stabilize the identity of the other actors it defines through its problematization. [. . .] But these allies are tentatively implicated in the problematization of other actors. Their identities are consequently defined in other competitive ways. It is in this sense that one should understand interessement. To interest other actors is to build devices

which can be placed between them and all other entities who want to define their identities otherwise. A interests B by cutting or weakening all the links between B and the invisible (or at times quite visible) group of other entities C, D, E, etc. who may want to link themselves to B.[76]

With regard to the Party, *Solidarity* was not only able to convince one million of the three million Party members of the merits of its platform and thus to join *Solidarity*. It also succeeded in driving a wedge into the middle of Party leadership and keeping the Communist hardliners in check, as shown by the replacement of Gierek by Stanislaw Kania on September 8, 1980. Kania worked toward a compromise. He advocated compliance with the Gdansk social contract and more democracy. With regard to the Kremlin, *Solidarity* could only try to stabilize the Kremlin's policy of non-involvement. It avoided all violence and drastic means such as a general strike. In addition, it counted on the support of the United States and NATO, both of whom had spoken out against a Soviet intervention. With regard to the Church, on the other hand, there was no one from whom its links needed to be severed. *Solidarity*, which was conspicuously Catholic in its appearance, was assured of the Pope's blessing. Thus, the image of Pope John Paul II graced the ballpoint pen that its leader, Lech Wałesa, used to sign the Gdansk Agreement. With regard finally to *Solidarity* itself, it was imperative to convince and integrate those activists in its own ranks and from smaller rival groups who demonstrated a willingness to use violence and/or to call for a general strike.

Both of these aforementioned moments of translation describe the process of dissociation from one's own respective position; Derrida clarified their conditions of possibility in linguistic terms with his reference to the disjunction between the subject of the proposition and the subject of enunciation. The next moment in this process stabilizes the Third Space of Enunciation in that permanent articulation—of both the dominant and the suppressed narrative—disperses both traditions and interweaves them:

> Enrolment does not imply, nor does it exclude, pre-established roles. It designates the device by which a set of interrelated roles is defined and attributed to actors who accept them. Interessement achieves enrolment if it is successful. To describe enrolment is thus to describe the group of multilateral negotiations, trials of strength and tricks that accompany the interessements and enable them to succeed.[77]

In our case, the designation of roles was rather easy because set interests made expectations clear to all actors. An institutionalization of the negotiations thus also came about, whereby Moscow only negotiated with the Party, while the Church negotiated with *Solidarity* and the Party: 'The particular solution, emerging from the discussions of 1981, was some form of council of national reconciliation in which each of the three main forces of the political arena—the Church, the Party, and *Solidarity*—could all be represented.'[78] In these discussions the pedagogical side continued to demand that *Solidarity* profess its allegiance to communism, whereas the performative side's negotiations bore in mind that particular recourse to the tradition of a folk nation that had been fundamental to its protest from the very beginning:

> During the long summer days of the strike, actors from the local *Wybrzeże* (Coastland) company were called to the shipyards to entertain the workers with readings of Mickiewicz, Słowacki, Norwid. Their Director was overwhelmed by the reception: 'We were rather fearful about employing our usual, professional routine, but it turned out that the texts were marvelously received. Mickiewicz's *Books of the Polish Pilgrimage* made an impact on the listeners as if it had just come hot from the author's pen.'[79]

That the continuing articulation of its tradition would eventually lead to its dissemination probably became clear to the Party sooner than it became clear to *Solidarity*, but at the very latest became clear once the Pope had adopted the Party's new slogan *Odnowa* (renewal) to designate social change.

With his *coup d'état* of December 13, 1981, Wojciech Jaruzelski terminated, on behalf of the Party, the search for a compromise. In this way, Jaruzelski temporarily destroyed the hopes of *Solidarity* and the Church. Yet at the same time, he also prevented a campaign of vengeance on the part of the more dogmatic members of the Party and the Kremlin. After the 'state of war' (martial law) in 1981/82, he refrained from restoring the regime and its Communist ideology and pragmatically limited himself to maintaining power. The forbidden *Solidarity* went underground and worked from there, whereas the Church was able to act as a good shepherd in a more or less unchallenged way. The breakdown of the Soviet Empire in 1989 was accompanied by the fall of the People's Republic. In the struggle for power, *Solidarity* eventually prevailed over the remaining communists. Now it was able to implement the fourth moment of the process of translation and mobilize its allies. That made it into a 'spokesman' that represented the results of negotiation on behalf of the remaining actors.[80] This mobilization took place at the ballot box. On December 22, 1990, Wałesa took office as President of the Third Republic.

Now that the Kremlin no longer played a role, the Communists found themselves integrated into the system, and the Church continued to play a leading role, there would have been a chance to constitute the country as a state-unified folk nation. This was further supported by the fact that though Poland had played no minor role in the liberation of Central Eastern Europe, its mission remained incomplete because Western Europe was still dominated by the no less despotic 'idol of interest' whose distorted secular capitalist visage had already been identified by Mickiewicz.[81] Things were meant, however, to turn out differently:

People who naïvely imagined that the victory of *Solidarity* and of its loyally Catholic leader, Wałęsa, would automatically lead to a Republic dominated by 'Christian values' were in for a shock. It took some time before the Church hierarchy realized that it could not dictate political developments as in old Ireland.[82]

In fact, the tradition of the folk nation had also been exposed to a dissemination. Without a doubt the insistence upon a common ancestry had served as an effective foil for identification in times of oppression. The negotiations with the Communist Party, however, must have made evident the structural affinity between ethnic commonality and an equality contingent on class status. Accordingly the concept of a folk nation had to appear outdated at exactly the moment in which a nation—now positively privileged within the frame of reference of its own state—was able to recognize the opportunity to bring about not only the equality, but also the freedom of its citizens. Ascribing superiority to the people must have appeared to be no more desirable than its ascription to a class, which had served to legitimate the curtailing of civil liberties and democratic procedures.

For this reason, the Poles got down to 'the construction of a political object that is new, *neither the one nor the other.*'[83] The constitutional process, which they had pushed forward in the 1990s, laid down the foundations for a third option, namely, that of a citizen nation:

> The final constitutional bill became a bone of considerable contention, uniting the SLD [Social Democratic Left] and the *Unia* [Union for Freedom] against right-wing groups, which thought it both 'anti-national' and 'anti-Christian.' In the eyes of the bishops, the Constitution lacked 'a soul.' But it was passed, and confirmed by a poorly frequented referendum. It reduced the powers of the President as practiced since 1989 and strengthened the Sejm and the Premier. It de-politicized both the army and the judiciary. Most importantly, it set up a principled, parliamentary democracy.[84]

CONCLUSION

As this analysis has shown, Bhabha's theory of nation is not only applicable to the typical contexts of postcolonial discourse but also to contexts in which power relations are by far more asymmetrical and in which, therefore, the possibility to articulate criticism is far from being a given. Here certain historical conditions could bring about a situation in which the ruling system is no longer able to prevent the expression of criticism and the creation of a Third Space of Enunciation in which a negotiation comes about in the sense of a Round Table. In the course of this negotiation starting positions will be translated in a way that amounts to a displacement. The driving force, which may, but need not be a minority, reformulates the identity of the actors involved, integrates them into a network of cooperative relationships, and ultimately—as an actor who no one can get around—achieves a representative function. This function puts the driving force in the position to formulate a new national narrative, which differs from both the criticized position and from its own original position, both of which had become disseminated in the course of the negotiation. This new narrative is neither the one nor the other but a third thing opposed to both. It works to establish the national subject in the sense of Lacan's *je* when this subject is brought into circulation in the grand narrative of the will, so that the people can give their consent in their daily plebiscite.

NOTES

1. Bhabha, Homi K., ed. *Nation and Narration*. London, New York: Routledge, 1990; Bhabha, Homi K. *The Location of Culture*. London, New York: Routledge, 1994.
2. Wagner, Gerhard. "Nation, DissemiNation und Dritter Raum: Homi K. Bhabhas Beitrag zu einer Theorie kollektiver Identität." *Dialektik* 1 (2006): 181–193.
3. Bhabha. *The Location of Culture*. 27.
4. Ibid. 145.
5. Anderson, Benedict. *Imagined Communities: Reflections on the Origin and Spread of Nationalism*. London: Verso, 1983; Hobsbawm, Eric J. "Introduction: Inventing Traditions." *The Invention of Tradition*. Ed. Eric. J. Hobsbawm and Terence Ranger. Cambridge: Cambridge UP, 1983. 1–14.
6. Bhabha, ed. *Nation and Narration*.
7. Bhabha. *The Location of Culture*. 145.
8. Ibid. 147.
9. Ibid. 149.
10. Austin, John L. *How to do Things with Words: The William Jones Lectures Delivered at Harvard University in 1955*. Cambridge, Mass.: Harvard UP, 1962; Habermas, Jürgen. *The Theory of Communicative Action*. Vol. 1 Boston: Beacon Press, 1984; Butler, Judith. *Gender Trouble: Feminism and the Subversion of Identity*. London, New York: Routledge, 1990; Tulloch, John. *Performing Culture: Stories of Expertise and the Everyday*. London, Thousand Oaks, New Dehli: Sage: 1999.
11. Bhabha. *The Location of Culture*. 147–148.
12. Ibid. 147; Gennep, Arnold van. *The Rites of Passage*. London: Routledge & Kegan Paul, 1960.
13. Bhabha. *The Location of* Culture. 147–149.
14. Lacan, Jacques. "Das Spiegelstadium als Bild der Ichfunktion wie sie uns in der psychoanalytischen Erfahrung erscheint." *Schriften*. Vol. 1. Olten: Walter, 1973. 61–70.
15. Lacan, Jacques. "Eine materialistische Definition des Bewusstseinsphänomens." *Das Seminar*. Vol. 2. Olten: Walter, 1980. 55–71, cf. 67.
16. Assmann, Jan. *Das kulturelle Gedächtnis: Schrift, Erinnerung und politische Identität in frühen Hochkulturen*. München: Beck, 2000. 18.
17. Suter, Andreas. "Nationalstaat und die Tradition von Erfindung: Vergleichende Überlegungen." *Geschichte und Gesellschaft* 25 (1999): 480–503.

18. Hobsbawn. "Introduction." 2.
19. Bhabha. *The Location of Culture.* 148.
20. Ibid. 27–28, 38.
21. Ibid. 25.
22. Ibid. 37.
23. Ibid. 25, 36.
24. Ibid. 35.
25. Ibid. 25–26.
26. Derrida, Jacques. "Limited Inc a b c . . ." *Glyph* 2 (1977): 162–254, cf. 188–190.
27. Ibid. 200.
28. Bhabha. *The Location of Culture.* 37.
29. Derrida, Jacques. *Dissemination.* London: Athlone, 1981.
30. Bhabha, ed. *Nation and Narration.* 291–322; Bhabha, *The Location of Culture.* 139–170.
31. Bhabha. *The Location of Culture.* 36.
32. Ibid. 28.
33. Renan, Ernest. "What is a Nation?" *Nation and Narration.* Ed. Homi K. Bhabha. London, New York: Routledge, 1990. 8–22, cf. 19.
34. Bhabha. *The Location of Culture.* 160.
35. Austin. *How to do Things with Words?* 5–6.
36. Renan. "What is a Nation?" 19.
37. Bhabha. *The Location of Culture.* 161.
38. Samek, Robert. "Performative Utterances and the Concept of Contract." *Australasian Journal of Philosophy* 43 (1965): 196–210; Parry, Geraint. "Performative Utterances and Obligation in Hobbes." *Philosophical Quarterly* 17 (1967): 246–252.
39. Plato. *Laws.* 2 vols. London and Cambridge, Mass.: Heinemann and Harvard UP, 1952.
40. Hobbes, Thomas. *Leviathan or the Matter, Form and Power of a Commonwealth Ecclesiastical and Civil.* Harmondsworth: Penguin, 1982.
41. Rawls, John. *A Theory of Justice.* Cambridge, Mass.: The Belknap Press of Harvard UP, 1971.
42. Lepsius, M. Rainer. "Nation and Nationalism in Germany." *Social Research* 71 (2004): 481–500. 495.
43. Renan, "What is a Nation?" 306, 309.
44. Tönnies, Ferdinand. *Community and Association.* London: Routledge & Kegan Paul, 1974. 88.
45. Ibid. 88.
46. Lepsius. "Nation and Nationalism in Germany." 496.
47. Lyman, Stanford M. *Postmodernism and a Sociology of the Absurd: And Other Essays on the Nouvelle Vague in American Social Science.* Fayetteville: Arkansas UP, 1997.
48. Habermas, Jürgen. *The Structural Transformation of the Public Sphere: An Inquiry into a Category of Bourgeois Society.* Cambridge, Mass.: MIT Press, 1989.
49. Ashcroft, Bill, Gareth Griffins, and Helen Tiffin. *The Empire Writes Back: Theory and Practice in Post-Colonial Literatures.* London, New York: Routledge, 1989.
50. Bhabha. *The Location of Culture.* 148.
51. Herder, Johann Gottfried. *Reflections on the Philosophy of the History of Mankind.* Chicago: Chicago UP, 1968.
52. Lepsius. "Nation and Nationalism in Germany." 485, 487.
53. Ibid. 487.

54. Ibid. 493–494.
55. Spivak, Gayatri Chakravorty. "Can the Subaltern Speak?" *Colonial Discourse and Postcolonial Theory: A Reader.* Ed. Williams, Patrick and Laura Christman. Hemel Hempstead: Harvester Wheatsheaf, 1993. 66–111; Spivak, Gayatri Chakravorty. *A Critique of Postcolonial Reason: Toward a History of the Vanishing Present.* Cambridge, Mass.: Harvard UP, 2000; Arteaga, Alfred. "Bonding in Difference: Gayatri Chakravorty Spivak interviewed by Alfred Arteaga." *On Other Tongue: Nation and Ethnicity in the Linguistic Borderlands.* Ed. Alfred Arteaga. Durkam: Duke UP 1994. 273–286; Young, Robert J.C. *Colonial Desire: Hybridity in Theory, Culture, and Race.* London, New York: Routledge, 1995; Werbner, Pnina, and Tariq Modood, ed. *Debating Cultural Hybridity: Multicultural Identities and the Politics of Anti-Racism.* London: Zed, 1997; Ashcroft, Bill. *Post-colonial Transformations.* London, New York: Routledge, 2001; Goldberg, David T., ed. *Relocating Postcolonialism.* Oxford: Blackwell, 2002.
56. Dirlik, Arif. "The Post-colonial Aura: Third World Criticism in the Age of Global Capitalism." *Critical Inquiry* 20 (1994): 328–356; Loomba, Ania. *Colonialism/Post-Colonialism.* London, New York: Routledge, 1998; Fludernik, Monika. *Hybridity and Postcolonialism: Twentieth Century Indian Literature.* Tübingen: Stauffenberg, 1998; San Juan, Epifano. *Beyond Post-Colonial Theory.* New York: St. Martin's Press, 1998.
57. Deleuze, Gilles, and Felix Guattari. *A Thousand Plateaus: Capitalism and Schizophrenia.* London: Athlone, 1988.
58. Callon, Michel. "Some Elements of a Sociology of Translation. Domestication of Scallops and the Fishermen of St Brieuc Bay." *Power, Action, and Belief: A New Sociology of Knowledge.* Ed. John Law. London, Boston, Henley: Routledge & Kegan Paul, 1986. 203.
59. Ibid. 223–224.
60. Disraeli, Benjamin. *Coningsby.* London: J.M. Dent & Sons, 1948.
61. Davies, Norman. *Heart of Europe: The Past in Poland's Present.* Oxford: Oxford UP, 2001. 14.
62. Wagner, Gerhard. "Nationalism and Cultural Memory in Poland: The European Union Turns East." *International Journal of Politics, Culture, and Society* 17 (2003): 191–212.
63. Weber, Max. *Economy and Society: An Outline of Interpretative Sociology.* 3 vols. New York: Bedminster, 1968. 391.
64. Ibid. 391.
65. Davies. *Heart of Europe.* 292.
66. Weber. *Economy and Society.* 934.
67. Mickiewicz, Adam. *Dichtung und Prosa: Ein Lesebuch.* Frankfurt am Main: Suhrkamp, 1994. 314–315.
68. Löwith, Karl. *Meaning in History:* Chicago: Chicago UP, 1949; Voegelin, Eric. *The New Science of Politics: An Introduction.* Chicago: Chicago UP, 1952; Walicki, Andrzej. *Philosophy and Romantic Nationalism: The Case of Poland.* Notre Dame: Notre Dame UP, 1994; Wagner, Gerhard. *Projekt Europa: Die Konstruktion europäischer Identität zwischen Nationalismus und Weltgesellschaft.* Berlin: Philo, 2005. 29–56.
69. Davies. *Heart of Europe.* 46.
70. Ascherson, Neal. *The Polish August.* Harmondsworth: Penguin, 1981; Michnik, Adam. *Letters From Prison and Other Essays.* Berkeley, Los Angeles, London: California UP, 1985; Mason, David. "Solidarity as a New Social Movement." *Political Science Quarterly* 104 (1989): 41–58; Piekalkiewicz, Jaroslaw. "Poland: Nonviolent Revolution in a Socialist State." *Revolutions of the Late Twentieth Century.* Ed. Jack A. Goldstone, Ted Robert Gurr,

and Farrokh Moshiri. Boulder: Westview Press, 1991. 136–161; Garton Ash, Timothy. *The Polish Revolution: Solidarity.* New Haven, London: Yale UP, 2002.

71. Callon. "Some Elements of a Sociology of Translation."
72. Ibid. 204.
73. Garton Ash. *The Polish Revolution.* 74.
74. Taylor, Charles. "Einige Überlegungen zur Idee der Solidarität." *Wieviel Gemeinschaft braucht die Demokratie? Aufsätze zur politischen Philosophie.* Frankfurt am Main: Suhrkamp, 2002. 51–63, cf. 56.
75. Davies. *Heart of Europe.* 16–17.
76. Callon. "Some Elements of a Sociology of Translation." 207–208.
77. Ibid. 211.
78. Davies. *Heart of Europe.* 17.
79. Ibid. 346.
80. Ibid. 214.
81. Mickiewicz. "Die Bücher des polnischen Volkes." 313.
82. Davies. *Heart of Europe.* 428.
83. Bhabha. *The Location of Culture.* 24.
84. Davies. *Heart of Europe.* 426.

*Translated by Karin Ikas

Contributors

Bill Ashcroft, a founding exponent of post-colonial theory, is presently Chair of English at the University of Hong Kong. Prior to that, he headed the School of English at the University of New South Wales in Sydney where he still holds a professorship. He has lectured and taught in several universities around the world including the island of Papua New Guinea. His research foci are post-colonial literatures and theory, Australian literature, Australian cultural studies, critical theory, African literature, S.E. Asian and Indian literature as well as Globalization Studies. His seminal study *The Empire Writes Back: Theory and Practice in Post-Colonial Literatures*, co-authored with Gareth Griffiths and Helen Tiffin (1989) was the first text to analyse systematically the back then newly emerging field post-colonial studies. His numerous publications have been translated into many languages and include: *The Post-colonial Studies Reader* (1995), *The Gimbals of Unease: The Poetry of Francis Webb* (1997), *Key Concepts in Post-colonial Studies* (1998), *Edward Said: The Paradox of Identity* (1999), *Post-colonial Transformation* (2001), *On Post-colonial Futures: Transformations of Colonial Culture* (2001). Bill Ashcroft co-edited (with Pal Ahluwalia) *Edward Said* (1999) and *Narratives of Colonialism: Sugar, Java and the Dutch* (2000).

Ulrich Beck is the British Journal of Sociology Professor at the London School of Economics and Sciences and Professor for Sociology at the University of Munich (LMU). From 1995–1998 he was Distinguished Research Professor at the University of Cardiff. He has been a fellow of several scientific institutions, among others the Institute for Advanced Study Berlin in 1990–1991. From 1995–1997 he was member of the Future Commission of the German Government. His most recent research activities include a long-term empirical study of the sociological and political implications of reflexive modernization, which explores the complexities and uncertainties of the process of transformation from first to second modernity. Specifically he is working on a sociological framework to analyze the dynamics and ambivalences of cosmopolitan societies. He has numerous publications that have been translated into various languages. His most recent major book publications include *The Cosmopolitan Vision* (2006), *Power in the*

Global Age (2005) and *World Risk Society* (1999). Beck is chief-editor of the journal *Soziale Welt* and of the book series *Edition Second Modernity* at Suhrkamp Publishing House.

Homi K. Bhabha, who advises among others the UNESCO Committee on Culture in the Third Millennium and the World Economic Forum in Davos, is discussed and celebrated worldwide as an essential figure in postcolonial studies, and, in fact, is seen as one of the so-called Holy Trinity of post-colonial theory (the other two being Edward W. Said and Gayatri Chakravorty Spivak). Born in Bombay, or what is today Mumbai, into a Parsi family, Bhaba received his B.A. at the University of Bombay and his M.A. and Ph.D. at the University of Oxford. He taught at the University of Sussex, and then moved on as an Old Dominion Visiting Professor to Princeton University. After a subsequent visiting professorship at the University of Pennsylvania, he was a Chester D. Tripp Professor of the Humanities at the University of Chicago and is now the Anne F. Rothenberg Professor of the Humanities and Director of the Humanities Center at Harvard University as well as Distinguished Visiting Professor in the Humanities at University College, London. His research foci include Colonial and Post-Colonial Theory, Cosmopolitanism as well as 19th and 20th century English Language Literatures and Cultures. In his study *Nation and Narration* (1990) Bhabha admonishes especially the trend to essentialize Third World countries into one homogenous identity, underlining that ambivalence is what characterizes the sites of former colonial dominance. Hybridity, liminality, interstice and mimicry are hence key concepts in his following book *The Location of Culture* (1994), where he incorporates insights of semiotics and Lacan's psychoanalysis to hold that only the most ambivalent cultural production is the most productive one. Besides numerous articles published worldwide, his publications include besides the above-mentioned books, for instance *On Cultural Choice* (2000), *V.S. Naipaul* (2001), *Democracy De-Realized* (2002), the co-edited *Cosmopolitanism* (2002) together with Sheldon Pollock, Dipesh Chakrabarty, Carol A Breckenridge, *Framing Fanon* (2005) and *Edward Said: Continuuing the Conversation*, co-edited with W. J. T. Mitchell. Forthcoming are *Measure of Dwelling* (Harvard UP) and the *Right to Narrate* (Columbia UP).

Karin Ikas has studied at the University of Texas at Austin and at Würzburg University, where she received her Ph.D. in English and American Studies, Cultural Studies & Didactics. Her dissertation on "Modern Chicana Literature: An Intercultural Analysis" won the prestigious Daimler Chrysler Foundation's "Academy Award for Intercultural Studies". She has conducted postdoctoral work at universities in Australia, South African, the USA and Canada, and is presently research lecturer at the Department for Social Sciences at Frankfurt (M) University where she also holds a teaching position in the Department of English and American Studies. She has published widely on English, Canadian, American, Australian, (Post-)Colonial, Gender and Jewish Studies. Her eight books include *The Canadian Nation in the Third Millennium* (2008), *Gender Debat/tl/ed: Gender and War* (2003), *Chicana Ways* (2002), *Die zeitgenössische Chicana-Literatur: Eine interkulturelle Untersuchung* (2000), *U.S Latino Literatures and Cultures: Transnational Perspectives*, co-edited with Francisco Lomelí, *Stories from Down Under*, co-edited with David Carter (2004), and *Violence and Transgression in World Minority Literatures*, co-edited with Rüdiger Ahrens, María Herrera-Sobek, Francisco Lomelí (2005). Forthcoming is 'A Nation Forged in Fire': *Canadian Literature and the Construction of National Identity*. Her current research includes *Constructing Gender in the Third Space*, *Victorians Abroad*, the *North American Novel*, also *Pacification Literature* and *Reconciliation and Literature in the Era of Sorry Politics*.

Britta Kalscheuer is lecturer at the Department for Social Sciences at Frankfurt (M) University. Her research work includes a "comparative study on credit associations in Germany and Taiwan" and an analysis of the "public understanding of science". She was a member of the interdisciplinary Graduates' College: "Cultural Hermeneutics in a World of Difference and Transdifference" (2001–2004). Her Ph.D. thesis with the German title *Inszenierte Interkulturalität: Die wissenschaftliche Produktion deutsch-chinesischer Kulturunterschiede* is a case study on German-Chinese cultural differences and examines selected intercultural approachesthat repeat the shortcomings of cultural comparison and hence contribute to the scientific production of cultural differences because of their neglect of postcolonial insights. She is author of several articles on intercultural communication and cultural comparisons and co-edited with Lars Allolio-Näcke and Arne Manzeschke, *Differenzen anders denken* (2005). With Lars Allolio-Näcke she further co-edited the two volumes, *Transdifferente Positionalität* (2007) and *Kulturelle Differenzen begreifen: Das Konzept der Transdifferenz aus interdisziplinärer Sicht* (2008).

Julia Lossau is assistant professor for cultural geography at Humboldt-University Berlin, a post she took after working as lecturer at Heidelberg University. Between 2001 and 2003, she was a Marie-Curie-Fellow (European Commission) at the Department of Geography and Topographic Science at the University of Glasgow. Her research examines the symbolic production of places and spaces, focusing particularly on postcolonial and, more recently, on aesthetic discourses. Presently she is working on the symbolic economy of cities, examining different forms of public art practices and their spatial effects. Books and articles include *Die Politik der Verortung: Eine postkoloniale Reise zu einer anderen Geographie der Welt* (2002), *Themenorte: Produktion und Durchsetzung von Raumbildern*, co-edited with Michael Flitner

(2005) and "Einfach sprachlos but not simply speechless: language(s), thought and practice in the social sciences", co-edited with Gesa Helms and Ulrich Oslender (2005).

Frank Schulze-Engler has taught at the universities of Frankfurt (M), Bremen and Hanover. In 2002, he became a professor at the Institute for English and American Studies at Frankfurt (M) University where he is now Head of the Department for New Literatures in English (NELK). His publications include *Intellektuelle wider Willen* (1992), *African Literatures in the Eighties* (1993), *Postcolonial Theory and the Emergence of a Global Society* (1998), *Crab Tracks* (2002), as well as numerous essays on African literature, comparative perspectives on the New Literatures in English, postcolonial theory, transnational culture and the cultural dimensions of globalisation. Forthcoming is his study *Shared Worlds: Experiences of Globalized Modernity in African, Asian and Caribbean Literatures in English*. He is the editor of *ACOLIT* (the Newsletter of the German Association for the Study of the New Literatures in English) and a co-editor of *MATATU: Journal for African Culture and Society*.

Edward W. Soja is Distinguished Professor of Urban Planning in the School of Public Policy and Social Research at the University of California in Los Angeles (UCLA) and Visiting Centennial Professor of Sociology in the Cities Programme at the London School of Economics. He was a visiting scholar at the University of Ibadan, Nigeria, and the University of Nairobi, Kenya, and taught at Syracuse University and Northwestern University. His major writings build on a critique of social historicism and focus on a reconceptualization of space and human spatiality. Besides a book co-edited with Allen J. Scott entitled *The City: Los Angeles and Urban Theory at the End of the Twentieth Century* (1996), he has written *Postmodern Geographies: The Reassertion of Space in Critical Social Theory* (1989), *Thirdspace: Journeys to Los Angeles and Other Real-and-Imagined Places* (1996) and *Postmetropolis: Critical Studies of Cities and Regions* (2000). His current research interests range from labour-community coalition building in LA to global urbanization processes and the New Regionalism. Currently he is working on *Seeking Spatial Justice*.

Gerhard Wagner is a full professor at the Department for Social Sciences at Frankfurt (M) University. Before he took that post, he taught at the universities of Bielefeld, Leipzig, Würzburg and Zürich and conducted research among others at Stanford University. His publications include a dozen of books, for example *Herausforderung Vielfalt* (1999), *Auguste Comte* (2001), *Der Fremde als sozialer Typus* (co-editor, 2002), *Projekt Europa* (2005), *Kultur in Zeiten der Globalisierung* (co-editor, 2005), *Eine Geschichte der Soziologie* (2007) as well as numerous essays on the philosophy of social sciences, the sociology of science, social and political theory, nationalism, and European integration. Currently, he is preparing the manuscript of the correspondence between Alfred Schuetz and Eric Voegelin for press with University of Missouri Press. Also forthcoming are the last three books of the five-volume edition of the collected works of Albert Salomon (co-edited with Peter Gostmann), of which volume 1 and volume 2 have already been published in 2007 and 2008 with the VS Verlagsanstalt. His most recent book is an introductory novel into sociology entitled *Paulette on the Beach*, published in German as *Paulette am Strand: Roman zur Einführung in die Soziologie* (2008).

Robert J.C. Young is one of the early pioneers and highly influential scholars in the interdisciplinary fields of Anglophone and postcolonial literatures that also cross over into areas of cultural studies, philosophy, anthropology, theory, and history. Currently, Robert J.C. Young is Silver Professor and Professor of English and Comparative Literature at New York University. Before he took this Chair at New York University in 2005, he was Professor of English and Critical Theory at Oxford University and a fellow of Wadham College. He also taught at Rutgers and Southampton universities. His long list of acclaimed publications include *White Mythologies: Writing History and the West* (1990), *Colonial Desire: Hybridity in Culture, Theory and Race* (1995), *Torn Halves: Political Conflict in Literacy and Cultural Theory* (1996), *Postcolonialism: An Historical Introduction* (2001), and *The Idea of English Ethnicity* (2008). He is also General Editor of *Interventions: International Journal of Postcolonial Studies* (Routledge) and was founding Editor of *The Oxford Literary Review*. His work has been translated into sixteen languages.

Index

27797191R00123

Printed in Great Britain
by Amazon